# LIFE'S A PITCH

*The Passions of the Press Box*

# LIFE'S A PITCH

*The Passions of the Press Box*

Compiled and Edited by
Michael Calvin

INTEGR8 BOOKS

Published by Integr8 Books 2012

A CIP catalogue record for this book is available from the British Library

ISBN 978-0-9566981-1-7

Printed in Great Britain by CPI Group (UK) Ltd, Croydon, CR0 4YY

Integr8 Books
An imprint of Integr8 Communications,
Higher Rads End,
Eversholt,
MK17 9ED

www.lifesapitch.co.uk

Twitter accounts: @BTLifesapitch @CalvinBook

# CONTENTS

Teamsheet                                                          ix
Team Talk                                                          xv

1.  Dear Me    **Michael Calvin**                                    1
2.  Life with the Bomb Squad **Adrian Clarke**                      16
3.  Feast and Famine **John Cross**                                 34
4.  Big in China **Dominic Fifield**                                46
5.  The Poet and The Penalty **Alex Hess**                          63
6.  Derby and the Tin Man **Tom Hopkinson**                         75
7.  Long Distance Love **Laure James**                              88
8.  The Ballad of Rodney McAree **Dave Kidd**                      102
9.  The Odyssey **Martin Lipton**                                  117
10. Stanley Victor Superstar **Iain Macintosh**                    134
11. We Will Never Die **Luke Moore**                               144
12. Every Club Should Have Two **Ian Ridley**                      159
13  Sgt Wilko's Barmy Army **Janine Self**                         173
14. The Liverpool Way **Rory Smith**                               188
15. The Tony Soprano of Old Trafford
    **Rob Smyth**                                                  201
16. Egg and Chips For Two **David Walker**                         214
17. When Torres Chose to Walk Alone
    **Dan Willis**                                                 228
18. Malcolm Crosby's Red-and-White Hankie
    **Jonathan Wilson**                                            242

Afterword **Marc Watson**                                          259
Team Huddle                                                        263

# Team Sheet

**Michael Calvin** is an award-winning columnist for the Independent on Sunday, who has covered seven Olympic Games, and six World Cups. He had the idea for this anthology, which he has compiled and edited, while hosting vodcasts for BT's website, www.lifesapitch.co.uk. His previous book, Family: Life Death & Football was nominated as Football Book of the Year in 2011.

**Adrian Clarke** played professional football for Arsenal and Southend United before becoming a sports journalist at the age of 26. He is now an expert analyst for Arsenal TV and BBC Radio Essex, and writes for numerous newspapers, magazines and websites all over the world.

**John Cross** has been reporting for the Daily Mirror since 1988, covering six major tournaments and three Olympic Games to date. Greatly enjoys contributions to the Life's A Pitch vodcast panels. He holds strong views, which helps. He's opinionated and passionate about the beautiful game.

**Dominic Fifield** was born in South Africa but raised a stone's throw from Selhurst Park. His passion for Crystal Palace was fuelled by Ian Wright's goals, Jim Cannon's moustache and a group of passing Millwall fans who threw bricks through the family greenhouse. He worked for the club before joining The Guardian. After six years as Merseyside correspondent, he now covers football in London, where regular trips to Palace compensate for a little too much Chelsea.

**Alex Hess** is an emerging writer who came to prominence through his contributions to the Fanzone on www.lifesapitch.co.uk. In between his misty-eyed dreams of Xabi Alonso, Alex is a freelance football writer who contributes to various websites, including Football365 and The Football Ramble.

**Tom Hopkinson** was a Derby County season ticket holder in the 1990s before work intervened. Since then he has written for the Daily Express, Sunday Express and London's Evening Standard, and is now a football reporter for The People.

**Laure James** is based in Belfast, and has written about football for more than ten years. She is trilingual, having both English and French heritage, and contributes regularly to the Daily Mail, Sky Sports and talkSPORT. She also presents The Social Club, Northern Ireland's only football podcast, and writes for Ulster editions of The Sun, Daily Mirror and Sunday Mirror.

**Tom Keeley,** who designed the book, is a creative consult-ant with more than twenty five years' experience in branding and corporate communications. He has worked predomi-nately within the world of sport including designing for the governing bodies of many of the UK's major sports.

**Dave Kidd** is Chief Sports Writer, Deputy Sports Editor and columnist at The People. He was previously a sports writer at The Sun. He's been supporting Fulham since the 1980-81 promotion season and is now trying to infect his 9-year-old daughter Emily and 7-year-old son James with the same affliction.

**Martin Lipton** has been Chief Football Writer of the Daily Mirror since 2002, having covered every major England game from 1994. Heartache, despair and penalty shoot-outs are, of course, his stock in trade. He's seen Liverpool, Manchester United and Chelsea win the Champions League. Sadly, not Tottenham. Yet.

**Iain Macintosh** is a freelance football writer and author. He writes regularly for The New Paper in Singapore, The Irish Examiner, SI.com, MSN and a variety of other publications and websites.

**Luke Moore** is a founding member, co-producer and co-presenter of The Football Ramble, the largest independ-ent football brand in the UK. He is also a well-respected writer and broadcaster and has contributed regularly to the likes of BBC 5 Live, BBC World Service, and ESPN.

**Ian Ridley** has written on football for The Guardian, Daily Telegraph, Independent on Sunday, Observer, Mail on Sunday and Daily Express. He is the author of nine books, including the best-selling Addicted, the autobiography of Arsenal and England captain Tony Adams. He also wrote more than 20 episodes of the Sky One drama Dream Team.

**Janine Self** is a freelance sports reporter based in the Midlands, where she worked for The Sun for 15 years. As well as covering football, including the 2006 World Cup and following the fortunes of the Wales national team, she has reported on Wimbledon, Formula One, Ryder Cup, Commonwealth Games and Olympics. Janine also co-wrote the autobiography of former football star Robbie Savage.

**Rory Smith** is a football reporter for the Times. Now based in London, he spent three years enduring the exquisite torture of covering Liverpool for the Telegraph, while his work has also appeared in the Independent and Four-FourTwo. He's not quite sure how he ended up a Liverpool fan, but apparently it's incurable.

**Rob Smyth** is a sports writer for the Guardian and co-author of Jumpers for Goalposts: How Football Sold Its Soul. His favourite players are Roy Keane, Ole Gunnar Solskjaer, Preben Elkjaer, Gerd Muller and Andres Iniesta. He's still haunted by his missed penalty against Swale Magpies in 1992.

**David Walker** is the sports editor of the Sunday Mirror. He returned to Fleet Street in 2005 after working in football as a director of Leeds United and Barnsley.

Before that he was the deputy sports editor of the Mail on Sunday, chief football reporter of the Daily Mail and also worked for The Sun.

**Dan Willis** is the editor of BT's football website, www.lifesapitch.co.uk, on which all the contributors to this book come together. Prior to this he was the sports editor of BT's TV service, BT Vision. Dan is a Liverpool fan old enough to remember when regular league titles were the norm at Anfield.

**Jonathan Wilson** is the editor of The Blizzard, a contributor to the Guardian, Fox Soccer, ESPN Star, Sports Illustrated and the Irish examiner. He is the author of six books on football, including Inverting the Pyramid: A History of Football Tactics, which was the NSC Football Book of the Year in 2009.

# Team Talk

Like many football writers of, ahem, a certain vintage, I was offered my first Fleet Street job in a pub. The King & Keys, the Daily Telegraph's local, was narrow, dingy, and enveloped by a mushroom cloud of cigarette smoke. It was a place of miracles and wonders, where anyone drinking less than five pints an hour was dismissed as a lightweight. After a good night, the ancient carpet had the consistency of fly paper. Inevitably, it was deemed the natural venue in which to prepare for the most important interview of my life.

Peter Eastwood was the Telegraph's managing editor. Meeting him was a cross between an audience with the Pope, and a Lightsaber duel with Darth Vader. Ted Barrett, the Sports Editor, gave me the big build up, but this white-haired, piggy-eyed despot held the power of life and death. He despatched summary justice, from behind a walnut desk with the dimensions of a full-sized snooker table. Eastwood enquired after my school (he wasn't impressed) and interrogated me on the contents of that day's newspaper. I prayed that Polo mints would disguise the fact I was on a performance-enhancing drug, Guinness.

Eventually, after an eternity, Eastwood went through my terms and conditions. I whimpered in abject gratitude. We both knew I would have signed for ten shillings, and a used first class stamp. He shook my hand, welcomed me on board, and issued a warning which echoes down the ages: "I do not know the colour of your politics, or your football team. Ensure I remain ignorant of those facts".

Wise words, as I am sure every contributor to this anthology will confirm. We may be an eclectic mix, but we have much in common. We all contribute to BT's football website, which gives this book its title and we've all been harangued for perceived bias by a succession of increasingly deranged strangers. Between us, we've been accused of a soft spot for the entire Premier League, Championship, and most of the mausoleum known as the Scottish Premier League. Some hardy souls have even been damned by association with non League clubs. My favourite involved an alleged allegiance to Luton Town, the club I knew simply as "the Scum".

Usually, revealing secret passions isn't worth the grief. But the Life's a Pitch writers are made of sterner stuff, and responded brilliantly to my invitation to bare their souls. You'll read protestations of man love for Roy Keane and Stan Collymore, who might just be the blind dates from Hell. You'll bounce between Red Top titans who straddle the North London divide. You want heroes? We got' em: Fernando Torres and Xabi Alonso; Ted McMinn and Malcolm Crosby, perhaps the only manager to be sacked by the Pools Panel. You'll be invited to share the lives of Bob and Jean Lucas. You'll share Portsmouth's pain, understand why Fulham fans don't take themselves entirely seriously. You'll be taken on a Chinese tour by Crystal Palace, and discover why Montpellier should be twinned with Belfast. If you need to understand Liverpool and Leeds, or relate to the young pro who fears his time at Arsenal is limited, read on.

I know I am biased, but this is a unique insight into what can be a rough old trade. We've gathered writers from national newspapers, and the blogosphere. Their offerings are in alphabetical order. I'll take one for the team by owning up to the most heinous crime a football fan can commit......

*Michael Calvin*
*July 2012*

*This book is dedicated to the memory of Danny Fullbrook,*
*chief football writer of the Daily Star.*
*Frank, Fearless, Fulham.*

## Chapter 1

# Dear Me

## Michael Calvin

This is a letter that must be written, but cannot be received, because I've not worked out the space-time continuum. It is addressed to myself, as a boy on the edge of adolescence. It covers love and loss, passion and betrayal. It features two football clubs, and a cardinal sin, the transfer of allegiance from one club to another. It sees a boy's world, through a man's eyes. It seeks to share the lessons of a lifetime. It craves forgiveness, because I will shatter the illusion of innocence, but there is nothing to worry about. I've been blessed.

Dear Mike,

Happy twelfth birthday. It's Sunday, August 3, 1969. The first face you see, as you wake in the top bunk of the bedroom you share with your brothers, is that of Colin Bell. It's a full page portrait, torn from Goal Magazine, and sellotaped to the wall, alongside images of Tony Book, Glyn Pardoe, and a mythical creature named Mike Doyle. They won the Football League for Manchester City in 1968, but you follow them by default. Mum bought you a City shirt, round necked and a size too big, last Christmas, because she liked its shade of light blue. It also had growing room.

Mums are practical like that. She has only the vaguest notion you support Watford, your home town club, who are beginning their first season in the Second Division. Their players do not get many photo-spreads in Goal Magazine, or in Charles Buchan's Football Monthly, the other drain on your paper round money. Only one, Keith Eddy, gets the full-colour treatment. His picture is posted above the bed. He's straight-backed, steely-eyed, a Prince in the guise of a lower League journeyman. Watford's captain wears the number four, and seems impossibly glamorous.

You've got Gola boots, because Adidas World Cups are too expensive, and you're not good enough to wear George Best's side-laced Stylo Matchmakers. Mum and Dad have three jobs between them, trying to make ends meet, but they buy your first sports book for your birthday. It's The Football Man, by Arthur Hopcraft. Neither they, nor you, realise this will shape your life. You will cherish it, memorise it, refer to it as the years roll away. You will never forget the last lines of the introduction: "This is not a gallery of heroes. I am a reporter trying to reach to the heart of what football is."

Dad is a Rugby League man. You watch his home town team, Whitehaven, on family holidays but much prefer to play endless games of football with your cousins, on a pitch at the end of your Grandparents' garden. It is, quite literally, in the shadow of the pithead. Haig Colliery is Cumbria's last deep-coal mine, and will not close until 1986. It leads down to a beach, where you pick black diamonds, washed-up deposits for the fire. Grandad, an imposing figure in belted trousers which extend to his armpits, sits in a high backed chair, and tells of being out of work, from the 1929 Stock Market crash to the Second World War. He fought, bareknuckled, in pubs for pennies, trapped rabbits for the stew-pot. As you grow older, you will discover the relevance of his reflections on the importance of honesty, humility and hard work.

The other important document, your Magna Carta, is at home, beneath your pillow. It is a letter, on headed notepaper, signed "R.E.Rollitt, General Secretary, Watford Association Football Club Ltd". It confirms the success of your application to be a Watford ballboy for the 1969-70 season, and requests that you report for duty, a minimum 50 minutes before home games. Your green rectangular pass, enclosed in a plastic wallet, is your boarding card for a journey which will take you to more than 80 countries.

You will watch football in Africa, in places like Bamako, the capital of Mali, where polio victims shuffle on all fours, chasing a ball made of rags. You will travel to the slums of Naples, to World Cups in Mexico, the United States and South Africa, to see its beauty, depravity and eccentricity encapsulated in one man, Diego Armando Maradona. You might not be fit to lace George Best's boots, but to cannibalise a line from an infinitely better writer than you, you will be in a succession of pubs to ensure no-one laces his drinks.

But, forgive me, we get ahead of ourselves. Let's dwell on what it means to wear those ancient, faded bottle green tracksuits, which chafe like Sir Thomas More's hair shirt. You luxuriate in the knowledge you are in The Show, on the inside. You change next to the home dressing room, and the smell of liniment is as evocative as the incense, released by your alter egos, the altar boys at High Mass. You check on the crowd through a frosted fanlight, and carry out boxes of metal numbers, to place on half time scoreboards which extend, from A-Z down the side of the pitch. Vicarage Road is pretty scruffy, to be honest. You've previously bunked in, via the allotments, to stand on the shale of the bend beside the Rookery End. Now you are within touching distance of heroes who still get the bus to work. You will never lose the thrill of the setting, the intimacy of the insight football provides into the best, and worst, of human nature.

You will make your first away trip, in a neighbour's motorcycle sidecar, to see Watford lose 2-1 at Oxford on September 6, 1969. You will pay a shilling for the programme, and throw up on the way home, because you eat a cheese sandwich. They didn't recognise food allergies in those days, did they? You stick to Bovril on match days after that. You listen to Sports Report, on the kitchen radio, when Watford embark on your first FA Cup run, winning 2-1 at Bolton Wanderers in the third round. First Division Stoke are beaten by a 30 yard drive by Colin Franks, who lives just down the road. The game is on TV, the equivalent of a state visit. When Gillingham lose 2-1, to two goals by new £7,000 signing Ray Lugg, a local photographer captures you hugging another ballboy, Keith Furphy, the manager's son. He is small, flaxen haired, and will go on to play professionally in the United States. He will get the plum job, operating behind the goal at the Rookery End, when Liverpool arrive at Vicarage Road on February 21, 1970, for the quarter final.

In the next century, when matches are beamed into satellite dishes erected on the sides of houses, and are regarded as minor wars, you'll wonder why you were so excited by the build up to the game. The Watford Observer – of which more, later – publishes a sixteen-page supplement, previewing the game. Watford are duly patronised as plucky outsiders, or blithely dismissed as relegation fodder by national newspaper men who can barely conceal their distaste at the ambitions of a team of such low breeding. Funny, that. You will love covering such ties, when it is your turn to make the long journey from Fleet Street to the real world.

On this day, you'll be stationed on the Shrodells' side, in front of a low-roofed eyesore which shields the hospital in which Gareth Southgate will be born, later that year. You'll see a grown man cry, for the first time. He's a Scouser, a crumpled figure in a donkey jacket who weeps as he sags into a wire mesh fence beside the wooden hut that houses the Supporters Club. Bill Shankly's team lose 1-0 on a pitch that consists of rolled mud, and you are centrally involved in the goal.

You collect the ball, in front of a sign advertising Double Diamond ("Works Wonders") and quickly toss it to Lugg, who takes a short throw to winger Stewart Scullion and moves into space to receive the return pass. He nutmegs Peter Wall, the covering full back, and delivers an out swinging cross, directly in your eyeline. It is met by a diving header from Barry Endean, who runs behind the goal to celebrate, and is ambushed by, you've guessed it, Keith Furphy. God, how you envy him, caught up in a scrum of men whose gold shirts, with a hornet on the left breast, are caked with dirt and suffused with sweat.

Life seems suddenly simple. You want a piece of this. You look into the crowd, and see men, lost in the moment. A football club, small and apparently insignificant, is woven into the tapestry of people's lives. You find it easy to express the emotions of the occasion, through the written word. You imagine the unity of strangers, and sense the spirit of that broken man, on the wire. You will meet Shankly, just before his death in 1981, and ask him about the defeat which prompted him to break up his first great Liverpool team. He will tell you, in that Ayrshire rasp, that it was "a bitter day, son. Bitter."

So, too, is Saturday, March 14, 1970. For some reason, lost in the mists of time, the semi final against Chelsea, at White Hart Lane, kicks off at 2.45pm. A fleet of coaches, carrying fans living in a twilight world of hope and disbelief, begins to leave Watford at breakfast time. Yours, caught in the inevitable jam, is eased to the side of the road, to let the team bus past, somewhere near Enfield. More than 40 years later, you will still be able to summon the freeze frame image of Eddy, sitting by the window and smiling at the forest of scarves being waved at him. He had suffered a cartilage injury, and will miss the biggest game of his life.

Some of your friends have stolen bedsheets, daubed them with gloss paint from the garden shed, and transformed them into banners. You wear a rosette, with a small silver-papered Cup at its heart. Your rattle, wooden, but with black metal gears, is so heavy it could stun a rhinoceros. Take a deep breath, and recite after me the team which played that day in full schoolboy shorthand: Walker, Welbourne, Williams, Lugg, Lees, Walley, Scullion, Garbett, Endean, Packer, Owen. Sub Garvey.

Names, faces, memories. Mickey Walker, who will go on to manage Colchester, Everton and Norwich (twice), has the piercing eyes and thin moustache of a spaghetti western villain. Duncan Welbourne, who will play 280 games on the spin, is a full back who looks like a Teddy Boy. He should, by rights, play in brothel-creepers. Tom Walley, who will develop into a brilliant youth coach and produce such England internationals as David James and Ashley Cole, will also become a family friend. Many years later you will discover Endean, the hero signed for £50, working as a builder in his native North East.

You are a water molecule in the sea of humanity which ebbs and flows around the lower tier of the main stand at White Hart Lane. It will, in time, become one of your favourite grounds, intimate and atmospheric. You have been to Rugby League and Amateur Cup finals at Wembley, but this is something more elemental. The stands seem higher, the noise louder. The pitch is fringed with dull, under-nourished grass, but is mainly mud, mixed with sand. Your silent prayer, that this will help Watford bridge the chasm in class, remains unanswered. Watford lose 5-1, but you are comforted by the fleeting euphoria of Terry Garbett's first half equaliser, struck from just outside the box. It will be 14 years, two months, and five days before Watford finally reach their first FA Cup final.

You will be there, in a different guise. That's because of another two line letter, which you will also secrete beneath your pillow. This, too, is on headed notepaper. It is signed, "E.R.Foster, Editor". He offers you a junior reporter's job on the Watford Observer. Mum cries. When you tell Keith "Trog" Turner, your headmaster at the local Grammar School, of your intention to abandon your A levels, he responds as if you have urinated through his letterbox. "Calvin", he intones, "this will lead to nothing." He's right, in a way. When, many years later, you are invited back, to contribute to his valediction, you find your diary is full.

Your great good fortune is to have, as your first Sports Editor, Oli Phillips. He introduces you to Bob Dylan, and fried tomatoes on toast. The latter is infinitely preferable to the former, who gives you aural indigestion. Oli is a talented writer, a warm and wise teacher. He gives you your first byline – Mick Calvin – for a report on the West Herts Bowls Club Dinner & Dance. You have your own page, to cover the Watford Sunday League, and are eased into the Vicarage Road rotation. Football is suddenly seen through a different prism.

Watford hit their lowest ebb almost as soon as you arrive. A 1-0 loss at Darlington, on August 30, 1975, leaves them 92nd in the Football League. You spend most of the season with the Under 18s, developing a working relationship with a quietly spoken lad of your age. His name is Luther Blissett. You will see him score a hat trick on his England debut, a 9-0 win against Luxembourg on the evening of December 15, 1982. AC Milan will sign him for £1m, and sell him back, for £550,000, within a year. He will end up as Watford's record goalscorer, 186 in 503 appearances. His is the first of many lives you chart.

You are sent to play darts against Watford's new owner, in the Supporters' Club bar. His name is, or was, Reginald Dwight. He dresses as Elton Hercules John, and arrives at the oche in platform boots, a pink satin suit, and scarf fashioned from peacock feathers. His glasses resemble diamante-studded dustbin lids. You can't hit the board, let alone find the treble 20, but something weird happens. You converse as fellow fans, share memories and emotions. Elton knows what he has to do at the end of the season. He sacks Mike Keen, rejects the chance to employ Bobby Moore, and recognises the potential of a young manager named Graham Taylor.

Your football education accelerates. Taylor is a force of

nature. He transforms your club, sweeps away generations of grime. He's empathetic, inclusive, sensitive, and utterly ruthless. He's a dream-seller, a scene-stealer. He insists his players live in the town and replies personally to all signed letters from fans. The season develops into a crusade. It is no surprise that Watford win the Fourth Division by eleven points, having clinched the title with six games to spare.

Elton had given Taylor five years to get into the Second Division. He needs two. You hitch a ride on a football special train to see Blissett score with two headers in a 2-1 win at Manchester United. This is getting silly. Watford are promoted for the second successive season, and reach the League Cup semi finals, where they are beaten by Brian Clough's Nottingham Forest. The following season is transitional, but highlighted by an extraordinary comeback. Trailing 4-0 from the first leg of a League Cup tie against Southampton, the First Division's form team, Watford win 7-1.

Your career matches the upward trajectory of your club. You cover your first Olympic Games, as chief sports writer for a chain of regional newspapers, in Brezhnev's Moscow in 1980, and begin to follow England around the world. Business can be matched with pleasure, because Watford remain a breaking story. Taylor builds a vibrant team around Tom Walley's products, like Blissett, John Barnes, Nigel Callaghan and Kenny Jackett, a kid from your council estate. As a fan, you bridle at Terry Venables' lazy description of Watford as long-ball Neanderthals. They reach the First Division in 1982, and win the FA Youth Cup for good measure. The mood of Venables, and his media acolytes, is not improved when Taylor is asked to oversee the England Youth team, on a part time basis.

Taylor has the common touch. When he criticises fans for lack of vocal support, they argue that it would help if the main terrace had a roof. He promptly walks out on to the pitch with a placard which reads "I'm sorry." There's not a lot to apologise for. Watford's initial season in the top flight is incredible. Blissett scores four in an 8-0 thrashing of Sunderland. Watford do the double over Arsenal, win at Spurs, and have home wins over Everton and Liverpool. They finish as runners-up, and qualify for the UEFA Cup. Not for the first time, or the last, Elton is in floods of tears.

Your year as a TV reporter allows you to follow your club into Europe. Kaiserslauten succumb at Vicarage Road. Watford win, in extra time, against Levski Spartak, a team run by Bulgaria's Interior Ministry. On a freezing evening 60,000 fans light bonfires to keep warm, and stage proletarian protests. The sleigh ride ends in the snow in Prague, where Sparta win 4-0, but the spiritual journey has yet to be completed. That happens in 1984, when Watford reach the FA Cup final.

You are working in Fleet Street, and permit yourself one last indulgence. You return home, drink in the estate pub before the game with your childhood friends. You envy your brothers their face paint and replica shirts, because you have to be suited and booted. You take your Mum to her first football match, on a Metropolitan line train which glows gold, and reverberates to Elton's Greatest Hits. Mum sits next to Freddie Starr at Wembley, near the royal box, and barely registers the result. You envy her sense of detachment.

You will neither forgive, nor forget, a posturing ninny of a referee named Roger Milford. This bubble-permed public- ity junkie unjustly sends Wilf Rostron off in the build up to the final, and costs a great pro the chance to captain Watford at Wembley. Andy Gray joins Milford on the hit list, although you will work with him, and like him, in later years. He knocks the ball out of goalkeeper Steve Sherwood's hands to score the decisive second goal in Everton's 2-0 win. Like Graham Taylor, you will never be able to watch a recording of the final. It is too painful.

Looking back, it is the end of innocence. Taylor's attempt to redress the balance ends at the semi final stage in 1987, when he is forced to select a wine waiter, Gary Plumley, in goal. The son of chief executive Eddie, Plumley is recruited because of injuries to Tony Coton and Steve Sherwood, and is predictably powerless to prevent Spurs winning 4-1. Watford couldn't even sell their full allocation of tickets. Taylor leaves at the end of the season, to be replaced, with disastrous consequences, by Dave Bassett.

We have entered the age of Heysel and Hillsborough. You are among the football hacks summoned to Downing Street by Margaret Thatcher. She has the eyes of a tawny owl, and clearly terrifies her Ministers, who dance attendance. She goes around the table, asking each visitor what they would do to solve football hooliganism. You might as well quote Afghani poetry, because her mind is made up before anyone opens their mouth. In her world, football fans are second class citizens, who have forfeited the right to trust and respect. They deserve to be caged, treated with contempt. You descend the staircase, framed by portraits of past Prime Ministers, with a sense of dread.

The more you understand the principles of power, and the closer you get to the sort of people who administer it, the more depressed you become. You are no longer prepared to take things at face value. Football is re-shaped by Super Sundays and institutionalised greed. The Premier League is marketed brilliantly, and spawns a counter culture of grasping agents, preening players, and celebrity nonentities. By 1996 Watford are back in the old Third Division. They have reverted to irrelevance, and you have turned on Taylor.

His failure as England manager is a self-fulfilling prophesy, even though he loses only one of his first 23 matches. He is too below-stairs for his most vindictive critics, and never recovers from his visit to the tabloid vegetable rack. Being lampooned as a turnip, following a European Championship defeat by Sweden, sets the tone. He cracks in Rotterdam, before the game which costs England a place in the 1994 World Cup. He loses his temper in the pre-match press conference, becomes embroiled in a row with a reporter, and comes across as paranoid, out of his depth. The Channel 4 TV crew, developing a fateful fly on the wall documentary, are doing handstands. You write a scathing piece, knowing the impact it will have on Taylor, his wife Rita, and his two daughters. You feel a little ashamed.

There are brief moments of rapture, which never quite rebuild bridges, but rekindle an old flame. Watford win successive promotions during Taylor's second spell as manager. You are in bed in Brisbane, howling at the moon and following the game on a ruinously expensive phone line, when they make the Premier League for the first time, on May 31, 1999. It is 3.36am, the following day, in Queensland when Nick Wright's overhead kick sets up a 2-0 win over Bolton in the Championship play off final at Wembley. The Sun hails Taylor as a national treasure. Go figure.

You still feel for the club, and ignore professional protocol that September, by standing in the old wooden press box at Watford, and punching the air to celebrate Allan Smart's winning goal against Chelsea. It is a rare highlight in a season which ends in relegation. Gianluca Vialli, Chelsea's manager that day, succeeds Taylor at Vicarage Road at the end of the 2000-01 season, and is as useful as an elephant on an ice flow. He lasts a year and Watford flirt with administration.

You are able take your sons to watch another Championship play off victory, 3-0 over Leeds United at the Millenium Stadium in 2006, but something still does not feel right. Aidy Boothroyd, in his first season as manager, is a media myth, quickly exposed in the Premier League. Watford finish bottom, winning only five matches. The cycle of recrimination and boardroom intrigue intensifies. The battery of devotion is dying, and you are unprepared for the identity of the recharger. He's Kenny Jackett, the kid with whom you played pick-up games on the estate.

He's Millwall manager, a Lion tamer. You contact him, in the summer of 2009, with an outrageous request. Give me complete access to your club, so I can search for football's soul. He agrees, and you report for the first day of pre-season training. You are on the substitutes' bench at Wembley, 333 days later, when Millwall are promoted through the League One play off final. You are unprepared for the intensity of the experience. It prompts you to question basic beliefs, realign your principles and allegiances.

Players reveal the reality of their trade, the insecurity which cannot be diluted by surges of adrenaline, or testosterone. They allow you to become part of the dressing room's fixtures and fittings. You get a sense of their professionalism, and the bitter cruelties of their trade. They are mostly family men, whose life is influenced by the vagaries of form and fate. Cut them and their nearest and dearest bleed. Jackett and his coaches give you the privilege of their trust, take you into their confidence. There are moments of tension and tenderness, anger and amusement.

Millwall remains a byword for strife, and a lack of social cohesion, but you look beyond the stereotypes. The club plays an integral role in a multi-cultural, multi-faith community. There are no fairytales out there, but you unearth reasons to believe in football's restorative powers. Good people are doing a good job, without fuss or fanfare. You begin to understand the precious nature of the link between players and their fans. These are not the corporate grazers of the Premier League, or the ogres of tabloid myth. They are true believers, your type of people. They agree with Grandad about the value of humility, honesty and hard work.

The deeper you delve, the more committed you become. You love the tall tales from the Old Den, where men were men, and opposing teams wished they were anywhere else. You meet club legend Barry Kitchener, the embodiment of a working class hero. Like most hard men, he has an affecting gentility, and dignity. By the time he succumbs to cancer, with tragic speed, in the spring of 2012, you have admitted to living a lie. Millwall is the football club best suited to your nature and experience.

Honesty is a double edged sword, which wounds when you return to Vicarage Road on the night of September 27, 2011. Your host, in the chairman's suite, is Graham Taylor. He is polite, attentive, but seems ill at ease with his duties. You guess why when Watford's new owner makes a late entrance. He is an interesting character, who changed his name from Laurence Bazini to Bassini when he was made bankrupt in 2007. Your antennae twitch. He's a little too glib, and doesn't endear himself to his guests with a guileless quip about Millwall fans ripping out the seats in the event of defeat. To be honest, you loathe him.

Watford come from behind to beat Millwall 2-1, without a hint of trouble. It is an abject game between ponderous, fretful teams. You are desolate, and realise that the club that enticed you into falling in love with the game's infinite possibilities no longer exists. It has betrayed the love of that boy with half-formed dreams, in the bunk bed. Taylor will eventually leave the club, on May 30 2012. Two months later Baz/ss/ini will sell Watford to the Pozzo family, who transform it into a feeder club for Udinese, in Serie A. Your instincts have been proved correct.

You wanted "your" team to lose when Millwall came calling. That's heresy, and you know it. Dare you share it? There's no option really, because it is what is expected of you. Be true to yourself. You know it makes sense. Repeat after me: "Mmmmmmiiiiiillllll"…

Best wishes.
Mike

## Chapter 2

# Life With the Bomb Squad

## Adrian Clarke

This is my recollection of the final season I spent as an Arsenal player...

### September 23, 1996

As a natural amphitheatre, it's not a patch on *The Globe* but this is a stage which has borne witness to more than its fair share of dramatic tragedies. I'm talking about a small, nondescript enclave - a patch of grass - to the rear of our changing rooms at the Arsenal training ground. Hidden on the opposite side of the car park, shielded by trees and a low set brick building that houses the treatment room, it's one of few areas which are free from prying eyes in the whole complex.

It is a natural home for in-house drama.

There are no banks of seats facing the stage. Just a row of old, rotting school benches, riddled with cracks and splinters backing on to the wall to our boot room, which in turn adjoins the shed that houses spare goalposts, nets and lawnmowers. To the left, a lush, neatly- manicured youth team pitch, while to the right, boot-cleaning brushes litter the floor around two dirty white porcelain sinks. Glamorous it is not, but if you'd had a season ticket for this spot in recent times, you would have been witness to some truly pivotal and frequently emotional moments.

First there was George Graham confirming to the players that he'd been sacked. Open-mouthed, we'd looked on as he smiled his way through what must have been an excruciatingly painful goodbye.

Then there was Paul Merson. Full of remorse and fighting back the tears, his confession to drug, drink and gambling addictions was heart rendering, if not entirely shocking.

Bruce Rioch took to the very same stage, just over a month ago. The sorrow in his eyes betrayed a proudly defiant final message he'd prepared for us, as the curtain called on his short spell in charge of the club. Next was Tony Adams, a man we all look up to, disclosing disturbing details of his double life, the public one and the one drowning in booze. He will come through it we hoped.

And finally, most recently, first team coach and interim manager Stewart Houston was compelled to follow in those illustrious footsteps, treading the same boards to reveal, rather less emotionally, that he was jumping ship to manage QPR.

Today, in the late September sunshine with glistening dew on the grass, our tall, slim and staggeringly articulate new boss - whom none of us had heard of a month ago – puts his head above the parapet. Bunched up on the benches like schoolboys, with some strewn across the grass, others sitting almost cross-legged, Arsene Wenger makes his introductions. As with everyone else who'd previously stood on the spot marked 'x', we listen, respectfully and in silence.

He's impressive.

Predictably, the sniggering begins as soon as our new gaffer's back is turned. 'He looks like a nerd', 'Is he a school teacher or a football manager?' are two of the more flattering observations to emerge as childish laughter echoes in the breeze. I join in, as you do, but this isn't time for me to take the piss. I need this guy to like me.

When he first claps eyes on me in action, he'll turn to Pat Rice and say, "Who is this Adrian Clarke? He is magnifique."

Well, that's the idea anyway.

### October 3, 1996

He's unusual, but definitely no school teacher in disguise. This is a man who knows what he wants. And exactly what he expects from us. Having tasted the best eight months of my life last year, I'm now enduring the worst. Unceremoni-ously dumped back in the stiffs, after a brief but wonderful sojourn with the big boys, my head has been spinning since February.

I've sulked, I've moaned, I've got angry and I've almost constantly felt disillusioned. But none of this has been in the open. I haven't talked to the staff about how I feel and they haven't particularly talked, not properly anyway, to me either. Wenger's arrival represents a fresh start. That's why I'm so pleased the new gaffer has involved me in his first couple of sessions. It's not exactly special treatment, as there must have been at least 30 of us, but a positive's still a positive. Those have been in short supply.

Aching in places I never knew existed, I enjoy the new stretching exercises the manager teaches us, and the plyo-metric circuit training too. I've never seen so many poles and medicine balls. The only frustration is that the ball work was focussed mainly on drills, and that means limited opportunities to catch his eye. Not that I'm the only one with the same idea. Everyone seems to have found an extra 10 per cent from somewhere. With each section timed to the second on the manager's trusty stopwatch, training is formulaic, but it's not boring. His sessions are fresh and they have opened our eyes.

### October 6, 1996

As auditions go, today's debut in front of Wenger was a six out of ten at best. Not good. Not good enough, anyway. It's just a really weird day. There we were, getting changed at Highbury before facing Luton Town in the Avon Combination, when this odd, clearly nonsensical rumour sweeps through the stadium, suggesting Wenger might have a paedophile background. It first appeared on a newswire apparently, and we later discover it is also repeated on the radio.

We don't know if it's all a wind-up, so perplexed, we carry on preparing as normal but the vibe is unsettling. It's obvious something is up and as the match kicks off, dozens of cameramen line the touchline with their backs to play, focussing their lenses on the new boss in the director's box. It must be awful for him, especially as it's all a load of made-up tosh.

Perhaps it's no bad thing that he's distracted though. We lose 1-0, and playing out of position at left wing-back – again - I don't especially shine. He won't have gone home thinking I was magnifique, that's for sure.

## *October 28, 1996*

Arsenal are unbeaten and flying under the new boss, but I'm nowhere to be seen. I blame myself as I've done little more than blend into the background. Lacking the staple ingredient you need to succeed in football – confidence - I've made it way too easy to be ignored. And the sad truth is, we're over a month into his regime now, and if Arsene Wenger and I strolled towards one another on Holloway Road I'm not wholly convinced he would recognise me.

Not a great sign.

When the boss trims his regular training group down to 18 bodies soon after the initial mass sessions, it's disappointing, but not entirely unexpected, that I don't make the grade. Unusually nervous, I haven't produced anything special for him to get excited about. So in essence nothing has changed. I was out of favour before he arrived and it's stayed that way. Mind you, it hasn't always been so depressing. This time last year I was even regarded as a something of a boy wonder.

Actually that's stretching it a little as at 21, I wasn't a boy, and I wasn't especially wondrous either, but certain newspapers and magazines did describe me as a 'whizz-kid' so I must have been doing OK. Training every day with the first team, and shining too, I was easily in the form of my life and sharing a day-to-day environment with the likes of Dennis Bergkamp, Ian Wright, David Seaman and Tony Adams felt amazing.

Little things were so different to how they are now. As a top priority, I'd leapfrog the queue to see physiotherapist Gary Lewin. Not now. The coaches would smile and say hello, instead of avoiding eye contact. My team-mates would be relaxed around me, happy to take the piss. OK, they still do that to be fair. Footballers can be ruthless bastards.

Off the pitch various agents would phone me up for 'chats' – although their motives were obvious. I've been spared those of late. The Nike rep would pull me to one side and hand me a bag full of free gear. Now, he puts his head down and looks the other way if we cross paths. Friends of friends would call me up asking for tickets and I'd be invited to various events. Even the press had got hold of my number looking for quotes. Some of it was good, some of it was downright annoying, but at least I was a wanted man.

I was an Arsenal first team player. 'Mr Popular'. It even got so 'bad' that the dressing room started calling me the *Son of Rioch* much to my feigned embarrassment of course. And then, without prior warning, everything stops. Just like that. We were facing Nottingham Forest away and having played well for 90 minutes against Coventry City the previous week, I'd fully expected to start at the City Ground. But I didn't start. I wasn't even on the bench. And no one said a Dickie Bird to me about it.

"Are you injured or something Clarkey?" I remember England's Steve Stone asking as we bumped into one another at the ground. "No mate. Think I'm just bombed," was my reply, rather transparently faking that I wasn't overly bothered. No doubt realising my bluff, Steve just said, "Really? Oh well, keep your chin up mate," and with a shrug of the shoulders he walked off.

I'd be lying if I told you I wanted us to win that day. It's a disgrace I know but I needed them to miss me. As it turned out they didn't, winning 1-0 and playing pretty nicely too. On the coach trip home I barely said a word. I was gutted.

Worse was to come as Rioch tinkered with a 5-3-2 system in training ahead of our next game, a League Cup clash against Aston Villa. As a winger that was very bad news for me. It meant Lee Dixon and Nigel Winterburn would switch from full-backs to wing-backs, with a centre-back and centre midfielder coming in for the two wingers. The team sheet went up and my name was completely absent for the first time in months. I hadn't even made the squad. From whizz-kid to unwanted in the space of a few days, my stomach did somersaults. I wanted to throw up.

"You've done very well for me Clarkey," the manager explained when I popped into his dressing room for an explanation a few days later. "But we've got some big games coming up and I feel you could do with a breather. Plus, with three at the back for the time being, I don't need a winger. Don't worry son, you'll get another chance."

'Dad' never did give me that chance.

### November 5, 1996

Having sat through a fascinating lecture on diet and nutrition by the manager's French biochemist Dr Yann Rogier a few weeks back in the canteen, I was genuinely excited at the prospect of improving my conditioning. I needn't have been.

The managers' favoured 18-20 players are the first to receive their diet plans and nutritional hand-outs, including energy tablets and tubs of creatine powder. And that's fine. But this week my fellow reserve team players, the other 'boy wonders' who've had a taste of the first team, guys like Paul Shaw, Stephen Hughes and Matthew Rose have been put on the plans too. It shouldn't upset me, because they're my friends. But it does.

They also train with the first team this week and the manager seems to take quite a shine to them. He and Pat

Rice are flirting with them, no question about that. Again, I shouldn't feel bitter about my pals being liked but every time I see or hear them all laughing with the staff it cuts right through me. Being ignored is turning me into a right miserable bastard.

### November 18, 1996

I need to shoot off. He looks in a mood. I'll wait till I have a good game. Where is he? I can't find him. Oh well, let's jump in the car and do it tomorrow instead. Asking your boss if he would mind having a quick chat really shouldn't be this hard. Yet, like a petrified teenager too scared to ask a girl if she'd like to go to the cinema, I've spent the last fortnight chasing Arsene Wenger and bottling it completely.

It's me all over. If an awkward conversation needs to be had, or if bad news is in the offing, I'll bury my head in the sand and hope the problem goes away rather than face up to it. It's really quite embarrassing. But there's only so much you can take isn't there?

Senior players like Paul Dickov, Eddie McGoldrick and David Hillier have already been sold, and the reserve team training group gets younger and younger with every passing day. I don't even know half of their names. I'm fast becoming the last reject standing.

People often talk about reaching a breaking point and today I reach mine. Watching on with envy as Shawy and Hughesy are beckoned to join in with first team is one thing but I can't complain too much, as they're just as deserving as I am. But when three youth team lads get the nod ahead of you something has to be said, doesn't it?

How I get through training without lumping someone I

don't know. Steam is puffing out of my ears and poor old Geordie Armstrong, our coach, doesn't know how to react, bless him. I know he feels for me, and I know he feels I've been dumped on, but this is humiliation on a whole new level. I've played nine times for Arsenal and although I might not have set the world on fire, I have never let them down. They're not even trying to be subtle with me now.

So finally, I get around to having that word.

Stalking him like a deer after training as he stands alone in the dimly lit dressing room corridor, I eventually pounced. "Excuse me Mr Wenger, would it be possible for us to have a chat please?"

Appearing slightly puzzled, certainly taken aback, his eyes open wider. "Yes. Yes, of course," he replies rather seriously. "I can't speak now but if you call my secretary and make an appointment, we can meet at in my office at Highbury later in the week."

So I did. It was done. I don't know what all the fuss was about.

### *November 21, 1996*

Wenger's first team continue to fly along near the top of the table. I don't know if it's all that creatine powder or his coaching but they've been a team transformed this season - without me. They're persisting with the damned 5-3-2 system too, but with the monkey off my back, the spring has been back in my step this week regardless. I train well and in general, I guess I feel less of an embarrassment. Playing second fiddle to a bunch of teenagers isn't great for your self-esteem but at least, and at last, I've tried to do something about it.

However, as I trudge up Highbury's beautiful marble staircase in readiness to introduce myself to Arsene Wenger properly, that ebullience is fading fast. I feel tiny. A far cry from less than 12 months earlier, when I'd bounced up the same steps, having starred in a 3-0 home victory over QPR on my full home debut en route to a post-match interview in the press box with Capital Gold radio's Jonathan Pearce. With smiles, pats on the back and bundles of warmth I'd felt at home there.

Not this time.

I knock on the huge oak panelled door and there he is, the man who will decide my footballing fate. Wenger smiled welcomingly asking me to sit down. "So, why is it that you wanted to see me Adrian?" He knows my name. It's a good start. He's smiling too.

"Well, it's just that since you became manager, I haven't really had an opportunity to train properly with you and I haven't been in any of your match day squads as yet either," was my straight-to-the-point opening mumble-stroke-gambit.

"No…that's true. I have to be honest Adrian and admit that I haven't seen much of you yet. It's been difficult to see everyone properly so far."

"I know, and I feel as if I haven't really shone when you have been looking but it's just that last season I trained with the first team all season, and obviously I played eight times and was an unused substitute lots of other times too, yet now I am not being looked at all. We're not playing with wingers, I'm not comfortable at wing-back and it's affecting my confidence. After you had players much younger than me in your group this week, I just felt I had to say something."

"Hang on," paused the manager. "You played for the first team?"

"Yes!"

"I did not know this. I am really sorry. If I had known you were a first team player I would have looked much more closely at you. I apologise."

Flabbergasted. How? Why? Had the staff really not gone through each player and informed the manager of their backgrounds? I've been an Arsenal player since I was 11 years of age.

It's not the time to dwell on the disappointment however. I have to build on the progress made and I think I do it well. With the manager's interest pricked, we talk about the Maths and English A-levels I'd sat in my spare time, my international caps at junior levels, how Gunners scout Steve Rowley had spotted me at a five-a-side tournament over a decade ago and so on. It's a lovely, lovely chit-chat.

"Thank you for coming to see me today, Adrian. I will watch you much more closely from now on."

"Thank you, Mr Wenger."

I feel fantastic.

### December 4, 1996

I'm on loan at Rotherham United.

Buoyed by my meeting with the boss, I go out and produce my best performance of the season by a country mile against West Ham reserves at Highbury, scoring one and making the other. I'm later told Arsene Wenger only managed to catch the last five minutes. In fairness to the manager he keeps his word by involving me in a couple of training sessions preceding the game and I do OK, but this match was the big one; my chance to show him how good I can be.

Rotherham had watched the entirety of the game, and were impressed enough to propose a month's loan, so here I am. Rock bottom of the Second Division they might be, but it has to be better than training with the kids I'd thought.

I'm starting to wonder.

For a start the manager Danny Bergara doesn't know who I am when I meet him. "Adrian, my chief scout has brought you in, so I must admit I haven't seen you play before," he confesses.

Great.

"Can you do a job for me in the centre of midfield tonight?"

Jesus Christ.

Being polite, I promised to do my best in a position I had pretty much never played in before, but it doesn't do me any favours. I would say that I played in our 1-0 home defeat to Stockport County last night but that's probably stretching it. I was out there. And I'll leave it at that. Certainly the hype I'd spotted in the local newspaper before kick-off proclaiming the club's coup in signing an 'Arsenal whizz-kid' has probably faded away already.

### December 24, 1996

Dropped to the bench for Rotherham's next game at Notts County, and left as an unused sub at home to Plymouth Argyle on Saturday, I decide to knock the loan on its head early. It's a waste of time. Bergara doesn't need a winger and he isn't prepared to give me a chance in that position, so I am best off leaving before my confidence sinks any lower.

The whole thing is a farce.

So here I am, back at Arsenal. Back, in the wilderness. No one's says anything to me about what has happened but I can tell they're not happy. I suppose I've let them down. In fact I'm so far down the pecking order now that they give me the Christmas period off, telling me I can stay at home. It's the first time this has happened since I was in the youth team.

Merry Christmas.

### February 14, 1997

Arsene Wenger's first season at the club is winning him widespread respect and it's hard to argue that he and his players don't deserve it. They're still playing ever so well. Sadly I'm still not feeling the love and this perpetual nightmare continues. To be frank, it's got much, much, worse since I came back from Rotherham.

For a start, the changing rooms burned down while I was away. Rumour has it one of the trainees left the tumble dryer on and it blew up, sparking a blaze. No idea if it's true but it is an amusing story. Not so funny is the fact that the 'bomb squad' (and that's what we're called by the way), have to get changed in freezing cold, character-less Portakabins sat in the car park. The showers are at best lukewarm. It's soul-destroying.

Where are the high-flying first team? They're changing at nearby Sopwell House Hotel, a luxurious countryside establishment close to St Albans and they bus it in to the training ground each morning once they are kitted up. Not starting until 11am, and finishing shortly after 12, us stiffs hardly even see them anymore. Geordie Armstrong has all but given up too. "You might as well go home Clarkey," he says, less than an hour into the session. "We've only got nine bodies and there's f*** all we can do with that number."

It's a sign of the times. A 'them and us' attitude is developing, and unless you're one of them, it's difficult not to feel unloved. The problem is, with Arsenal playing well and unquestionably improving under the new regime, it's not even as if I have a right to complain. Why would they change things?

### February 17, 1997

And I thought Patrick Vieira was good.

Today I play with this 17-year-old French kid called Nico. His full name is Nicolas Anelka, I believe. He arrives just before kick-off against Norwich City reserves, wearing jeans and a t-shirt, but definitely no smile. As he sits there looking disinterested and lost, we assume he's just another moody trialist but it's obvious from Geordie's fawning that here's a player that is of interest. And in fairness to him, he doesn't actually speak any English.

And just as it did in September when I played alongside Vieira on his club debut for the reserves, Nico's football speaks for itself. After his registration comes through during the opening 45 minutes, he comes on at half-time and leaves an indelible mark on all of us who witness it. Fast? This kid is pure lightning. A step above any other 17-year-old I've ever seen that's for sure. He's set to sign next week I believe, and alongside Vieira, it's clear that Wenger's standards are incredibly high.

I wonder - being completely honest with myself - if I am actually up to that standard. I know I've moaned and groaned this season and there's no question I've been hard done by, but these two players are younger than me, and appear to be quite a bit better than me too. Never before have I felt as if I wasn't good enough to be an Arsenal player.

It's a worry.

### March 26, 1997

In my kit and just about to go out for my warm-up at the Vetch Field ahead of a game away to Swansea City, Geordie runs in out of breath with a message. "Clarkey, Southend are on the phone. They want to take you on loan for the rest of the season."

Good news.

"Ronnie Whelan's waiting for you on the line, do you want to speak to him?"

Of course I do!

"Adrian, how are you mate?" It's definitely Ronnie Whelan's voice, putting pay to a momentary fear that it's a wind-up.

"Not too bad thanks Ronnie."

"Do you want to sign for us till the end of the season, like? I know we're bottom of the First Division and it isn't looking great for us but we've got some good players and I think you'll fit right in."

"Yes, it sounds good. I'm keen."

"Do you like a drink?"

I pause. What's the right answer? Is it a trick question?

"Er, yes I guess so. On a Saturday night I'll have a couple. You know, nothing too crazy."

"Right," he pauses, in that familiar Irish-Scouse accent of his. "It's just that we've got a cracking set of drinkers at the club and there's all sorts of banter flying about the place, you know. I think you'll have fun."

"Count me in Ronnie, I'll see you tomorrow."

So, a bit different to Arsene Wenger then!

### May 9, 1997

The loan spell goes fantastically well.

OK, as expected Southend get relegated but I'd play all seven First Division games in my favourite position as a left winger, and I acquit myself pretty well. As Ronnie had promised, it's also a lot of fun too. Happier as a player and as a person for the experience, I approach today, D-Day, in a pretty good mood, even though I've been summoned to Sopwell House to learn my fate.

Arsenal have finished third and qualified for the UEFA Cup, proving unequivocally that I haven't been missed. With less than two months of my contract to run, I know the chances of a surprise renewal are slim in the extreme. I drive quietly; resigned to the likelihood I'll hear bad news. News that if I'm honest, 18 months ago and stretching back over the last decade, I never expected to hear. I thought I would be a Gunner forever.

But I am 22 now. I'm an excellent player, good enough to have been treated better this season, certainly. I showed last year that I have the ability to play with the very best and hold my own but at this level, talent alone isn't enough. And football's changing. The game seems to be embracing power and pace more than ever before and I have neither in abundance.

Am I honestly capable of making a real difference to Arsene Wenger's fast developing side next season? No, I am not, and although it pains me to admit it, I know it's true. That's a job for kids like Patrick Vieira and Nicolas Anelka. So bizarrely, and even though I've been part of the furniture for 11 years, the prospect of being told it's the end of the road for me at Arsenal isn't that scary at all. In a strange way, being put out of my misery might be a relief. The club's already moved on without me, it just needs rubber stamping.

On time and with butterflies knotting my stomach nevertheless, I enter the restaurant as planned, to meet with my master, Arsene Wenger. Probably, for the final time.

"Adrian, I hear that you did well at Southend, did you enjoy it?"

"Yes boss, I had a great time. It was a fantastic experience."

"Well…" this was it, I sense it. "Even though you did well, I am not going to offer you a new contract with Arsenal."

I hide my disappointment with a resigned nod.

"At your age, you need first team football and I'm afraid that you don't figure in my first team plans for next season," he continues. "I know that Southend would like to keep you, but they don't have a big budget to pay us a fee, so we have decided to try and make it easier for you by not asking for compensation. I hope that this helps you find a new club, whether it is there or somewhere else."

"Yes that's great of you…" I smile. "Thank you. Thank you for everything. I am sure I will sort myself out and who knows, I might even prove you wrong."

He stands. I stand. We shake hands and he wishes me good luck.

So there it is. After no more than three or four perfectly amicable minutes, my long-standing relationship with Arsenal is officially over. Shaking a little, I stroll out of the restaurant, passing Luton Town's Matthew Upson in the foyer as I calmly head towards my car. One in, one out I think with a wry smile.

I look around the car park and back into the hotel entrance, and no one is looking. Everyone going about their daily business, there are no goodbyes. I unlock my car and deliberately place the key into the ignition. I pause with a deep breath. And then, from nowhere, I cry my eyes out.

## Chapter 3

# Feast and Famine

## John Cross

Being an Arsenal fan has been a thrilling roller coaster ride under Arsene Wenger. Incredible highs and depressing lows compete for attention in the home cinema of the mind. From the day Arsenal won their first trophy under Wenger in 1998, the club went on to enjoy seven years of feast, quickly followed by seven years of famine.

Wenger was a revolutionary, a relative unknown in English football who transformed the most traditional of Premier League clubs into being a Continental team, full of flair, trophies and drama. Gone was the Arsenal known for the boring 1-0 wins, the Bank of England club with a resistance to change and foreign influence. Suddenly, Arsenal were becoming known as one of the best footballing teams in Europe who were sweeping all before them in England.

Two Premier League and FA Cup Doubles, two more FA Cups, a fixture in the Champions League and, most impressive of all, the Invincibles season of 2003/04 when they won the title while unbeaten. It is hard to believe that, since those glorious seven years of success, nothing has followed. Title challenges and cup finals have come and gone without success. It must go beyond the quality of player. If Wenger was able to spot players before, then why not now? Where have the athletic giants of the Invincibles era gone? Is it a mental problem which is holding Arsenal back?

One player who arrived during the glorious era and departed after the last trophy - the 2005 FA Cup - had been won is Sol Campbell. He is brutally honest about Arsenal's current failings on the pitch, but perhaps an anecdote from the Invincibles season is even more instructive. There has to be a win-at-all-costs mentality in a successful team whereby the wrong attitude is not tolerated by team mates.

Arsenal's finest year was, of course, the Invincibles' season. And they clinched the title at White Hart Lane, home of their great rivals Tottenham. But, rather than win it in style with a victory over their bitter neighbours, they threw away a 2-1 lead and drew 2-2. Temperamental keeper Jens Lehmann lost his cool after Robbie Keane wound him up and conceded a penalty.

Campbell, the former Spurs captain who defected across north London, was in no mood to celebrate and had to have it out with Lehmann before the lap of honour began: "I was pissed off. We should have won that day but Jens was stupid. Robbie Keane tried to back into him, wind him up and stepped on him. Jens just lost it. We were 2-1 up, it was game over and yet that let them back into it and they scored with a penalty.

"We had a massive argument in the changing rooms. That's me. I want to win. I wanted to win the game. You know, a draw was enough but I wasn't happy at all. It was me in the dressing room, Jens and Arsene Wenger. Believe me, I wasn't happy. We'd won the Premier League - and yet I wasn't happy at all. I respected Jens and we had it out and then went back out to celebrate on the pitch."

It is clear that Campbell respects Lehmann but that flash

point tells you everything you need to know about the spirit in the camp. Winning was essential. Everything else was a disappointment. When they had a little wobble after going out of the Champions League to Chelsea in April, up stepped their big players. Thierry Henry, almost single-handedly, rescued a topsy-turvy game with Liverpool at Highbury when they twice went behind. Henry scored a brilliant hat-trick and took the game by the scruff of the neck.

Contrast that to 2011/12 season. Arsenal had the chance to go eight points clear in third place when they played struggling Wigan at home. They conceded two early goals, lost Mikel Arteta - such a calming and experienced influence - to injury and then took just three points from their next 12 games. Arsenal had the mother of all wobbles and, despite his outstanding season, Robin van Persie was unable to steady the ship as captain. Wenger's men eventually clinched third and that was seen as success even though it completed a seventh season without a trophy.

There have been slim pickings for Arsenal of late. Wenger has gone for youth, speed and development. Back in the Invincibles era - and when the Double and FA Cup were won in 2002 and 2005 respectively - they were a team of giants in every sense. Campbell, Patrick Vieira, Lehmann and Henry. They also had such talent - Robert Pires, Freddie Ljungberg, Kolo Toure and Dennis Bergkamp. You could take your pick out of those players for world class talents and also a wonderful mentality, having gained success and experience on various levels. Been there, done that, won it.

Campbell refers to the missing quality of today's generation as "the edge." It's something that perhaps defines the difference between the golden era and the era of nearly men since 2005. The football remains spectacular, there is always drama and a story. But van Persie has carried the team at times and Campbell insists that they will not get back to the previous heights without a major sea change.

Campbell provides a fascinating insight into what made the Invincibles special. Not just one danger man like van Persie, but five, six or seven. Henry, Bergkamp, Pires, Ljungberg, Jose Antonio Reyes, Kanu, Sylvain Wiltord. These days Campbell looks on and compares the current team with a wry smile and regret. He firmly believes they need more quality to start winning trophies again. Straight talking, winners, tough training and sheer determination.

"If they don't buy players then it will be the same again. With the team they've got, even with everyone fit then I still don't think it's enough. They need some more players who can make a difference. They need players who can give them the edge. It's all about the edge. Who has got the edge? If you haven't got enough players on the pitch who can't make a difference or provide that edge then it's never going to be enough.

"Any team can lock down a team who only has even just two players who are a little bit different and can provide something different for the team. If a team has got four or five players who can make a difference plus maybe two on the bench then you always have a good chance of winning something in any season. When I was in the Invincibles, it was an incredible experience to play in that team. Talk about players who had that edge!

"It was fantastic. The team was full of great guys, played fantastic football and we had a really strong spirit there. Sometimes we had our arguments but sometimes that's good because it clears the air and you go again. I love the game of football, training, banter and going in to win. You can't beat that winning feeling. But you have to lose to learn to win. We had a lot of players who had strong minds in that Arsenal squad and that's what I like about it. We had players who could say something and say it to a team mate, who wouldn't start crying in the corner because they couldn't take it.

"As long as it was founded and valid it was accepted. That's what I liked. The qualities of the squad and the players were immense. We had guys in there who weren't coming to the end of their careers but they were 30, still tremendous athletes, great guys and always had the will to win. It didn't matter who scored the goal, who won the game for the team. That's what you want because you are together as a team. Every day you try hard in training, keep on improving, keep on excelling and keep on pushing yourself. It was fantastic at that time. Arsene just had to sit back and control a few things while everyone got on with it. But you need that to produce that sort of consistency."

Arsenal had a wonderful consistency during the glory years. They also had a knack of signing top class players. In fact, not just top class players but World Cup winners.

Arsenal's former vice-chairman David Dein took great delight in introducing Gilberto Silva on a pre-season tour in 2002. "Meet our new World Cup winner, Gilberto Silva." Dein was and is a shrewd political operator. His relationship with Wenger remains strong largely thanks to the fact he brokered the deal to install the Frenchman at the club after meeting him at various football functions. They met at Cup draws, technical meetings and formed a powerful alliance.

Dein had a persuasive manner with Wenger, not just in installing him as manager. He influenced him to bring in players and get them to sign with his "lucky pen." The pen was used to recruit Henry, a flop at Juventus, but a World

Cup winner with everything to prove and Arsenal goalscoring records to break. The Campbell coup, signing him on a free from Tottenham, was another audacious transfer. Vieira was recruited from AC Milan reserves. Emmanuel Petit was attracted by Wenger's pulling power and their French connection.

They were not always big players in terms of reputation, but Arsenal had a particular niche in the market. If Wenger was reluctant to go the extra yard for a player then Dein would push him over the line. Since Dein's departure, the club has increasingly become more about a business model than building a dream team. Chief executive Ivan Gazidis runs a tight ship. He runs the club cautiously and is a brilliant administrator. Wenger has also signed up to that model.

Wenger loves to develop players. But at a club like Arsenal, there is an impatience for success. It is almost like there have been two eras of Wenger's management. The feast of 1998-2005 and the famine ever since. Great promise, but a failure to realise potential. Again, Lehmann offers an insight into what is required at a club like Arsenal and what is needed to deliver success: "You have to have something extra to play for Arsenal, something special and the right mentality. You can be a good player but it has to be a good player who is a winner and knows how to win trophies. When we had that unbeaten run we just didn't know how to lose."

There can be no doubt after the glory of 2004 and 2005 Wenger changed direction. He did stick with a 4-4-2 system all the way to the Champions League final in 2006 when they lost to Barcelona. Wenger will always claim they were 13 minutes away from victory with just ten men, just like they were a Nicklas Bendtner miss away from knocking out Barcelona in the Nou Camp in 2011. But there have been too many near misses to think it is bad luck. Arsenal were genuine title contenders in 2008 and yet fell short.

Time and again, Arsenal players have left blaming the club rather than themselves for a failure to win trophies. That says much about Samir Nasri and Gael Clichy. But in joining Manchester City, clearly the belief had gone that Arsenal could deliver the trophies in the way they used to. Wenger dismantled the great teams of 1998, 2002 and 2004 and built again with varying degrees of success.

Do not forget the humiliation of 2001, when Arsenal lost 6-1 at Manchester United. Arsenal's response was to sign Campbell, Gilberto and Giovanni van Bronckhorst. The latter was not a great success but went on to reach a World Cup final. However, Arsenal's defeat at Manchester United in August 2011 was followed by a supermarket sweep which brought in Mikel Arteta, Per Mertesacker and Andre Santos. Arteta has been a fabulous unsung hero and has the sort of attitude which has been much needed. But none of them are World Cup winners like Gilberto or experienced campaigners like Campbell.

The change does not just stop there. Wenger has switched to a 4-3-3 system. It's all about smaller players, intricate passing movements and subtleties. Sometimes they over-played and over-elaborated, but it was good to watch. However, if an opposing team didn't play fair then Wenger would pick up his ball, go home and sulk afterwards. There was a bite to go with the flair in 2004. But with Vieira's departure went that ferocity and instead it was about small ball players who struggled to mix it.

The 1998 team's attack was based around Bergkamp, an ageing Ian Wright and Nicolas Anelka who was poached from Paris Saint Germain for just £500,000 and turned into a striker who went onto play for Real Madrid, Liverpool and Chelsea in a chequered career. That's fine when you have the fans' confidence. But when that is being tested, they get fed-up with bargain buys of potential and want the ready made article to provide the answer.

Back in the earlier days, Wenger was prepared to spend big. Henry, Reyes and Wiltord all cost above £10m. Arsenal still seem to have a problem going much above that figure. They have been left behind in the transfer market while other clubs have improved their scouting network and Arsenal are no longer picking up the relative unknowns and turning them into big stars.

Kolo Toure was a great example. Came from nowhere - he was born in Ivory Coast and was signed for just £150,000 from ASEC Mimosas after a trial - and yet became a legend in the Invincibles. Who was the last one like that? Maybe Robin van Persie. But he was signed from Feyenoord as a hot head who had played regularly for the Dutch junior teams. Hardly a fair comparison.

That avenue has been shut down. And yet people for years marvelled at the way Wenger plucked players from obscurity and had them winning trophies months later. That was part of his charm. It became part of the Arsenal way. Yet during the barren years, the wonder has turned to frustration among the fans. If he does sign a smaller name or a gamble then the fans are in uproar because they want a bigger name who will deliver instant success. They are fed up waiting, fed up with the promise of jam tomorrow.

Quite simply Arsenal have become a selling club. The philosophy has changed. The Emirates Stadium is magnificent and 60,000 flock to most home games. However, Arsenal are tied to their mortgage and, despite having the best match day turnover in the country, they are a club who need to pay the bills. In recent times, the exodus has become frequent, painful and annual. Henry went to Barcelona but since then there has almost been a direct line to Manchester City. Emmanuel Adebayor, Gael Clichy, Samir Nasri and Kolo Toure all went for big money to the Etihad.

Other players regard Arsenal as no longer big players in the market. One former player put up his status on his Blackberry Messenger as: Leave Arsenal Win Trophies. It's hard to disagree.

Wenger used to enjoy parading the trophies to Islington Town Hall. They were heady days and great achievements. Great football, too. Arsenal were transformed from being the boring team under George Graham which ground out 1-0 wins, to being exciting and successful under Wenger. He won the Double in 1998 after winning at Manchester United, hauling back a seemingly impossible points deficit to win the title for the first time in seven years.

But Arsenal did it in style, too. Wenger inherited the famous back four of Dixon, Bould, Adams, and Winterburn and had David Seaman. Vieira and Emmanuel Petit ruled midfield, Marc Overmars on the flank and world class strikers up front. It was a superb team. But when Petit and Overmars were sold, Arsenal rose again and Wenger built again. They won the Double in 2002 and clinched the title at Old Trafford. Wiltord was bought for big money, Campbell signed on a big deal and Henry and Pires had also been brought in.

They blew it in 2003 - in those days the FA Cup was seen as a disappointment and beating Southampton barely warranted a celebration dinner - and yet grew strong in 2004. By the Invincibles' season, Arsenal only had to trot out onto the pitch to frighten the opposition. Even Sir Alex Ferguson has admitted he redefined the identikit of his ideal player after seeing the Invincibles beat up their team once too often.

Arsenal made history that season, going through the whole campaign unbeaten. Wenger had claimed it was possible the previous year and got laughed at. That humiliation only inspired him to prove people wrong the following year. The unbeaten run reached 49 games before United got rough, Wayne Rooney dived and Arsenal lost their sequence at the hands of their biggest rivals. Jose Mourinho arrived on the scene and Chelsea began to dominate. Arsenal won the 2005 FA Cup but that season was all about a hangover in the league from losing that record. Arsenal have struggled to recover since.

Arsenal reached the 2006 Champions League final and came close - even with ten men - against Barcelona. Wenger, true to form, began to break up the team. Tomas Rosicky, Alexander Hleb and Cesc Fabregas made up the midfield. They were all about being small, skilful, intricate and full of flair. Wenger had been there, done that and won it with the Invincibles and this was a new challenge with a new style. And yet it didn't work.

They fell further behind. Chelsea bullied and beat a mix-and-match Arsenal team made up of some younger faces and first team old hands in the 2007 Carling Cup final. It was a close final, but Chelsea were miles ahead in the league. Didier Drogba, Michael Essien, Ricardo Carvalho and John Terry were powerful and made Chelsea look unbeatable. Arsenal were falling behind. They came back in 2007/08 to mount a serious title challenge which fell away after Eduardo broke his leg in horrific fashion at Birmingham.

Their challenge fell away from the moment they conceded

late on and drew 2-2 at St Andrews and the Eduardo injury was blamed in part. That excuse typified Arsenal in that they did not have the leaders or mental strength to recover. Arsenal were selling and replacing with players who were not as good as their predecessors. They have struggled to find the midfield general to replace Vieira or even Gilberto. When you are not winning and selling then it is almost as if you are inviting the biggest names to sulk and get away. Fabregas, Nasri and Adebayor did just that.

Wenger still has a clever knack. The signing of Bacary Sagna was barely heralded but he has been the best right back in the Premier League since his arrival. Sadly, Sagna may end up going the same way. Alex Song was transformed from hopeless into sought after midfield giant. If all of his team mates go, then who can blame him if he wants to go next? That's what happens at a selling club.

Arsenal went close to ending the barren run in 2011 when they reached the Carling Cup final and were red-hot favourites. But they fell behind, came back to level and then blew it in the final minutes when a mix up between Wojciech Szczesny and Laurent Koscielny gave Obafemi Martins an open invitation to win it for Birmingham. They hardly had a team of proven winners, but they beat Arsenal. It's not so much that teams need a winning mentality but belief would be a start. Arsenal have lost that belief.

Wenger has always disregarded the Carling Cup as something of a pointless exercise. But it meant a lot in 2011. Arsenal's season unravelled after that Wembley heartbreak in late February. Their rather optimistic hopes of a quadruple soon went. Their league form nose dived, they crashed out of the FA Cup and even a win over Barcelona at the Emirates was forgotten because they lost in the Nou Camp and crashed out. It's become a rather familiar Arsenal excuse from fans to say they have beaten Barcelona, the best team in Europe. That's all they've had to cling to for far too long. Near misses, pretty football and waving goodbye to hero after hero.

Wenger refuses to give up on his principles. Playing good football, not paying over the odds on contracts or transfer fees and giving youth its chance. Perhaps the flirtation with mid-table mediocrity in the 2011/12 season gave Arsenal fans a timely reminder that you cannot take a Champions League place for granted. But it's not a trophy. The accusation is that Arsenal have become more obsessed with the balance sheet than the football.

Arsenal are in a healthy financial state but don't compete any more with the likes of Manchester City, Manchester United or Chelsea either in terms of finance or success. In the early Wenger era, Arsenal came back after barren seasons to enjoy new success. With each passing season the good old days seem harder to remember and the hope of new success seems further away than ever. Wenger is unquestionably the finest manager Arsenal have ever had. But in a different age and era when money rules the roost over traditional management skills, he is struggling to keep up.

## Chapter 4

# Big in China

## Dominic Fifield

Mid-afternoon in Manchuria, and Daqing, an ugly industrial outpost that scars the Heilongjiang wilderness, sweats in the blistering heat. To the north, hidden in the haze, lie the virgin forests and rugged mountains of the sub-Siberian wasteland. Lost from view to the west stretch the steppe of Inner Mongolia. The whiff of petroleum clings in the oppressive heat, betraying this far flung region's practical function to the State, though the locals have grown used to the stench. Today they have at least been offered a distraction from the monotonous grind, flocking in their thousands to the municipal stadium, klaxons blaring and flags waving, with the ground heaving at capacity. It has been for four hours.

It is 15 July, 1999, and the hooters are bellowing in celebration of the most high-profile sporting event to have been staged in this remote corner of north-east China. The week to follow will be dominated locally by the Daqing Games, but it is the curtain-raiser that has fired the imagination. The acrobats and dancers, performing in traditional dress as platoons of brass bands parade the running track and stony-faced soldiers ring the pitch, are the *hors d'oeuvre* to the main event: the first visit of a western football team to this politically sensitive province. The stadium is the size of the average League One ground back home but, today, it sighs to the hubbub of 30,000 people, all of whom thrill at the prospect of welcoming household names to their home town. The quirk is this is no visit from Manchester United or Real Madrid, the adoring chants going up not for David Beckham or Raúl but for Lee Bradbury and Clinton Morrison. Crystal Palace are in town.

Looking back, the whole scenario still feels unlikely. Palace, of the Nationwide First Division, were a club gasping in administration, their daily financial affairs overseen by the corporate recovery specialists Moore Stephen Booth White, a firm of insolvency practitioners who had been installed in the Portakabins at Selhurst Park earlier in the year when Mark Goldberg's money had run out seven months into his chairmanship. The club creaked under onerous debts, their best players flogged at knockdown prices and 46 members of staff sacked. They did not own their stadium, revenue streams had dried up, and no prospective saviours had been earmarked. The situation felt vaguely hopeless. Remarkably, the administrators would remain in charge until the summer of 2000. And yet, in China, this team on its knees were pioneers. Even trailblazers.

Admittedly, English clubs had visited before. In May 1995, a year after the Chinese league had turned professional, Arsenal had played a friendly against Beijing Gou'an in front of 60,000 fascinated fans at the capital's Workers' stadium, the locals prevailing 1-0, presumably much to the relief of the organisers given the government dignitaries in attendance at the game. Go back even further and, in 1978, West Bromwich Albion travelled east in a trip best remembered for the midfielder John Trewick's apparently tongue in cheek reaction to his first sight of the Great Wall. "Impressive, isn't it?" he was caught on camera saying. "But once you've seen one wall, you've seen them all." He has never been allowed to forget that quip. United, Treble winners the previous season with memories of their unlikely European Cup success in Barcelona still fresh, would make a whistle-stop visit to Beijing before the summer of 1999 was out.

Yet, despite those previous flirtations with top flight sides, no English club had embarked on a tour as far-reaching as Palace's, a two-week expedition into the unknown that took in the relative comfort and familiarity of Beijing and Shanghai before venturing off the beaten track – via a series of hair-raising internal flights – to Kunming in the steamy south and Daqing nearer the Russian border in the north. A year later they would return, with a squad further stripped to its bare bones by 16 months of cost-cutting, to be welcomed in the cities of Xi'an and Nanchang though, by then, it already felt old hat. In Daqing, which literally translates as "great celebration" but is a town founded on and sustained by oil, the team had been granted rare access to a region that has no reason to be on the tourist trail. It was not geared for high-profile visits. Foreigners spotted in the city tended to be presumed to be smugglers or, worse still, spies. Daqing's population tops three million and yet it is omitted on most maps, its Wikipedia entry revealing it is, somewhat bafflingly, paired with relatively glamorous Calgary in Canada and, maybe more appropriately, Luhansk in Ukraine. It is nondescript. Grey. Freezing in winter, baking in summer. A working city in the workers' country.

It had taken the team's three minibuses four hours to chug up the potholed road from Harbin, with its Russian-influenced onion topped buildings and emerging downtown, a journey offering panoramic views of fields stretching to the horizon and few clues that this is China's industrial heartland, a region that has been occupied by the Russians and the Japanese in recent times and repatriated by the Chinese at a bloody cost. The convoy of vehicles flitting through the croplands was an oddity for those agricultural workers shaded in wicker hats who cared to glance up, their daily slog interrupted by the growl of the distant engines.

The squad arrived to find Daqing in the midst of a full-scale building project – hotels, garages and factories rising all around – with their own accommodation at the Zhing Ping Zunlian Ji Di centre distinctly basic even if the welcome was warm. The water would run murky brown in most of the rooms, the kit man forced to sleep wrapped in a wet towel when his air conditioning unit coughed and spluttered before ceasing to function altogether. The building, draped in red and blue in the visitors' honour, doubled up as the national table tennis centre, six-year-old prodigies patting their ping pong balls metronomically through training bouts in the foyer. But there was no internet connection available and only one telephone capable of making international calls – the bill was bicycled round from the post office some 24 hours later to be settled – with mobile reception, at best, sporadic. It was hardly the ideal location for the administrator, Simon Paterson, to conduct his search for prospective new owners.

The welcome reception comprised a five-course banquet, staff lining the walls of the dining room to peer, intrigued, at the motley crew of track-suited players melting in the heat. Some of the more hyper-active members of the squad, Morrison principal among them, had their hosts in fits of the giggles. The striker has been a blur of energy throughout his professional career but, in China, his antics took on added comic value: whether it was the impromptu break-dancing; the constant chatter in broad Sarf London; or his stroppy reaction to being reprimanded by one of the coaching staff, or beaten by one of the local table tennis talents. The staff at the Zhing Ping Zunlian Ji Di found him a novelty, but they could not do enough for him. The visit of an English football club had taken on huge political significance. It was an event for an otherwise forgotten city to cherish, with the game, against Dalian Wanda from the Liaoning peninsular to the south of the province, to be broadcast via satellite television to millions.

The visitors' unlikely popularity owed everything to two local faces within the Palace ranks. Back in the autumn of 1998, when Goldberg's grand vision had seen Terry Venables installed as manager and all the chairman's personal money poured into an ill-conceived transfer policy, the South London club had negotiated the purchase of the China national captain Fan Zhiyi and his compatriot Sun Jihai from Shanghai Shenhua and Dalian, ground-breaking moves sanctioned by the Chinese Football Association for a fee of around £950,000. While Sun, who would return to England with Manchester City later in his career, was a youngster still forging his reputation, Fan was already a national icon who enjoyed status comparable to that of the fresh-faced Beckham.

His image stared down from billboards in his native Shanghai, his sponsorship deals extensive and lucrative even within the heart of modern Communism. Fan could click his fingers and, as Palace discovered numerous times on the tour, even representatives of the State would busy themselves cutting the red tape. When the internal airlines had sought to charge the tourists £500 for every skip of dirty kit or bag of footballs, fees the administrator could neither justify nor meet, the China captain had intervened and the charges were suddenly waived. His influence was considerable.

The centre-half had married an air hostess who, overnight, had effectively become China's first lady of football, a WAG before her time, and the 27-year-old had been eager to experience the west. Whether a semi-detached in East Croydon and 88 games with a club in the second tier of English football fulfilled his ambitions is not clear, but his standing soared regardless. "I don't think any of us quite realised just how much he is admired," said the Australian midfielder Nicky Rizzo at the time. "They just follow him, staring at his every move. He's mobbed on every street corner, gets VIP treatment wherever he goes. What he says, they do. That's just the way it is. He's a local hero, a football star and the Chinese captain. A celebrity. Palace don't have very many of those."

The club had spied a marketing opportunity. Football was growing in China, enthusiasm for the game swelling as the national team, briefly coached by the Englishman Ted Buxton, steadily ascended the Fifa rankings. It was overtaking table tennis as the nation's favourite to the extent that, when China failed to qualify for the 1998 World Cup, a formal apology had to be issued to the Chinese people for such unforgivable under-achievement. They would reach the tournament four years later, failing to glean either a point or a goal in their group, but, by then, their powerhouse potential was established.

Clubs and politicians alike in the United Kingdom had been keen to cash in. The Prime Minister Tony Blair, seeking to forge links with the globe's fastest growing economy, had visited a few months after Palace took the plunge with Fan and Sun, leaping on the bandwagon to promote "football diplomacy". He departed heartened, even if he had been denied the chance to enjoy the PR coup of a kick-about for the massed cameras by overzealous security guards. Even so, the business strategy to tap into Chinese football felt basic, revolving initially around Shanghai Shenhua's shirts being sponsored by Perkins Engines of Peterborough.

Even so, Palace had bought into the concept. The impact made by Fan and Sun on the pitch over their first season in the Nationwide League was rather wrecked by disciplinary problems – both players were sent off twice, Fan's second dismissal coming after he shoved the referee, Paul Rejer, in a 6-0 loss at Loftus Road – with communication clearly an issue, but Palace, rarely higher than mid-table and eventually in administration, had never enjoyed such positive exposure. When Sheffield United, then sixth, visited Venables' 19th placed side in the September of 1998, the game was broadcast to an audience of more than 100m people back in China through Chinese Central TV, a subscriber channel, and the pay-per-view Shanghai Cable. More people watched the home side win 1-0, courtesy of a Sasa Curcic goal, than tuned in for the Super Bowl that year. At the time, Palace were perceived to be bigger than United or Liverpool, Milan or Juventus, albeit only in the distant single-party and politically repressive People's Republic.

Had the market truly been tapped thereafter then the club's potential could have dwarfed that of any oligarch's play-thing but, just like Palace's "team of the 80s", this would all prove a false dawn. Some clubs have succeeded in making money from China, Real Madrid taking in around £10m from sales of replica shirts and tickets from their tours in 2003 and 2005 and the Italian Football Federation occasionally taking its Super Cup game to Beijing, but the figures are not dramatic. Certainly not in the context of those organisations' turnovers. In May 2011, Chelsea hired ECN Management, a company claiming to have expertise in China, to find branding opportunities for the likes of Fernando Torres and 17 of his team-mates, whose image rights were owned by the London club. There has been exposure since, and pre-season matches in Macau and Guangzhou, but the sense that the world's most populous country – with its emerging wealth, political influence and burgeoning economy – is untapped lingers still. As Palace discovered over a decade ago, China can feel impenetrable.

The tour conducted in 1999, more so than the follow-up a year later, probably amounted to Palace's only significant money-making achievement in their unlikely dealings with Asia, and then only because the event was sponsored by Richard Branson's Virgin, who were keen to promote their success in pipping British Airways to the new Shanghai to Heathrow route. The entrepreneur, accompanied by Eddie George, the governor of the Bank of England, had met the squad on the tarmac upon arrival at Shanghai Pudong international airport, with Fan duly shoved to the foreground in most of the PR photo-calls. Virgin's involvement cut down on major travel costs and maximised the kitty from associated sponsorship deals.

Indeed, the club made certain they returned in profit, if lighter in numbers, by selling Sun back to Dalian while on the trip, ensuring one debt of around £525,000 was wiped out. There were monies left over to meet the summer's wage demands and fund the administration until the start of the domestic campaign. "The injection of cash into the coffers will keep the wolves from the door for the near future," said the managing director, Phil Alexander, as the deal for the full-back was finalised. Officially, Sun was homesick. In truth, Palace needed the money and Dalian, bottom of the domestic league, had come under pressure from the town's mayor to re-sign their talisman. Everything boiled down to politics. The British embassy in Beijing had welcomed Steve Coppell's side as "ambassadors for English football", suggesting this was about more than future sponsorship deals, prestige friendlies and some share of the take from television revenues. As it was, most of Palace's own heady aspirations ended up being dashed.

What those on the four-match trip did gain was an unexpected insight into a country which, at the time, still felt secretive. It was as if the squad – complete with their novice media officer, recently taken on as a trainee by *The Guardian* but now charged with everything from conducting press conferences, keeping a record of the trip on the disposable cameras purchased at departures in London (another reminder of financial constraints), informing players of any rumours of interest from rival clubs that had surfaced back home, and filing from the tour on the club laptop when internet connections permitted – had been deposited unwittingly into the script of a Carry On film. Palace had traditionally spent pre-season rattling up cricket scores against amateur teams in Scandinavia, easing their way smoothly and efficiently into the domestic calendar. There was something comfortable about those trips to Iceland and Sweden. It felt like gentle preparation. In contrast, upon arrival in Shanghai on 4 July, 1999, the squad tumbled into new territory.

It had all started as it would go on. The minibus transporting the coaching and back-room staff from Beijing Capital international airport to the team hotel broke down at the junction of two three-lane super highways with a passing policeman, his mood best described as livid once he'd realised Fan was not on board, ordering the passengers out into the 35 degree heat and on-rushing traffic while the panicked chauffeur poked nervously at the steaming engine. The driver, to his immense credit, did eventually manage to restart the bus but clearly felt he could not risk stalling again, meaning every red traffic light thereafter was run as those terrified in the back choked on the plumes of black smoke that filled the cabin. It felt appropriate that a trek into the unknown should begin in such hair-raising manner.

This was a trip of contrasts: from the relatively western-ised Shanghai and central Beijing, complete with Las Vegas style hotels on the drag up to Tian'anmen square; to the up-and-coming Kunming in the fertile plains of the Yunnan plateau; and the rough and ready Daqing. Everywhere the tourists went, the locals were in awe. That clearly owed much to Fan's presence, but Palace's other players, many of whom had yet to establish themselves in the second tier of the English game, were genuinely known. The likes of Steve Thomson and Wayne Carlisle enjoyed a status above their status. The players and staff, including the media officer, were mobbed wherever they went, perfecting their autograph techniques in the process. There were elaborate welcoming ceremonies to accompany the press conferences at the hotels en route, banners fluttering in the streets depicting the likes of Hayden Mullins and Andy Linighan, Attilio Lombardo and Matt Jansen (both of whom had been sold in the mid-season cull the previous year). Most of the squad would have gone unrecognised back in South London – some might have done so out on the turf at Selhurst Park – with this a taste of how the other half lived.

The players, the odd predictable grumble aside, flung themselves into the experience. They plodded up and down a stretch of the Great Wall, returning laden with tacky souvenirs – Morrison purchased a decorative sword which he insisted was a gift for his mother though, unsurprisingly, it did not make it through customs – and even tucked in with relish to the local delicacies served up on the regular welcome banquets. Pre-match meals at Palace normally consisted of baked beans on toast. In China, there were seven-course formal dinners involving roasted bats' wings and griddled forest dog. There were explosive incidents after brushes with duck's eyeballs, boiled whole chickens – complete with heads – and mallard's brains, the richness of the local delicacies costing three players an appearance against Gou'an as they spent their days bent double over their hotel room toilets. Rizzo, who had previously escaped any cramps, ended up sprinting out of one training session having been caught decidedly short. He ended dismayed that the dressing room cubicles had not been restocked with toilet roll, a sense of pained anguish later shared by the kit man.

There was a snake dish to celebrate Coppell's 44th birthday midway through the trip, a meal spent in the roof bar of a little restaurant opposite the hotel and interrupted by a large rat which scurried across the terrace disturbing chairs and tables. The manager was fascinated by the culture into which he and his squad had been flung. He kept the younger members of the party in check as best he could, reprimanding two, who have both since gone on to play in the Premier League, for spending more time engrossed in their handheld games consoles than the splendour of their surroundings on one visit to the tombs of the Ming dynasty outside Beijing.

Coppell also had practical concerns. The start of the new league campaign was less than a month away and some of the training facilities in China were, at best, basic. In the sticky heat of Kunming the squad had travelled to the National Sports Centre, on the banks of Lake Dian Chi, with high hopes to work at the Chinese equivalent of the Football Association's St George's Park complex only to find the pitches saturated after heavy rainfall, the team wading through the session as if playing on a paddy field. Throw in the fact that the Yunnan plateau lies 2,000 metres above sea level, making breathing difficult, and the reality that the hedged perimeter to the pitch had been colonised by a mass of sinister looking spiders – hanging menacingly on the webs as if casting judgement on the accuracy of the players' shooting – to make retrieving balls an anxious process, and there were times when the coaching staff despaired. These days, with western powerhouses regular summer visitors, one suspects facilities may be rather more opulent.

\* \* \*

That was then. This is now. The Chinese Super League is currently enjoying its third coming. Previous attempts to establish the league have been undermined by corruption and even hooliganism, a strange concept in a society that can feel well regimented and obedient when witnessed at first hand, and those problems have not been entirely exorcised. The perception remains that Chinese league games are regularly thrown, meaning gamblers' money pours instead into foreign markets. An undercurrent of violence simmers on and off the pitch, with one of Nicolas Anelka's first games for the now money-flushed Shanghai Shenhua after his move from Chelsea in January 2012 turning into a free-for-all brawl. But key to the success of the latest renaissance is the level of funding now being poured into the game. Anelka is on £200,000-a-week with his transfer likely to open the floodgates. The money thrown at Didier Drogba to join him was considerably more. The CSL may be in its infancy, but its backers' deep pockets are established.

Shenhua's funding stems from Zhu Jun, a dot-com entrepreneur and chief executive of The 9 Computer Technology Consulting, an online game operator. At the time he purchased the club from the Shanghai municipal government, merging it with Shanghai United FC – which the then 37-year-old had already boasted in his portfolio – he was ranked the 66th richest man in China. Anelka is understood to have signed two contracts: a playing deal with Shenhua, and the second an agreement to endorse Firefall, a game developed by Zhu's company. The bulk of his earnings stem from the latter agreement, hinging upon promotions and endorsements.

Rival clubs, owned by a mixture of government-linked bodies and private companies, are striking similarly ambitious deals. Guangzhou Evergrande are owned by the real-estate developer Apollo and are currently paying the Argentinean Dario Conca, signed for £8m from Fluminense, around £9m-a-year. Lucas Barrios is due to join for nearer £10m from Borussia Dortmund and will be coached at the Southern China Tigers by the former Italy World Cup winning manager Marcello Lippi, who agreed a two-and-a-half-year deal worth £25m in May. The numbers are mind-boggling, making the Premier League seem almost financially sound.

The motivation behind the lavish expenditure is the State's desire to make inroads on the international scene – primarily, to claim a World Cup – with China's ever growing pool of billionaires charged with reinventing the image of the game in the country, marred as it had been by corruption scandals involving everyone from club to match officials. Marlon Harewood, the former West Ham and Nottingham Forest forward who spent time with Guangzhou R&F gaining promotion to the Super League, likened standards to those in the Championship, "but it's bound to rise".

Back in 1999, it had some way to go. When Palace visited that sweltering summer, the professional league – the Jia A division – was only five years old and still attempting to establish itself, the salaries offered meagre in comparison to today's staggering figures and the foreigners recruited into the domestic game merely journeymen with nowhere else to go. Coppell's side had arrived in Beijing to play Gou'an, the local top flight team, to find themselves barred from training on the turf at the stadium – there were only eight well kept football pitches in the city at the time – and forced to undertake their sessions on the running track, sharing the lanes with a grizzled Italian who might have doubled as a body-builder and a veteran Uruguayan, both of whom were hoping to earn themselves contracts in the Chinese capital. The pair had a week to prepare for fitness testing: all foreigners hoping to play in Jia A had to be able to run 3,200 metres (eight laps) in 12 minutes otherwise they would be barred from competing. Effectively, they were being made to run for their visa. As it was, both hobbled off injured in the friendly at the Workers' stadium a day later, their brief sojourns in China curtailed.

In the tropical climate of Kunming, "the City of Eternal

Spring" albeit also the venue where dissidents were sent after the Revolution as punishment, the tourists confronted a Yunnan Hongta side complete with three gargantuan imports from the Ivory Coast. The visiting players suffered at the hands of the trio, departing the Zhidong stadium with a collection of bloodied noses, split lips and bruised egos. The African trio, the Hongta manager claimed, had been recruited to try and "out-English the English", which seemed fairly primitive if effective. Outside the arena the tourists shuffled away in the shadow of an imposing billboard depicting idyllic fields of wheat and other crops, the sun beating down from a glorious blue sky. The caption across the foot, written in English, read: "Working towards a prosperous future for our planet." It was an advertisement for the local brand of cigarettes.

The tourists had grown used to the acrid smoke puffed by the locals around the clock. Internal flights were spent peering through the smog of the cabin, tobacco hanging heavy in the air. Journeys on Yunnan Airlines, to and from Kunming, were eventful. One plane was delayed due to "mechanical problems", spreading panic among the more nervous fliers in the party, while the sight of locals merrily chatting away on their mobiles as the aeroplane either lurched up the runaway or touched down again with a thump became commonplace. If never reassuring. The flight from Kunming to Harbin involved a stop over at Jinan where those joining the journey included, among others, five chickens who were allowed to roam freely around the galley, clucking contentedly in the aisle, and a mother carrying a nappy-less baby. A hole had been cut in the infant's trousers at the rear, offering ventilation, though Dean Austin, exposed in the window seat, spent the trip praying junior would be facing the other way if the mallard's brains kicked in.

For the reporter in the ranks, this was a rare insight into a different world. Travelling in training kit associated the media officer with the team and, as far as the locals were concerned, designating the man with the laptop and the pasty legs a player simply in need of some intense pre-season cardiovascular work. Coppell and the staff guffawed at the very idea, with good reason, even if the pressman needed educating. In Shanghai, the team bus's departure for the stadium ahead of the friendly against Shanghai 02 was delayed because the media officer had risked 40 winks after lunch and promptly overslept. Kick-off was delayed by 15 minutes as a result. Coppell was waiting at the front of the coach and the memory of the look on his face prompts shudders of apprehension even now. Such an offence would normally carry a fine or worse, as was made patently clear, though the fact the culprit was working for nothing rather kiboshed any notion Simon Paterson might have had of raising some petty cash.

Yet the role had plenty of perks, too. Meeting the needs of the autograph hunters, who would clutter the hotel lobby every morning in search of anyone wearing Palace training kit, was a pleasure though the supporters' misguided adulation went further at times. In Daqing, back under that searing sun, the players and staff had strolled on to the turf to survey the scene a couple of hours before kick-off with the pre-match celebrations in full swing. The stadium was crammed, those in the stands behind each goal whooping in a choreographed chant of the visiting team's name. The drone of the hooters was deafening but the scene was hypnotic. The players eventually trotted off in search of the shade of the dressing room, the management staff meandering away to discuss selection and the dreadful state of the turf, leaving the media man daydreaming in the centre-circle and, transfixed by the swell of pitch all around, ambling subconsciously towards one of the goals.

It was only as the cheers went up, a raucous "Hello" chorused by the masses crammed on the open tribune, that reality clicked back in. The applause was directed at the one figure still loitering on the turf. The rookie press officer masquerading as a professional footballer. I'd like to think there was a brief moment of hesitation, a quick contemplation over just how to react, but, as Steve Coppell had stressed, Palace were acting as ambassadors in the Far East. Ignoring the masses was not an option. So, shamefully, up went the wave. It should have ended then and there but, as the shrieks of appreciation built, out came the obligatory footballer's clap of appreciation above the head. To the length of the end. Back and forth.

Pleased with myself, my popularity clearly established, I turned with a smile and began the strut of one who belonged back to the tunnel... only to find Coppell and his assistant, Steve Kember, staring at me. Their smirks said it all. Looking back, it's a close run thing to determine which was the more misguided notion: that Crystal Palace could conquer China, or that their press man could work the crowd. Both parties have since stumbled across some level of realism.

## Chapter 5

# The Poet and the Penalty

## Alex Hess

In today's *tiki taka*-infused footballing landscape, there's a maddening tendency for a bit of calm precision in a midfielder – especially one with an Iberian surname – to be over-praised. It's all Xavi Hernandez's fault, really. If it wasn't for the delicacies served up by his all-conquering Catalan and Spanish sides of recent years, the appreciation of the discreet, ball-playing central midfielder may have remained a niche practice. Xavi and his band of possession fetishists, though, have made the admiration of football's subtler arts painfully trendy. 'Metronomic' is often the adjective given to his new breed of unruffled playmaker, whose inevitably-quoted pass completion stats prompt nods of scholarly approval from the game's analysts. Be it Andrea Pirlo or Leon Britton, the understated passer has become an over-appreciated spectacle. This tribute to Xabi Alonso, then, feels trivialised as a transparent act of bandwagon-mounting.

And yet I was there first.

Way back in 2004, this approach to midfield play was still something of a novelty to an English footballing culture that defined itself by the raucousness of Rooney rather than the subtlety of Scholes. As a teenager whose own playing experience consisted of a weekly exchange of elbows with the fellow patrons of one of north London's less cordial five-a-side leagues, physicality, rather than finesse, had always seemed the game's natural core. So when a little-known Spaniard arrived on Merseyside that August, though my Liverpool idols had ranged from looming centre halves to jinking wingers, I was yet to witness anything like the guile and ingenuity I'd grow to adore in Xabi Alonso. By the time we parted ways half a decade later, not only had Alonso established himself as one of the world's finest midfielders, but he had also sauntered just ahead of Sami Hyypia and Steve McManaman as my favourite wearer of the red shirt. Three years on from his departure, he remains an idol.

Prior to his spell at Anfield, Alonso had made a name for himself as a classy young midfielder for Real Sociedad, the Spanish minnows whose improbable title challenge during the 2002/3 season had enthralled an entire nation, until its climax of final-hurdle heroic failure. Sociedad's exploits had entered my orbit through weekly viewings of Sky Sports' La Liga roundups, and so I was quietly intrigued when another idol-in-waiting, Rafael Benitez, succeeded in bringing Alonso to England. It wasn't long before this intrigue developed into something deeper. Nor did it take much time for the club's fan-base at large to take to a player who showed a vision and artistry not seen at Anfield since the days of Molby and Barnes. Crucially, he represented a welcome antidote to the midfield-bypassing football that had tainted the increasingly Owen-oriented Houllier regime. Despite being often touted as 'unsung', no-one really doubted the class of Alonso during his time at Anfield. He glowed with quality, and showed a will to seek victory through intelligent possession that was in keeping with the club's much-touted but recently compromised ideology.

As popular as he was among the entirety of the Anfield faithful, though, I like to think (completely mistakenly, of course) that my own affinity for Xabi Alonso is unique. Despite the fact that he is, in all probability, not the most innately gifted player I've seen in Liverpool red, and certainly not the most typically inspiring or exciting, it is Alonso, far and away, who stirs the most fondness. Yes, he was of course a magnificent footballer, but I have seen a few of them. Somehow Xabi is different. Perhaps, I think, what helps him afford the place he occupies in my heart, more than just his poet's understanding of the game, is the fact that he's the player who best embodies Rafael Benitez's time at the club.

You see, my relationship with Liverpool changed during the Benitez years. It had always been a central preoccupation, but as I entered Sixth Form around the age of sixteen, my support of the club entered a new phase. Not in terms of its obsessiveness (that, as with numerous kids, had been there since day one, when I could reel off Jason McAteer's reserve appearances, or Patrik Berger's favourite breakfast cereal) but in its intensity. What was previously an innocent attachment quickly evolved into an emotionally-driven fixation. The reasons behind this rash emotional investment are anyone's guess, but the exploits of Liverpool Football Club and its various protagonists became a narrative that gained equal, and often greater, meaning than more immediate and far more logically important goings on.

To compare sports fandom to drug addiction is to enter much-visited and dangerously tedious territory, but even the worst clichés are born from some truth. Given that every

Liverpool result during this time supplied me with a buzz unmatchable until the next match day arrived, the parallel is somewhat unavoidable. I'm fully aware that this doesn't speak towards an overly healthy psyche – form your own theories about adolescent emotional displacement and the like – but the Benitez years, for better or worse, marked the point at which supporting Liverpool assumed its central role in my life.

If I'm to play a quick round of the blame game, there's no doubt that my Grandad is ultimately responsible for this whole mess. It was he who handed me my Anfield debut in the Christmas of 1995, where at the age of seven I would watch a cocky Scouse kid called Robert Bernard Fowler stick a casual hat trick past David Seaman. It was also he who, shortly afterwards, obtained the scruffy autograph of then-demigod Ian Rush – in a parallel universe unconceivable to my young self, they belonged to the same golf club – that would adorn my bedroom wall for the next few years. These were the truly formative events that effectively marked the beginning of the end, and my Grandad is fully culpable. But Benitez should not be let off the hook either. Rafa changed the way I saw Liverpool.

Being in my mid-teens when he arrived on Merseyside, I had thus far grown to know my club as being carried largely by local heroes in Fowler, Michael Owen and Steven Gerrard, but one that, with the exception of the 2000/01 season, had come to be defined largely by its penchant to underwhelm. Now, call me a fairweather fan (or, actually, aim the allegation at my teenage self), but dull underachievement just wasn't cool for a football club during my school days, and especially not in north London, from where the exhilarating tide of Vieira, Henry and Pires was sweeping away all in its path.

After the great treble at the turn of the millennium, Gerard Houllier's latter teams were badly devoid of menace or inspiration and desperately one-dimensional. Let-downs like Kewell, Cheyrou and Diouf littered the squad, and the hoofs encouraged towards the antiquated Heskey-Owen partnership meant the ceding of any meaningful possession. Benitez, all in all, was not left with a great deal to work with. Despite this, though, he quickly converted his remnants into a team truly worthy of the term, and although they initially struggled for results, Benitez's Liverpool looked like a club going places. With Alonso an ever-growing influence, they passed and probed with intent if only sporadic success. The wildcard flair of Luis Garcia added a splash of continental excitement. Rafa's modernisation project rekindled my enthusiasm, and a year into his reign, with Liverpool implausibly European champions, I was well past the point of no return. I no longer simply supported the club, I was dependent on it.

In letting myself in for this, I had effectively given Benitez licence to dictate my emotional wellbeing, and he took me on quite a ride. And, now I'm able to reflect on this journey, it's fair to say that no player better encapsulates the delights and frustrations I experienced in the club's six years under Rafa more adeptly than his Basque playmaker. Though Gerrard's individual blossoming under Benitez was stunning, and his centrality to the regime's two trophy wins form the more iconic images of the portly Spaniard's time at the helm, Gerrard's heroics began well before then, and would continue after. And while Fernando Torres' arrival and subsequent form neatly mirrors the era's ambition, excitement and eventual disappointment, he wasn't present for the team's greatest victory. Alonso, though, very much *was* there in

Istanbul - Rafa's finest moment was also Xabi's, and the two men are for me forever associated.

As well as arriving at the point at which I became 'serious', for want of a better word, about my fandom, Alonso's five years at Liverpool also coincided with my transition from the late-adolescent social flounderings of sixth form to the frantic admiration of the 'cultured' that marked my move into undergraduate studenthood. This probably explains my love for the man as much as anything else, and indeed watching Alonso play was a far more refined footballing experience than I was previously accustomed to. I was raised on a diet of mazy McManaman dribbles, Fowler rockets, and Gerrard's (in)famously 'Hollywood'-style distribution. The only Liverpool players I'd seen adopt the approach of a true passing midfielder had either been marginalised (*à* la Danny Murphy, who could never quite play his way into the centre), fleeting in appearance (like Gary McAllister, whose sporadic displays of technique and vision were largely lost on my earlier teenage self), or indeed both (in this case Jari Litmanen – criminally underused by Houllier, I'm told, and he didn't hang around for long as a result).

With Alonso, though, it was different. His station in the middle of midfield reflected his utter centrality to the team, and his offerings were obvious. Even on his debut, a low-key 1-0 defeat away to Sam Allardyce's charming Bolton side, the disparity between Alonso's quietly effective prompting and Gerrard's often maddening over-ambition was quickly noticeable. His touch and technique stood out as a cut above the norm, even if his speed of distribution needed improvement, and I was seduced from the outset. Over the next few years, as Alonso bedded in and matured to near-perfection, Benitez assembled a side whose heart didn't thunder along to the frenzied reverberations of Gerrard, but instead ticked happily away to the patient – and, yes, metronomic – rhythm of the young Spaniard. Not only was his restrained passing game hugely effective, but Alonso's ethereal approach aligned nicely with my own desperate attempts to seek out and extol the world's more artfully subtle offerings. Alonso was something of a footballing George Orwell to Gerrard's Dan Brown; *The Godfather Part II* to Owen's *Matrix Reloaded*, and his overwhelming preference for subtlety over spectacle no doubt appealed to the pretentious student in me as much as his halfway line wondergoals appealed to the Liverpool fan. At a time when I was desperate to overstate my worth as a connoisseur of understated sophistication, Xabi was on hand to provide exactly that – and in the most important realm possible. My own intellectual vanity aside, though, Alonso was a masterstroke of a signing, and his unique brand of anti-dynamism was crucial to the long-term remodelling job that Benitez undertook.

The beauty of Alonso is that he belongs to the rare breed of player that rewards a close viewing. He deals in small moments of skill not instantly apparent – taking an awkward pass in his stride with his weaker foot, for instance, or his knack of pinching the ball off an opponent just as it arrives at their feet. Small moments – or moments made to look small – but moments that count, that change things, that form the bedrock of success. If Al Pacino was indeed right about the inches that add up to a victory being there all over the field, then Alonso was a master at quietly gathering them up. Not that Alonso was averse to the spectacular – as his oft-repeated strikes against Luton and Newcastle will testify – but he never indulged for its own sake. In fact, almost as skilful as his famous 60-yard lob over Steve Harper is the way he steals the ball from Charles N'Zogbia in its immediate lead-up. Sidestepping firmly into the path of the flying Newcastle winger, Alonso terminates his opponent's run and emerges with the ball, before launching it on a route to goal via the skies. Small moments, but moments that matter.

Orchestrated by Alonso, Liverpool's midfield under Rafa began to think again, and retaining the ball regained rightful priority above hammering it hysterically at the forwards. Despite the often revisionist accounts of Benitez's Liverpool as an unadventurous side, when they clicked into gear (which only happened consistently for one season) they were a far more intricate and exciting outfit than the club had offered in a long while, and with 77 goals in 2008/09 they boasted by far the most effective attack in the league. The names of Gerrard and Torres invariably decorated the scoresheets, but their athleticism and clinical sniping was propelled, of course, by the Basque brain behind them.

It was in May 2005, though, well before he had reached his peak, that Alonso underwent his most enduring moment as a Liverpool player. The Champions League final against Milan was far from his finest performance for the club, but his contribution on that monumental night will last long in the memory. Not only did he shoulder responsibility, at the age of 23, for one of the most high-pressure penalties imaginable, but *he actually missed it*, before, thank Christ, sticking in the rebound. Xabi wasn't just present in Istanbul, he was at the very heart of the most profoundly dramatic moment in my short time as a Liverpool fan.

I distinctively remember – quite notably, in fact, as I can't recall much about watching the match at the time – the television camera lingering on Alonso as he waited to take that penalty having spotted the ball. Alonso stands inside the

D, hands on hips, manically shifting his weight from one foot to the other and, in a bizarre tic of nervousness, alternately licking his lips and spitting on the turf. It's fair to say that he's an absolute picture of barely suppressed terror – and rightly so. Like the rest of us, Alonso was shitting himself.

Equally memorable is his response to scoring the rebound (a deceptively well-taken finish lifted cannily over the stricken Dida). Lurching away from the goalmouth, one arm attempting a kind of drunken windmill action, the other askew in a rigid downward diagonal, he quickly runs out of steam and is floored by a Milan Baros headlock, at which point he tumbles in a uncoordinated spiral of elbows, hits the turf, and then simply remains face down, dead still. It all happens in the space of a few seconds, but it's distinctly at odds with his default mode of gliding elegance. It's a celebration, I think, that completely betrays a moment of undistilled joy coupled with absolute psychological exhaustion that every Liverpool fan was also experiencing. It still pangs within me when I watch it today. I think it's a salient point, given the alienation that much of today's fans feel from the millionaire players we pay to watch, that Alonso didn't, couldn't, run towards the byline pulling any of the self-congratulatory poses that have now become standard goal celebration fare: the badge thump, the knee slide, the shirt over the head. He simply collapsed, and stayed collapsed. In that instant, Xabi was us, and we were him, and we were all spent. It was a moment emblematic of a player who, throughout his time at Liverpool, displayed none of the ego and self-indulgence that tends to mar much of the Premier League populace. Benitez may have orchestrated that comeback, and Gerrard may have instigated it, but Alonso realised it. He delivered it.

Of course, the memories of the Benitez era aren't all glowingly nostalgic, and it's just as important to Alonso's association with that period that he illustrates its tragedy and misjudgement as much as he does the triumph.

Say the words "Gareth Barry" to most football fans, and you're unlikely to cause much offence. The midfielder is akin to a dinner of beans on toast, or an episode of CSI, in the utmost indifference his name inspires. A scathing recollection of his doomed, lumbering pursuit of Mesut Ozil in Bloemfontein might be the extent of any resentment harboured his way. Mention his name to a Liverpool fan, though, and it's a direct reminder of a Kop idol's most terrible act of misjudgement.

The summer of 2008 was sullied by another doomed pursuit involving Gareth Barry, though this time he was the target of the chase with Rafa Benitez openly courting him in the apparent hope of shipping Alonso off to Turin. Over those few months, figures were exchanged, transfer requests were handed in, and Benitez was scribbled furiously off Martin O'Neill's Christmas card list. Barry, however, remained at Villa. And so Alonso stayed at Liverpool. And, though he was coming off the back of a below-par season, those of us with an active collection of brain cells breathed a quiet sigh of relief. Benitez's summer cravings seemed increasingly inexplicable as the ensuing season went on, as I saw, for the first time, a delightfully balanced Liverpool side mount a genuine title challenge, losing just two league games all season and amassing 86 points, the club's best figure for two decades. Alonso, inevitably, showed his finest run of sustained form so far, dovetailing wonderfully with Javier Mascherano at the base of midfield, and providing a fertile supply line for the explosive and reassuringly homoerotic partnership of Gerrard and Torres ahead of him. The Promised Land was not quite reached, but it was well within sight. Despite losing out on the title, and despite the occasional foreboding hint of boardroom gluttony from Stateside, things were looking up, and the club's yearning for Gareth Barry was a distant and easily discarded memory.

But then Real Madrid came knocking. And, just like that, he was gone. With typically minimal fuss, Alonso returned to Spain for the sum of £30million – a huge amount for a holding midfielder, but scant consolation for the sense of sheer loss I felt as his rumoured departure quickly became an inevitability.

Of course, we'll never really know if things would have actually transpired differently had Rafa never have devoted the previous summer to whispering sweet nothings in Gareth Barry's direction. A contract with Real Madrid, after all, is not offered to just anyone, and at 27 would have been hard for Alonso to decline whatever the circumstance. There can be little doubt, though, that leaving Liverpool was no easy decision for him, and that his criminal undervaluing, exposed by the Barry saga a year earlier, certainly helped make up his mind.

Upon Alonso's departure that summer, few foresaw that his loss would be felt quite as greatly as it was, but none doubted that it was a great player the club was losing. Although the club's parasitical ex-owners, rather than comparatively trivial managerial decisions, are ultimately to blame for Liverpool's decline, Alonso's sale nonetheless marks the definitive point at which the previous season's title challengers hurtled round a hairpin bend and ploughed into the quicksand of mediocrity in which they're still flailing. (Though if there was any silver lining to Alonso's exit, it's that Barry never did arrive as his replacement, which would have been akin to divorcing Scarlett Johansson to marry Delia Smith).

Although he wasn't technically present during the disastrous campaign that followed his exit, Alonso was very much there *in absentia* during 2009/10. His spectre loomed large over the now-shrunken Anfield pitch, recoiling in disgust at every shanked, tempo-disrupting pass from Gerrard and Lucas. His absence was painfully obvious – especially with his supposed replacement spending far more time nursing injury and illness than actually playing football – and it is Benitez's role in Alonso's disenchantment that's most often touted as having sown the seed of his eventual downfall. That all of it – Alonso, Benitez, the lot – could, just maybe, have been prevented is what stings the most.

Heart-wrenching conclusion aside, though, Alonso's five years as a red were largely wonderful, and his own affinity for Liverpool also seemed genuine and deep-seated. His remarks about the club during his time there consistently reached beyond the standard PR-friendly vacuousness that footballers generally recite about their employers, and he is occasionally spotted in the Anfield stands in the years since his departure. "I am still a Liverpool fan and will be forever, absolutely", Alonso declared fully two years after leaving. "The experiences I had there are deep in my heart". Well, Xabi, I'm still an Alonso fan, forever and absolutely. As hard as our parting was to accept, anyone will tell you that it's important to remember the good times. And so, I still on occasion find myself gazing into the middle distance, picturing *that* strike sailing over Steve Harper and towards me behind the Kop end goal, and my heartbeat briefly flutters ahead of its normal, steady, metronomic rhythm.

## Chapter 6

# Derby and the Tin Man

## Tom Hopkinson

With its dangerously high, almost vertical wooden stands, the Baseball Ground always seemed like a magical place to me. It was 20 years since the stadium had played host to Derby's heyday by the time I started going to matches, yet still it felt, particularly at night, as if the ghosts of great players and legendary managers filled the air every time we crammed ourselves inside. The proximity of the stands to the pitch meant there was always an air of tension in the ground which I never really trusted. But it was one I revelled in all the same.

While I might have missed the glory days of title triumphs and European football, of Brian Clough, Dave McKay, Archie Gemmill and Kevin Hector, the stadium was still the setting for so many happy childhood memories. And, as anyone who followed Derby week in, week out in the late 80s and early 90s will attest, there were some that weren't quite so happy as well. But as the old adage goes, 'The older I get, the better I was', and so, too, are my recollections of the Derby teams of my youth. The older I get, the better they were. We must just have been unlucky.

When I first started kicking around ideas for this book, I

wondered whether I should focus on a particular game from that period, a time when my fanaticism was at its peak. The 3-3 draw with Sheffield Wednesday in the FA Cup quarter-finals in 1993 was an incredible night on which the pendulum swung both ways and back again. I must have driven my mum mad in the weeks that followed as I watched and re-watched the moment Shane Nicholson put Derby ahead with a 35-yard free-kick which rattled the crossbar, hit despairing goalkeeper Chris Woods on the back and rebounded over the line. "Nicholson! 3-2... It's falling apart for Wednesday." I can still hear the commentary today.

A rampant 7-0 victory over Southend in the second round of the League Cup in 1992 heralded the coming together of a young team expensively assembled by chairman Lionel Pickering; and three weeks after that came a 1-1 draw with Arsenal in the same competition. There was the FA Cup third-round trip to Burnley at the start of that year which was abandoned at 2-2 because of fog; trips to Grimsby and the town's famous Steels Corner House for as tasty a portion of fish and chips as you'll find; to Barnsley, on the Roadrider, the supporters' bus, for my first away game without an adult in tow; and to Tranmere in 1995, where Igor Stimac marked his arrival from Hajduk Split with Derby's goal in a 5-1 defeat. Nobody cared too much about the result that day; we were all too busy falling under Igor's spell.

I contemplated basing this chapter on him. When he played he was arrogant, he was brash and he strode around the Baseball Ground and Pride Park as if they belonged to him. At times it felt like they did. Sometimes he would drive us crazy trying to play his way out of trouble rather than booting the ball into touch, but you couldn't stay mad for long, he was that good. By the time he arrived at Derby, we were crying out for a new fans' favourite. We hadn't really had one since the Tin Man, Ted McMinn, had left the club a couple of years earlier and we immediately took him to our hearts. In 2004, a BBC poll asked supporters of each team to name their all-time cult heroes and Stimac topped ours ahead of McMinn and Dean Saunders, which would have been my top three as well.

I'd made the occasional visit to the Baseball Ground with my dad in my very early years, but it wasn't until I turned 13 and stood on the Pop Side with a mate that I really became a fan. We stood on the old Vulcan terrace for the first time against Manchester City in 1990 and watched Saunders earn a 1-1 draw with a goal which remains one of the best I have seen. The Vulcan erupted as it flew in and so, too, the Colombo to our right. Opposite them, the C Stand went up as well and my love affair with Derby County had begun. Not so long ago, I enjoyed a round of golf with Saunders. "There's some shit on the end of your club, Tom", he told me as I stood over a shot on the eighth. "Not that end," he added, laughing, as I stared at its head. They say you should never meet your heroes but Deano, just like Igor when I met him in Poland during Euro 2012, didn't let me down.

Nor, for that matter, did Ted McMinn, when we met to speak about his colourful life for these pages. He was adored by the Rams faithful, was Ted, and, almost two decades after he last crossed a ball for Derby, the good feeling towards him remains. He'd fly down the wing - as best he could on that bog - and seemingly get the end product horribly wrong almost as often as he got it beautifully right. We loved him for both in equal measure. I could have wasted hours pondering a sentence or two which would best tell you why there was such love for McMinn as a player and not come up with anything better than the reasons given by two Derby fans when they voted in that poll.

'Not for his talent, but his cheeky, impudent way of pushing a ball past a full-back, running into him and getting a free-kick virtually every time,' wrote one. 'He would then wink at the crowd after doing so. A throwback to the days of characters and entertainment.' The other was more succinct. 'Did things he wasn't capable of.'

That right there was the joy of Ted McMinn. They'd loved him at Queen of the South, Rangers and Seville before he joined Derby and, after he left us, he thrilled fans at Birmingham and Burnley as well. He was voted No.3 on Burnley's list of cult heroes, and the fact their fans and Derby's still hold him dear remains a source of great pleasure to this day. "It cost me a fortune phoning up," he says, laughing. "But to get in the top three at both clubs was great. Even at Rangers, I've been away from Glasgow for 25 years and to be, not so much recognised, but remembered when I go back, it's brilliant. When I go up to Scotland, people still say, 'I remember that game you played against Celtic...'

"I was only at Burnley for two years after I'd left Derby, but I was third behind Jimmy McIllroy and Leighton James. To have been in the top 100 at clubs like that would have been fantastic, but to be in the top three at Burnley and top two at Derby... Sometimes you think, 'Hang on, there were a lot better players than me', but people maybe think I did something different." He did something different all right, even if it wasn't always to everyone's liking. Graeme Souness, the man who sold him from Rangers, famously said, 'How can I tell Ted McMinn what to do when he doesn't know what he's going to do?'

McMinn went on: "I don't think anyone can go out and

have a gameplan. Jimmy Sirrel would do his match report on Derby's opponents and then our manager, Arthur Cox, would say, 'The full-back doesn't like people coming inside'. But that was never comfortable for me. If anyone told me to do something, I was like a kid. 'Don't go near the fire.' I'd go near the fire. 'Go inside.' I'd go outside. Sometimes people would ask, 'How did you do that?' And I'd think, 'I haven't a clue'. It was instinct. Half the time it would come off, the other times I'd end up on my face. Wingers were hit and miss, you could be different from one week to the next. There aren't wingers any more, but that's what they used to be.

"At Rangers I remember going to cross the ball with my right foot but poking it out with my left while my right was still swinging. I ended up flat on my face with 40,000 people singing, 'Ted McMinn'. If they'd booed me I'd have been looking for a hole to crawl into, but they realised it was accidental. It was the same at Derby, they just wanted to see people trying. For me, crossing the ball was what a winger was there to do. I never had a trick. I had a bit of pace. I really, really worked hard at crossing because, early on, I struggled. So when I came to Derby I'd just cross balls to the kids and practice for hours. My leg would be killing me, but it would give me confidence and I'd know what I could do. I knew I was never the most gifted player in the world, so I was always first in training and last away, although that was probably because I'd have to go back to my missus," he adds, chuckling mischievously.

McMinn wasn't sure whether he was joining Derby or Newcastle when he arrived back in Blighty from Seville in 1988, but Gordon Guthrie, the Rams' long-serving physio, bundled him into a car and drove him to the East Midlands, where Cox and his assistant, Roy McFarland, made sure he'd put pen to paper before showing him the pitch. "I'd have never signed for Derby if I'd seen the ground first," he says. "There was a little strip of grass along each touchline where the linesman runs and I was thinking, 'Yes, I'm a winger and I've got a wee bit of grass to work with here, but through the middle I've got no chance'."

McMinn's relationship with Cox and Guthrie would define his Derby career every bit as much as his relationship with the fans. "Gordie was always there for me, because I spent so much time in his room. If I got in trouble at the weekend, his phone would ring. You knew it was the gaffer. Gordie would just say, 'Yep, he's here', then give you the nod. You'd walk into the gaffer's room and take your fine. Then you'd get back in and Gordie would just say, 'Right, back on the treatment table'. He had three beds, a set of scales, a tube of Deep Heat, an ice machine, an ultrasound and a heat lamp. They were Gordie's tools to get people fit, no matter what injury they had."

Cox, just like Jock Wallace had been at Rangers and Seville, was a father figure to McMinn at Derby. "I got in so much trouble, but he would always mask it up. He'd give me a fine, then tell me it was suspended. I wouldn't have had a wage every other week if he hadn't. He would think, 'He has two kids at home, a mortgage and, if I fine him, he'll be in trouble'. We still speak. Like Jock, Arthur had been in the army and he would manage his players that way. When I did my knee, I'd been in the best form of my life. I'd been having an operation for five hours one day, my leg was practically hanging off and I was about to miss my opportunity to go to the 1990 World Cup. Arthur walked in, put the television on and showed me pictures of kids who hadn't got any food.

'There you go, there's somebody worse off than you', he said. I was devastated, but he was right."

McMinn's body took some punishment in his playing days - nothing like what it would take after he retired - and perhaps the fact he would be missing for large periods made it that bit more of a treat when he played. It didn't do any harm in our eyes either that his feelings for that lot in red along the A52 were the same as ours. "When we played against Nottingham Forest, for some reason - I don't know why, maybe it was like the whole Rangers-Celtic thing - but I got so hyped up. Maybe it was because Mark Wright would come back from England duty and say, 'Forest in a couple of weeks... Pearcey says he's going to do you'. When we played Forest, within the first five minutes Stuart Pearce always got booked. He'd come through you, lean over and say, 'You get back up and I'll be back'. Then he'd nip you, or try to pick you up by your sideboards, the back of your hair, or stand on your toes. He actually bit me on the chest once. I fell on top of him and he just bit me. I'm lifting my shirt, asking the referee if he saw it and he just said, 'Get on with the game'. He'd be up for assault these days, but it was part of the game then.

"In one game, I'd been having words with Nigel Clough and, in the end, me and Wrighty were substituted before we were sent off. We were losing 2-1 and getting a lot of abuse in the dug-out from the Forest fans. I said to Wrighty, 'I'm going to get Cloughie at the end of this game'. Wrighty knew what I was like. 'You're not going to do anything'. I said: 'I will, but what about Pearcey?' He said: 'I'll look after Pearcey'. We were forgetting he ran straight down the tunnel at the end, rarely shaking hands with anybody. So the final whistle goes and Wrighty says, 'Right, go down the tunnel, stand behind the door and I'll tell you when Cloughie's coming'.

"So I stand behind the door, and I jumped out and grabbed him. It's all ready to kick off and there's the copper who'd just warned us in the dug-out that if we misbehaved once more we'd be arrested. So Cloughie's saying, 'Have you seen that?' There's a wee skirmish - nothing, handbags - but the police have stopped it and I've got reported. Brian Clough is trying to calm it all down, so he went into the Forest dressing-room and they're still singing. He asked Nigel what had happened. 'He called me Daddy's Boy'. He made Nigel come and shake hands with me. We gave it a cursory shake. After that we never really spoke or acknowledged each other in games. He was a Red Dog and I was a Ram. But when I did my knee, Cloughie Senior was walking down the tunnel at Derby one day and he stopped and said, 'Young man, the game needs good players like you. Get back soon'. I'll never forget that."

That injury kept McMinn out for 14 months, but when he returned he was quickly back to his best. In the 91-92 season he was Derby's player of the year as we reached the play-off semi-finals, losing to eventual winners Blackburn. "The play-offs were probably the biggest disappointment of my time at Derby. We were 2-0 up after 10 minutes but were beaten 4-2 by a good Blackburn team. They were just starting to spend money. We won 2-1 at home in the second leg and I scored, but it wasn't enough. That was my last goal for Derby and it wouldn't have been far off my last game. Everything just turned around, the first team that season ended up being the reserves the year after. Martin Kuhl had signed, Mark Pembridge, Marco Gabbiadini, Paul Kitson. So the old school were on their way out and I was one of them.

"Arthur was straight to the point. 'I don't want you

knocking on the door every five minutes saying, 'Why have I not been picked?' Play in the reserves for a year and bring the kids through, Mark Stallard, Martyn Chalk, but don't come knocking'. He gave me a new contract and a bit more money, he knew I was good in the dressing-room even though me and Gabbi didn't get on. Me and him had a bit of a bust-up at training one day. Gabbi would rub people up the wrong way and some people could hack it, some couldn't. He wasn't my cup of tea. I got on with Kits, Tommy Johnson, Shane Nicholson. Shinner (Nicholson) was a good lad."

McMinn joined Birmingham a year later and then Burnley. He had a short spell in Australia before ending his playing days at Slough Town. He had thrilled fans the length and breadth of the British Isles and, for a short time, on the other side of the world with a right leg that some days could be likened to a wand. A right leg he no longer has. He contracted a mystery infection in 2005 - it remains as much today - and, after having half of his right foot amputated, went on to have the leg removed below the knee.

"It's not grown back yet," he says, chuckling, as we sit in the front room of his home. He has lived in Derby for 23 years. "The surgeon who did my leg said it could have been the injections at Rangers, the cortisone at Derby. I scratched my hand once. I had a blister on a heel and burst it. Somehow, something had got in and eaten my bone. It could have been in my body for years and there was something that triggered it; it could have crawled in when a needle mark wasn't covered up. I'll never know. But it got to my bones and started eating them. We went on holiday once and I walked through sewerage. I got a cut on a holiday to Corfu, it could have been as recent as that. But if it was as recent as that then it ate through my bones at one hell of a rate.

"They took the toes away and sewed the sole back on to the top. I didn't have any toes, so when I walked, I rolled because there was nothing to stop me. A woman said to me the day after the operation, 'Have you thought any more about amputation?' I said, 'I only had it done yesterday!' She said, 'No, the next stage'. I said, 'I'll tell you now, I'm not having any more done'.

"But my son was down to see me and we took the bandage off and he said, 'Dad, that's horrible. It's like a samosa'. It was like a triangle, there were no toes, there was nothing but the sole. I went home and went fishing, and I nearly fell in the pond. I just said, 'That's it'. I phoned the guy and asked when he could get me in. He said five weeks and I said, 'Can't you do it tomorrow?' They did the operation, shaved the bone so it's rounded and doesn't pierce the skin when you put pressure on it, sewed it up and two days later I checked myself out. I started walking seven days later."

It took McMinn two months before he felt like popping out for a pint. "I'll never forget walking into the Malt Shovel in Aston after having it done. You never know how everybody's going to be. I walked in and this guy just shouted, 'Peg leg, what do you want?' The whole place went silent. Everybody was waiting for a reaction. So I just said, 'Get me a Budweiser', and everybody started laughing."

A tribute game to McMinn was organised between Rangers and Derby legends at Pride Park in 2006 and the attendance, 33,475, remains a record for the stadium. Nearly half of those packed into the ground were from Glasgow. To coincide with the match, McMinn cycled 300miles from Ibrox to Pride Park and raised £15,000 which was split between the David Murray Foundation and Derbyshire Royal Infirmary's limbs unit.

"When I had the first surgery done, the guy said to me, 'What do you want to do?' I said, 'I want to walk again and I want to play golf'. He said, 'Get your leg cut off and you can play golf and walk again, you can cycle, you can lead a lot more normal life than you think you can. But if you stay like that you're not going to have a normal life. You're going to have people opening doors, people feeling sorry for you'. And that was the last thing I wanted."

It wasn't too long after the second operation that McMinn, with his prosthetic limb and working at Derby as kit man, was back on the golf course. "The Derby boys would come for a game. Luke Varney would play a bit more because he wasn't really getting a game and he'd say, 'Ted, me and you are having a wager'. We'd go to my course and I had general knowledge of it, but I'd only got one leg. 'How many shots are you going to give me, Luke?' I'd go for the sympathy vote.

"One day I got to the seventh hole and my prosthetic leg broke. My foot snapped and Luke's there claiming the victory. He's saying, 'You walk off, or hop off, and I win the £20'. I wasn't having any of it. 'No, no, no. I ain't walking off'. I was using a buggy, parking it where my ball was. I was playing my shot on one leg, trying to stand still on my swing, but I'd fall forwards or backwards. What Luke didn't know was that I'd phoned my wife, Marian, and asked her to bring my spare leg to the course. His face was a picture as we came off the ninth and she pulled up alongside us. She opened the car window, handed it to me and I gave her the broken one. Luke's going, 'I've never seen this before - a replacement leg on the 10th'. He's thinking, 'I've won this', but then Marian turned up and I won. I would never let anybody beat me at golf: Luke, Robbie Savage, Paul Jewell... My lad was three-up with six to play recently and I beat him. Whatever I play or whatever I do, I ain't going to be second. I'll never let anyone beat me."

Nor has he let amputation beat him. These days McMinn is the kit man for Derbyshire County Cricket Club. His old mate John Morris, the club's former head of cricket, wanted a more football-like feel in the dressing-room and he knew McMinn was the man to get in there, get the banter flowing and instil that mentality in his players. McMinn wasn't sure if the club would want him to stay after Morris was sacked, but the players loved having him about the place and he was kept on.

You only have to see - or hear - him around the County Ground for a minute or two to realise the job is perfect for him and that he's perfect for the job. He feeds off his love of being around and part of a team. He always gave the impression that was the case whenever he pulled on his Derby shirt as well. He loved to play football and we loved to watch him enjoying himself.

In many ways, there are huge similarities between his personal life and his career. He has done his fair share of winding people up - four marriages will attest to that - but at the same time has taken a lot of knocks and kicks of his own. Whatever he has been faced with, though, he has picked himself up, dusted himself down and cracked on with a wink in that cheeky, impudent and very likeable way of his.

"I always said there was nothing I'd have changed about my life when I was writing my autobiography," he says, as we start to bring the interview to a close. "I'd have changed the way I was in life because I've been married four times and I've hurt a lot of people. When I had my leg done, I thought I was getting punished for all the bad things I've done. But would I change my football career for this not to have happened? No, never. I loved every minute of it."

And we loved every minute we watched him as well.

## Chapter 7

# Long Distance Love

## Laure James

Extend arm out, twist to a right angle at the elbow, hold hand horizontally before the eyes and calculate the trembling. The minor pulsations, the internal Richter scale of clattering nerves, signals the happy trauma from which no football fan, on a history-making match day, is either immune or wants to be.

On the morning of, and in the days leading up to, la 38ème journée, or the final day of Ligue 1 2011/12, Montpellier's shape had shifted. The city's Mediterranean climate had been replaced with heavy clouds and persistent rain. Its culture and art was suddenly awash with blue and orange flags, flares and fits of excitement. Montpellier were just one point away from winning their very first top division title. It was an exceedingly strange and electrified time for a club whose band of supporters had, over the years, become used to being, and following, the unknowns.

As a young girl, when asked which team I supported, the best I used to hope for in response was "Cantona played for you, right?" and the worst: "Don't you mean the rugby team?"

Back in the mid 1990s, the vague, thin knowledge of

Montpellier Hérault Sport Club which English football fans demonstrated was miserably sufficient. Indeed, you could have said the same for most French people. Even when Stade de la Mosson hosted eight World Cup games in 1998 and all-time top scorer Laurent Blanc recorded his 76th goal – yes, *that* Laurent Blanc, the centre-back - Montpellier was still cursed with something of a drifting, ignorable existence. They were in the overbearing shadow of Montpellier Hérault Rugby, Pro D2 (2003) and European Shield (2004) champions, apart from a brief elevation in football's consciousness when Eric Cantona joined on loan from Marseille in 1989. The football club had a habit of clambering with an almost naive but unbreakable eagerness up and down the divisions. Even King Eric's contribution was marred by a dressing room incident. Six years before his infamous kung-fu attack on Matthew Simmons, he had battled with team-mate Jean-Claude Lemoult, hurling his boots in his colleague's face and slicing what had previously been quite a peaceful Montpellier team in two. Half the squad demanded his immediate ejection, whereas Blanc and Carlos Valder-rama, then the club's most recognised if not revered player, defended his case to stay.

Despite being hit with a ten-day ban from going anywhere near the ground, Cantona's loan arrangement was kept in place, a decision which pleased the fans. Even his tarnished reputation had little effect on his unshakeable form. He was instrumental as the team went on to win la Coupe de France in 1990, defeating lower-league RC Paris 2-1, albeit only in extra time.

From 1994 onwards, under returning manager Michel Mézy, the club regained confidence, attracted greater attend-ances and attained fleeting respect. Overall, though,

Montpellier's reputation was tepid and mediocre. Mézy quit the club for a second time in 1998 and by 2000, MHSC had tumbled back to Ligue 2. Then followed a three-year, making-up-the-numbers return to Ligue 1. Montpellier's inclination to yo-yo became clear.

As for me, memories of the Coupe de France semi-final against derby rivals Nîmes in 1996, and having to be consoled after our 1-0 defeat, continued to haunt, only dissolving in time for the 1998 World Cup. A schoolfriend's father had been drafted in to help with the reconstruction of Stade de la Mosson and one of the happiest, yet curiously strange, experiences for young supporters of la Paillade, as Montpellier are known, was watching Italy take on Cameroon. Almost 30,000 people saw Italy win 3-0, comprising an opener from Luigi di Biagio - and an unforgettable assist from Roberto Baggio - followed with a brace by Christian Vieri. Nevertheless, it only papered over the splitting cracks of an increasingly tenuous relationship between girl and club, and by the start of the new millennium, Montpellier had plunged head-first back into obscurity. As usual, nobody noticed.

Five years in Ligue 2 did little to restore much faith among the fans and an embarrassing tumble into Le National, the third tier of French football for one season, did even less. Salvation came when a 1-0 win against Grenoble on the final day of 2006/07, courtesy of a penalty converted by Victor Hugo Montaño, proved sufficient for Montpellier to claw themselves towards moderate respectability.

Another considerably bigger statement of intent came, once again, on the last day of the season, this time on May 29, 2009. Strasbourg had taken a surprise lead but the Montpellier team's attitude, unity and strength accounted for everything. Yohann Carasso saved a penalty and attacking midfielder Tino Costa scored twice in the final few minutes to achieve promotion back to Ligue 1. Such recent struggles and inconsistencies, therefore, make the club's ascent and René Girard's accomplishments all the more masterful, but predominantly surprising. Regretfully, even the more painful returns to history are, for me, merely anecdotal.

That decade of instability was endured from afar but, eventually, my relationship with MHSC became strained purely by distance. My family relocated again and again, each time in a furthermore westerly direction from France. I grew physically more detached from the blue and orange and, when I eventually moved to Northern Ireland aged 20, my status as a fan had threatened to disintegrate. Working as a football journalist made it increasingly difficult to circumvent the Irish Premiership's fixtures for a stolen weekend away in le Midi. The irregular flight schedules were maddening (if any airline route co-ordinators are reading this, consider it a lobbying plea for something even semi-direct) and the months without Montpellier grew into years.

I couldn't take it any longer. With each passing year, the guilt deepened. Season after season, I watched fathers and uncles bring their children to Irish League games, scolding them loudly for dropping their chips. It summoned memories of the filled baguettes served on French domestic terraces. I began to scan through squad lists and programme articles. They made me yearn with a renewed nostalgia. So, after years of absence, each available holiday had a trip to la Mosson shoe-horned in. I could walk down the same grassy banks and winding pathways, watch the same men sweep their scarves over their shoulders and relieve themselves in long grass and attentively listen for new terrace chants, or opinions on our latest signings.

Then there's the chairman. With a combination of Ken Bates' longevity, the spotlight-hunger of Maurizio Zamparini and the unhinged personality of Aurelio de Laurentiis, Louis 'LouLou' Nicollin has been a cult synonym of Montpellier since becoming président in 1974. Owner of Group Nicollin, an enterprise which specialises in household waste and environmental planning, Nicollin is certainly seen as a man you could relate to. When asked about the prospect of winning the domestic championship he replied with: "Champions? What I am more concerned about is if we were to qualify for the Europa League. That would really piss me off. What a rubbish competition."

He is prone to plenty of other, PR-free comments. One of the first things I'll always ask my uncle Paul, who still lives in the Hérault region, is: "What's fou-fou LouLou done lately?" Nicollin is such a part of the team that opposition players will not swap, but give their shirts to him after a match to add to his collection, as Yann M'vila did after Montpellier's 2-0 win at Rennes in the 36th match of the 2011/12 campaign.

That trip to the north was unusual for LouLou, a superstitious man who stayed home for most of the away games of the season. While this habitual absence is always countered by his ever-guaranteed availability for a robust verdict via TV link, the sight of him in the stands, a blanket on his knees, hands knotted in his lap and the nervousness clear on his face, showed him as a surprisingly vulnerable figure, a fan like any other.

This, too, was the match where Souleyman Camara, who had missed a last-minute penalty in the chaos of the 2-2 draw at home to Evian the previous week, received his President's support. "You are going to score," LouLou whispered in his ear as he walked out of the tunnel to take his seat. Camara's ninth league goal of the season – and his first away from home – followed in the 26th minute. Nicollin still has the Midas touch.

Football's a tribal game and there are fans who tend illogically to obsess about the vendettas, conspiracies and simmering hatred they believe journalists have harboured and directed at their clubs. When Lisburn Distillery sink to the lower reaches of the Irish League, or Linfield map out the blueprints of yet another double league and cup victory, I'm often asked where my allegiances lie.

"I don't have a local club," I answer honestly.

"Rubbish, who do you support?"

"Montpellier."

"Who?"

In the interests of being understood, I have been slowly repeating myself for 15 years. "Mont-pell-ee-air," as each monotone syllable lost its quickened French flair. The effort was worth it.

Amid the rain and on unfamiliar territory, everything changed. On May 20, 2012 the final day of the season and in the most chaotic way possible, la Paillade teetered on the brink of lifting their maiden crown. Montpellier had to secure just one point from relegated Auxerre, who had nothing but a party to spoil. Simultaneously, Paris Saint-Germain, outsiders, but overwhelming favourites back at the start of the season, were sitting three points behind MHSC in Ligue 1. The multi-million euro-backed team would stop at nothing to defeat Lorient.

Just reaching this point had been nerve-wracking enough;

in the discussions whether Montpellier could hold on or would fade away, disciplinary problems also played their part. Away at Nancy, two red cards reduced the visitors to a stubborn rearguard action but they still very nearly equalised in the final minutes, eventually losing 1-0. They bounced back with a 3-1 victory at a shaky Marseille - a team out of sorts, a management team not communicating, and a fanbase mostly on strike – where, roared on by the travelling support, Younes Belhanda's bicycle kick third offered a timely illustration of his talent.

At home to Evian a week later, he demonstrated his impulsiveness. Montpellier had a golden opportunity to go eight points clear at the top of the table but after Belhanda opened the scoring shortly before the break, from the penalty spot, Thomas Kahlenberg equalised. In the second half, Evian's Kevin Berigaud produced a second, leaving the weight of the world on Olivier Giroud's shoulders. He delivered, scoring six minutes from time. Montpellier's luck continued when they were handed a penalty four minutes into injury-time after Remy Cabella was fouled in the box but at this key moment, this pivotal test of focus and fortitude, everything appeared to collapse. Belhanda, who should have been concentrating on the penalty, and Cedric Mongongou were dismissed for fighting. Instead, after five minutes of unsightly pushing and shoving, it was Souleymane Camara who took the spot-kick. Saved. Now Montpellier would not claim the victory and be without their playmaker, banned to the end of the season. Belhanda lashed out in interviews afterwards against Giroud for not taking responsibility for the penalty. The men who could have shown the rest of the league how to do it right, had only demonstrated how to shoot themselves in the foot.

Then came the game against Rennes, themselves fighting for a place in Europe. Montpellier prevailed with 38 per cent possession. Cabella stepped in for his suspended colleague, and bounced the second goal in off the post behind stranded goalkeeper Benoit Costil. The final home game of the season, against a Lille team still with a slim hope of the title, was a sell-out; massive banners rolled down from the stands, ultra group Butte Paillade '91 celebrating their anniversary, the Kop Wolf group welcoming Champions League football to Mosson.

Wave upon wave of stewards and firemen were added to the human drama as the game stayed goal-less, and external factors seemed intent on disturbing Montpellier's chances. A half-time floodlight failure meant that the only light in the stadium came from the flares glowing red in the Etang de Thau. At the last minute – always, it feels, at the last minute – there was a goal. Giroud, hovering just inside his own half, broke, cut the ball back, and Ait-Fana finished. It was still on, but again, nobody could shake the instinct of looking over their shoulders for the moment it could be off.

That same anxiety pounded continually in me, a dull throb for the week that followed. On the final day of the season, my Lyonnais partner and I were at Stade Gerland, watching Lyon v Nice. It seemed perverse that, on this rare trip back to France, I was to be watching l'OL rather than my beloved Montpellier. As my partner feared for Hugo Lloris' confidence ahead of the Euros – the French captain let in four preventable goals – I was seized by nerves, guilt and impatience. The PA was grainy, my mobile phone's capacity to access Twitter had disintegrated and the last news we had was Auxerre against Montpellier, the game that would decide my club's fate, had been suspended.

The barrage of tennis balls, toilet rolls, tomatoes and any other innocuous yet disruptive missiles which Auxerre supporters could lay their hands on and promptly launch, meant the game fell behind by 15 minutes. The last minutes mirrored Manchester City's title decider just the week before. Montpellier, aware of PSG's 2-1 victory away to Lorient, knew exactly what was needed and, ignorant of much of the game I had gone to see, I implored them to see it through. The Parisians anxiously scoured updates from Auxerre – who had taken a 1-0 lead through Olivier Kapo - just as compulsively as I.

Carlo Ancelotti's players shuffled uneasily, deflecting the immense tension expelled from the small away end of la Stade de Moustoir. Back down in Lyon, tapping my feet, wringing my wrists and trembling, I felt bundles of sensations, light-headedness, agitation, expecting the worst and preparing for glory. Lyon had by then been defeated 4-3 and rather than awaiting the outcome of the league, the Lyonnais hung around for a fireworks display, ignited from what looked like four, enormous poster beds on the pitch. French TV showed the PSG team awkwardly crowded around a television screen, their reporter gamely trying to interview a sunken-eyed Sirugu, who could say nothing. Three times the game at l'Abbé Deschamps was stopped; twice the players were ordered back to the changing rooms. Montpellier's goalkeeper Geoffrey Jourdren tried negotiating with the bitterly angry Auxerre fans behind his goal, but it took the CRS to clear the stand to stop the interruptions. Would their nerve hold?

By the time John Utaka's equaliser went in, texts from friends in Northern Ireland, who had tuned into fragmented online streams, were my lifeline. My eyes widened, my heart began to thud and my skin prickled. I was in a stadium with more than 32,000 others, watching one firework explode after another, in an agonising wait for history to be written. Nobody noticed. The Lyon fans, muttering with indifference, shrugged at their 3-4 loss. Les Aiglons celebrated marking their season finale with three points away from home. It was utterly surreal but in no way diluted my swathes of pride. Then John Utaka scored again. Cue delirium from one exiled girl from Herault surrounded by disconsolate and baffled Lyonnais.

Montpellier's success is impossible to overestimate Indeed, it cannot be justified in terms of figures. For once, established parallels between big budgets and silverware do not apply. The club had never won the domestic title before, with a third-place finish in 1988 their previous best effort. Their average attendance is eighth highest in a league of 20 and their propensity to spend is even less favourable. They have only the 14th highest annual budget in the French League. Millionaire (or richer) consortiums are a relatively new phenomenon in France, but welcomed by LFP, the league's governing body, chiefs who long to see the country challenging once again at the top level, namely the Champions League.

What they had never bargained for was a small, provincial club devoid of any point to prove, racing to the top of the division. And staying there. Even by the business end of the season, many dismissed the possible fairytale. Printemps, or springtime, belonged to PSG. Moreover, not only had Montpellier forged a meaningful title challenge with modest assets, the club's legacy is only now truly established. Suddenly, Montpellier could cling to real achievement: a league title, a place in the Champions

League, a revenue stream, a star on their chest and a buoyant future.

Silhouettes of thousands of fists, punching with all the fearless conviction of militia who had believed in their cause from the beginning, penetrated red fog. Tens of thousands watched victory unfurl in la Place de la Comédie, the city's main square, while flags whipped and jubilant screams bulldozed through the throng of supporters. The noise from the Comédie on that final night was a roar that swept out through the town, the wide boulevard down to the station, the Esplanade out to the Corum, the web of sidestreets and alleys of Ecusson and the Quartier Gare. It bounced off walls and roofs while the musky stench of flare-smoke travelled on the tingly spring wind.

Then, there was the trophy parade. An utterly unique, stomach-swilling spectacle at which barely a few years ago, most would have chuckled, with an underdog's self-depre-cation. Reports of just how many people witnessed the fervent homecoming range from 10,000 to 100,000 and, while the more inflated estimates match those expected of a major European title win, the conservative figures more accurately reflect the city's football following.

Montpellier is not a football city. It never has been. Culturally aware, spiced with a greater number of theatres and concert venues per capita than anywhere else in France, the fastest-growing metropolis in the Languedoc region is also home to a young, liberally-minded, well-educated population. So, given the magnitude of the rugby team, are René Girard's men criminally under-supported because 98 per cent are egg-chasers? No. From experience of the city's magnificently varied make-up, a little more than half follow the rugby, while a third are either profiting from their art-house cinema membership or fiercely parading Moroccan flags in areas of deprivation. The rest may be heard, albeit louder than ever before, to be crying "allez, allez!" from Avenue de Heidelberg.

Many, however, were on the Comédie, committed to the cause in the drizzle. Generally reserved for café culture, markets, music in the day and dance groups and street theatre at night, the bars had stashed tables and chairs safely away and others had enterprisingly set up external counters to serve beer in plastic cups. As the heaving assembly awaited the (delayed) team bus, people scrambled for vantage points; on the roofs of the tramstop, on the towers of the flood-lights, on the fountain of the Three Graces. There were flares, of course, lighting the gloom, and flags – those of Algeria and Morocco among the Tricolores – and the Languedoc cross. Again, roars echoed around the streets as the trophy was presented, and the celebrations continued into the night.

The next, already festering question is whether rising to become champions of France will also prove to be a kiss of death. Will the squad, following more exits of note than acquisitions during the transfer window, be canon-fodder on the Champions League stage? Losing top scorer Giroud, destined to emerge as a household name since signing a significant four-year deal with Arsenal, represents more than the sacrifice of 21 goals in a trophy-winning season. Erudite and charming, youthful and an epicurean, Giroud rebuffs football stereotypes and instead exemplifies the city of Montpellier's popularity – and population. Crediting his father for developing both his superlative taste in wines and interest in buying up Pic St Loup vineyards, the striker embraces life's finery. He illustrates why Joe Cole became a

Francophile and achieves, with perfect grace and humility, what Joey Barton can only plagiarise.

We also must consider manager René Girard's future. Is he likely to be prised away given the job he's done? Or will he remain, at the head of a club's coaching pyramid which also boasts academy success, and a strong scouting network which has the ability to spot a bargain? What will propel Montpellier to further successes and what, in addition to Giroud's departure, could jeopardise the momentum?

But discussions on whether the future will bring minor disintegration rather than sustained prowess are unlikely to trouble Montpellier fans. The championship has brought with it a recognition, at least throughout Europe, upon which it is impossible to place a value. It feels like a distant acquaintance remembering your name. It sparks a sense of pride and validates your obsession, your adoration – not as if it were needed, of course. Now, with the 2012/13 campaign underway in Northern Ireland, Belfast slurs of "here, wee girl, you must have been happy with your French boys!" greet me and I'm asked for Ligue 1 betting tips.

Regretfully, I often think about the culture shifts. How one family's 'anglofication' meant their eldest daughter swapped summer nights of watching her beloved football team run out, with anything from amateur sleeve badges to Ligue 1 credentials, for cricket. It was difficult to adjust to. I was the first to volunteer to wear a bib during skills sessions, if only to conceal a Manchester United shirt which had been bought by my anxious parents in an attempt to ingratiate me with other children, and inconveniently alienate me from the Arsenal fans.

For my own social interests, I eventually chose to forget my club. Moving to Belfast didn't make it any easier. I felt the same indifference, imposed by circumstance rather than choice, creep back. I even became more concerned about how Sammy McIlroy, Lawrie Sanchez and Nigel Worthington were handling life at the helm of Northern Ireland, rather than occupying myself with the fractious relationships within the French national side and their growing habit of under-performing. But while Northern Ireland paid my bills, France - and crucially Montpellier – had nestled long ago in my heart. Fanaticism, like true love, can wilt as quickly as it deepens, or fold as inconspicuously as it cements. But it never really disappears. And now, from afar, my team are champions.

## Chapter 8

# The Ballad of Rodney McAree

## Dave Kidd

This story begins at the end. Well somewhere close to its end, certainly at the climax. It is Thursday 18th March 2010 at Craven Cottage. Fulham, little cosy old Fulham, are entertaining Juventus, one of the grandest clubs in European football, in the last sixteen of the Europa League. They are attempting to overcome a 3-1 first-leg defeat, which, within two minutes of kick-off, had become a 4-1 aggregate deficit. Yet thanks to one goal from Bobby Zamora and one either side of half-time from Zoltan Gera, as well as the sending off of former World Footballer of the Year Fabio Cannavaro, Fulham are on level terms and beginning to believe in the impossible.

Dickson Etuhu passes to Clint Dempsey, who receives the ball with his back to goal near the corner of the penalty area on the Fulham right. The Texan turns and produces a chipped shot of stunning accuracy which arcs over the bald head of keeper Antonio Chimenti and dips beneath the crossbar into the far corner of the net. From the moment the ball leaves Dempsey's boot, I swear it's a goal. Yet as a Fulham supporter of 30 years' standing, I also know that this sort of thing doesn't happen to my club.

But as delirium breaks out all around me in the Johnny Haynes Stand, a tear stings my eye for the only time in my football-watching life. I turn to my left, to the electronic scoreboard hanging from the roof of the Putney End, and see the words 'Fulham 4 Juventus 1, 82 mins'.

Instantly, my mind races back 14 years. I am looking at that same Putney End, then a crumbling open terrace, overgrown with weeds, with large sections cordoned off as a health-and-safety hazard. There are a dozen Torquay fans, performing a Conga as they celebrate their club's late winner over Fulham in a Third Division match.

A few months earlier, Torquay had been bottom of the entire Football League and Fulham were next to bottom. Craven Cottage, a uniquely beautiful football ground, even in its days of disrepair, had been living in the shadow of the wrecking ball for as long as I could remember. It had been in the clutches of property developers, desperate to build bijou apartments on its prime Thames-side location, for more than a decade. Our local rivals Brentford would turn up every year and sing 'they're building flats on the Cottage'. We've never forgiven them. Only three or four thousand of us cared enough to watch the truly awful football regularly served up there between 1986 and 1996, as Fulham plummeted from English football's second flight to its basement, via various FA Cup humiliations at the hands of non-League clubs.

So, as the referee blows for full-time and Juventus are beaten, I hope each and every one of those hardcore supporters are inside Craven Cottage to experience scenes of such unfettered joy. Roy Hodgson's men had already knocked out the holders, Shakhtar Dontesk, and went on to defeat the champions of Germany, Wolfsburg, before

another fine comeback accounted for Hamburg and somehow Fulham had reached a European final they would lose,
deep in extra-time, to Atletico Madrid. Yet Dempsey's chip
was the defining moment of that astonishing European
journey - because it is so rare that a goal combines sublime
beauty with supreme significance.

Later that evening I am reminded of the only other
Fulham goal to compare with it, in my memory at least.
Outside a pub in Fulham High Street, amid scenes reminiscent of the Liberation of Paris, a knot of supporters break
into a chorus familiar to Fulham's diehard element:

"Who put the ball in the Carlisle net? Rodney McAree!
Rodney Mac-a-ree, Rodney Mac-a-reeeeeeeeee!
Who put the ball in the Carlisle net? Rodney Mac-a-ree!"

* * *

This is not the story of Roy Hodgson's Europa League run,
which, despite its magical quality, was partly the product of
the millions lavished upon the club by Mohamed Al Fayed
since he purchased Fulham in 1997. The team of 2009-10
may have over-achieved admirably and scaled unimaginable
heights yet they were still a team of richly-rewarded internationals. No, this is the story of Fulham's Third Division
promotion-winning team of 1996-97. The bunch of waifs
and strays which kick-started the club's rise through the
divisions, when there was barely a pot to piddle in.

Men like Rodney McAree, a little Northern Irish midfielder who made just 22 League starts for Fulham and netted
three goals. Even in the small squad assembled by young
manager Micky Adams in the summer of 1996, McAree was
a fringe player. He was injured for much of the promotion

campaign and made just eight appearances, scoring only once. Yet when you mention the name Rodney McAree to Adams, a spade's-a-spade Yorkshireman not given to hyperbole, his one-word answer is 'legend'.

McAree was fitting windows for a living back in Northern Ireland long before Cannavaro and his team-mates were being humbled at Craven Cottage. Yet without McAree and his colleagues, Alessandro Del Piero, David Trezeguet & Co would never have set eyes on Craven Cottage. That's because the single goal McAree scored was the one which virtually ensured Fulham's elevation from Division Three. It was the winner against promotion rivals Carlisle at Brunton Park on a filthy old day when more than 3,000 Fulham supporters had made the seven-hour journey to Cumbria. A 25-yard exocet of a half-volley, with beauty and significance written all over it. Folklore is an inexact science. In the popular mythology of supporters, McAree's goal transformed Fulham Football Club.

Yet the Carlisle victory was not the result which actually secured promotion - that came in a 0-0 draw at Mansfield three days later. And Adams tells me that, directly after the Mansfield game, a director informed him Fulham were about to be bought by a wealthy man who would change the club for ever. A couple of months later that man turned out to be erstwhile Harrod's owner Al Fayed. So if McAree had not unleashed his thunderbolt at Brunton Park and Fulham had drawn at Carlisle, they would still have been promoted and Al Fayed would still have bought the club.

Yet to use such cold, hard logic would be to misunderstand what makes so many of us decide to support football clubs other than Manchester United - the overwhelmingly elusive search for glory. McAree's goal was the single most glorious moment of that promotion campaign and the fact that McAree scored it, and not one of Fulham's regular first-team starters, is perhaps what makes it so appealing to the memory. The YouTube footage of his goal is so grainy that it looks as though it had been scored 25 years earlier, in the early days of colour television.

Adams, then in his first job in management and now a veteran of more than 600 League games at the helm of eight different clubs, remembers it as though it were yesterday. Football managers tend to recall those little selectorial masterstrokes which make all the difference. Adams said: "Rodney was at Fulham because of a relationship our director of football Ian Branfoot had with his dad who was, as Rodney is now, manager of Dungannon Swifts in Northern Ireland.

"Rodney was a wiry midfield player, eight-stone wet-through. We went up to Carlisle. It was windy and cold and horrible. The team talk was 'you lot probably won't fancy it today'. But I picked Rodney ahead of somebody, Martin Thomas maybe, who was more of a digger. I wanted someone to get on the ball and play which Rodney could do. We went a goal down to Rory Delap, Micky Conroy equalised for us and then - the moment. It was a great strike, corner of the net, it just flew. We had thousands of fans there and they went berserk. They still sing songs about Rodney McAree at Fulham now and that is absolutely fantastic. That team was special and those who were there recognise that. They recognise what we achieved when we had nothing and we were nothing."

McAree himself, who had failed to make the grade at Liverpool and Bristol City, is well aware, and enormously touched, by the standing his Carlisle goal has given him at a club now long established in the world's richest League. He said: "I'd been out injured for a good few months and my dad, Joe, had been at a youth tournament in England and he rang to tell me they'd be passing by Carlisle on the coach that day, on their way back to get the ferry to Northern Ireland. He asked if I'd be playing and I told him that I was pretty sure I wouldn't even be on the bench, so he didn't bother going.

"Then, Dad's literally travelling past Carlisle on the M6, when it comes over on the radio that I've scored! I didn't score many so I didn't know how to celebrate a goal like that. Even though there were 3,000 Fulham fans behind the goal I'd just scored in to, I ran the wrong way! The journey back was memorable. We'd all had a sweepstake on the Grand National on the way up - but it had been cancelled because of a bomb-scare so we put all the sweepstake money into re-stocking the fridge with beer at Birmingham.

"We all had to be at a family open day for supporters at the Cottage the next day and, despite the hangovers, it was fantastic to see what it meant to people; the goal, the win and the fact that we were virtually promoted. I went back to Fulham as a guest of the club for the game against Spurs in late 2011. My wife Adele and my parents were with me and it meant to so much for them to hear the crowd singing that song they sing about me, fifteen years later. I didn't win a whole heap of medals in my career but to know that I played a small part, but which is so fondly remembered, in what Fulham have gone on to achieve, means an awful lot."

To understand what that promotion meant to Fulham supporters you must go back to the mid-1980s and the ownership of hated property developer David Bullstrode who wanted to sell Craven Cottage and merge the club with

QPR to make Fulham Park Rangers. Relegation from the second to the third tier was followed by the club's first ever demotion to the Football League basement in 1994, courtesy of a final-day defeat at Swansea, which is remembered as keenly as the Carlisle victory, yet with entirely different emotions. Branfoot was then appointed manager with his former Southampton player, Adams, handed a player-coach's role.

For a year and half, though, Fulham's downward spiral continued. In January 1996 a club-record lowest attendance of 2,176 watched a 3-1 home defeat by Scunthorpe, which left the west Londoners next to bottom in the football League. Four days later, they were beaten at Torquay, the one club beneath them. A week after that, Adams took over as manager, with Branfoot moving upstairs. Fulham stumbled to 17th place, their lowest-ever finish but the summer of 1996 would be a time for change. Although not without Adams winning hard-fought battles for hearts and minds.

Adams said: "I went to Fulham as player-coach to Ian Branfoot, but it was sold to me on the basis that I'd eventually get the manager's job. By the time we dropped to 91st in the League, Ian was moved up to director of football and I got the job. Ian had a philosophy about playing the long ball and turning teams around but I wanted to put my stamp on it. Sometimes we hit it long but I wanted us to play too. Yet When a club gets into a downward spiral, people look after themselves and don't work as a team.

"The day I took over, I told the groundsman I wanted to play on the deck more than Ian did, so let's get plenty of water on the pitch so the ball is zipping around - he said 'yeah, okay' then he scarified it and drained it so the pitch was all bobbly. There was a group that had an executive box at Fulham called 'Manager Out' and all they did was moan about whoever the manager of the day was. And our groundsman was part of this group. Eventually we got him out - the twat.

"That just summed up where Fulham were at the time. The club was in the doldrums, the ground needed money spent on it but the club didn't own the freehold. We had no training facilities, training kit and hardly any balls. I can't tell you the amount of times we'd come back from a training session and all our jewellery and wallets had gone. There was a train station next to the changing room, people would hop off the train, nick our stuff and hop back on again.

"For years the players had ruled the roost there. Stalwarts like Jim Stannard and Glen Thomas would travel round the M25 from Essex for training. When Don Mackay was manager, if they got stuck in a traffic jam they'd say 'we can't get in Gaffer - we'll see you Thursday'. It was a crazy football club. Janice the club secretary ruled the roost and she could be evil. In the summer of '96, I cleared the decks. I studied how Gillingham had won promotion the previous season under Tony Pulis - three big centre-halves - eight or nine six-footers - Tony's philosophy hasn't changed to this day. I thought 'yeah that's how you have to be successful at this level'.

"You had to be physical and put importance on set-pieces. I recruited Paul Watson (a young full-back with the crossing ability of a lower-league Beckham), Richard Carpenter (a classy midfielder and dead ringer for Jurgen Klinsmann) and Darren Freeman (a shaggy-haired, empty-headed workaholic striker) from Gillingham reserves - I got them for under 50 grand at a tribunal. We got in Rob Scott who had a great long throw-in. He and Freeman played either side of Micky Conroy in a front three.

"Conroy was already at the club but had been having a tough time in terms of goal-scoring, so we got the ball forward to him more early and more often. Glenn Cockerill was important to me in midfield, I'd played with him at Southampton and he was an older head I could rely on. At the back there was Robbie Herrera from Torquay (a Rene Higuita lookalike nicknamed 'The Colombian Drug Dealer', despite being a mild-mannered Devonian). In the middle were Mark Blake, Terry Angus (a hulking terrace hero and possibly the nicest man in football) and Nick Cusack, who was a terrific footballer. He was a centre-forward and I turned him into a sweeper.

"But the most important one of the lot was the captain, Simon Morgan. Initially he wouldn't accept my ways. We used to go to Epsom Downs on a Tuesday and run up the hills at the racecourse. He didn't like that. We lost at Hartlepool early in the season and he was sulking on the bus and I had to pull him. I said 'I need you big time' - we got a result the game after and the game after that, we got a bit of momentum and he bought into it."

Morgan was the only one of that promotion-winning side who had experienced Fulham's relegation three seasons earlier - and, apart from the young trainee Sean Davis, he would be the only player still at the club when they were promoted to the Premier League under Jean Tigana in 2001. To me, Morgan was Mr Fulham. When the club handed him a testimonial against Tottenham, and I was covering the match for The Sun, I went through the turnstile and handed over my tenner. The only time I've ever paid to do my job. Morgan was special. He'd played in the top flight at Leicester but as well as being a superior player to most of Fulham's basement team, he also seemed to have the dedication and loyalty to the club which makes me surprised to hear from Adams that he was a notoriously bad trainer.

McAree said: "We had some valuable experience in that team and Morgs was immense. It's testimony to him that he remained at Fulham for so long. Alongside him was Cockerill, the Rod Stewart of Fulham, he did most of the singing on the team bus - along with the keeper Mark Walton."

After that defeat at Hartlepool in the second game of the season, Fulham won five in a row and remained in the promotion places for the rest of the season. Having watched Fulham so regularly throughout the bad, old years, it was sod's law that 1996-97 should be my first season reporting on a national newspaper for The Sun, so my attendance at the Cottage was restricted to midweek games, holidays and the odd occasion when I could twist the news editor's arm to send me to cover my own team.

Yet on the way back from covering a match at Charlton in September, I remember the moment I became convinced that change was afoot at Fulham. As I listened to Five Live's Six-O-Six phone-in, a succession of Darlington supporters were ringing in to complain about the visiting team who had apparently kicked their boys off the park that afternoon. The result: Darlington 0 Fulham 2. For years, I'd been complaining about away teams turning up at the Cottage, booting lumps out of us and heading off with three points.

Adams recalls: "Yep. Andy Crosby, now assistant manager of Southampton, was one of three Darlington players to be carried off in the first half hour of that game. If teams wanted to fight, we'd scrap them but if they wanted to play us at football, we'd do that as well. We showed them we had the mental strength to go up to places like that and win. We had, as a club, been the ultimate southern softies for years before that."

The beautiful game it may not have been but I was full of anticipation before my first Cottage visit of the season. Your club's ground is the only place you refer to as 'home' when you are seven and, God willing, still call home when you are seventy-seven too. The first visit of the season always gets the emotions going. Yet this turned out to be the defeat by Torquay, and the subsequent conga, which I recalled so vividly on the night of the epic Juventus triumph.

Still this was a mere blip. My next visit brought a 2-1 comeback victory over Scunthorpe, with the attendance more than doubling since the previous season's nadir against the same opponents. There were goals from Conroy, the Scottish journeyman who was Fulham's top scorer that season with 23 goals, and a winner from the relentless Freeman, who that night became my new favourite player. With his long curly goldilocks, his manic workrate and a lack of intellect which was always mercilessly exposed in captain Morgan's programme notes, Freeman was a vastly popular character.

"Darren wasn't the sharpest knife in the drawer and usually the butt of all jokes," said McAree, "but he was priceless to us that season. He and Rob Scott had the pace and strength to set up so many goals for Mick Conroy." And Adams recalls: "Freeman was Forrest Gump. I remember one game, God's honest truth, he picked up a ball and started running towards our own goal. We were screaming at him - YOU'RE GOING THE WRONG WAY! DAZ, WE'RE KICKING THE OTHER FUCKING WAY!' He was attacking our own back four. He wasn't the brightest in footballing terms but he's done very well for himself now, he's a property developer. He should have had more confidence in his own ability but he was a star that season and when I took him to Brighton as well. He's in the folklore down there too."

Victories came thick and fast in a long, consistent run stretching in to the New Year. I witnessed wins over Brighton and Barnet, as well as a 6-0 rout of Darlington - with no kicking involved this time as our former starlet Paul Parker, who had won League titles with Manchester United and played in a World Cup semi-final for England, returned for a brief spell. Then came Fulham's only serious poor run. Four defeats in five matches, which included a rare live Friday-night appearance on Sky and a 4-1 home thrashing by Cardiff.

Adams said: "I picked myself for that Cardiff game, as we were without a left-back, and I had a nightmare. We were on a poor run and it looked as though we were never going to get a result again. One day I just stopped training and sent them all home - because I just couldn't see it. Then we were 1-0 down at home to Swansea, one of our promotion rivals (I was there, on my birthday). Little Paul 'Bozzie' Brooker came on and transformed the game for us. We went on another run after that and didn't look back. He was a fans' favourite Bozzie, but in the trenches - forget it. I ended up taking him to Brighton, though, and he was fantastic there."

The Swansea win would be the start of an 11-match unbeaten run, culminating in the Carlisle victory and the promotion-sealing draw at Mansfield. After his heroics at Carlisle, McAree earned a fractured cheekbone from a stray elbow at Mansfield and had to drink his celebratory champagne through a straw. The final game of the season was a wonderfully Fulhamish anti-climax. Adams's men won 1-0 at Cambridge but were denied the title because Wigan's victory left the two clubs level on points. Fulham had the better goal difference but Wigan had scored more goals. For a few seasons, Football League positions were decided on goals scored rather than goal difference. And who's bright idea had that been? Why, Fulham chairman Jimmy Hill's, of course.

Covering the Cambridge game for The Sun, I decided to quiz a well-refreshed Hill about how he'd managed to deny his own club the title. He told me he was reluctant to talk to The Sun at all, because they had supported Labour in the General Election, which had ended in Tony Blair's landslide victory in the early hours of the previous morning.

As a lifelong Fulham and Labour supporter, who had previously experienced nothing but Tory rule and football misery, this was a heady time. Naively, I expected Britain to be transformed, rather than Fulham. But while Blair changed little, Al Fayed proved a more revolutionary leader. Adams was sacked within three months, despite a decent start to life in Division Two. Kevin Keegan arrived as director of football, with Ray Wilkins picking the team.

As a rookie 23-year-old reporter, Adams was one of the first professional football men I got to know and he remains a good friend. Keegan, however, soon took offence at a light-hearted criticism I had written about the pre-match entertainment at Fulham's 0-0 draw with Bournemouth - an Abba tribute band, which suggested that some of the changes at the club might not be entirely to our liking.

That perhaps one-day there might be a gaudy tribute statue to Michael Jackson, tainting football's most beautiful ground ...

Keegan, who had a contract with The Sun to provide a

number of ghost-written pieces at that time, became the first famous person ever to rant down a phone at me (it sounded so much like his infamous 'I'd love it' explosion that I was convinced it was one of my mates taking the piss). Then Keegan rang my boss, and staged a repeat performance. I was a young freelancer at the time. A lesser boss would have fired me and left my career stone-dead. Your boyhood heroes are often not what they seem, kids.

Adams reflects: "The night we got promoted at Mansfield, I was told by the director Bill Muddyman there was a buyer coming in who was going to change Fulham forever, he couldn't tell me who it was - but he was right. When Al Fayed came in there were people linked with my job on, literally, a daily basis. Then there were pictures of Kevin Keegan and Ray Wilkins in the stands at Craven Cottage while I was still in charge. Listen, that's football. I'm proud of what I did there but it became a different club.

"I don't think it happens in too many football clubs that a successful manager and group of players are moved on so quickly, maybe Manchester City has been similar in recent years.

"I signed a five-year contract when Mr Fayed came in and I was told I'd be the Alex Ferguson of Fulham. Three months later he sacked me. If I ever get cynical about what people tell me, that's why. But he had the money to get whomever he wanted and he wanted Kevin Keegan, I can understand that. I don't think Al Fayed would have bought the club if we hadn't won that promotion from Division Three, though. He wanted to get to the Premier League quickly and we had got the club one phase closer to where he wanted to be."

I took far less delight in the Second Division Championship season which Keegan masterminded in 1999 - before he left for England and ended up quitting in the Wembley toilets. Then came Tigana's wonderfully cavalier side which swept us into the top flight as runaway champions in 2001. Initially, Al Fayed invested big in the Premier League - £11million for Steve Marlet anyone? - then fell out spectacularly with Tigana. For four years, Chris Coleman admirably kept the club up, despite consistently having to sell his best players. After the brief and miserable reign of Lawrie Sanchez, came the Roy Hodgson years. A miraculous escape from relegation, a club-record seventh-place finish and that mesmerising run to the Europa League Final.

That goal by Dempsey. The euphoria outside Craven Cottage as the Juventus players skulked on to the team bus. Walking on air up to Fulham High Street. And outside the pub, that knot of supporters reeling in the street.

And singing: "Who put the ball in the Carlisle net? Rodney Mac-a-reeeeeeeeee!"

## Chapter 9

# The Odyssey

## Martin Lipton

It all started, for real, for me, in 1972. Our first colour television, to watch the Munich Olympics. My first full year at school. Another brother on the way. And, fatefully, the first football match I can remember. The day my dad took me to White Hart Lane and set me on the true journey through life. A journey that has had many twists, false turns, moments of doubt along the way.

Throughout that journey, I've sustained the faith that made me believe, against all the expectations fostered by events, that one day I would be rewarded. It's a day I am still waiting for, a day that may never come. Yet a day that, despite all those facts, I still believe in. Even when I find myself walking away from Wembley after a 5-1 thumping in the FA Cup semi-final, or when I was coming back from Cardiff when they have conspired to lose to Blackburn, BLACKBURN, in the Worthington Cup Final.

How do you sum up what it means to be a football fan? For me, it is about the life lessons it brings. Learning to veer between belief and frustration, to cope with the reality that disappointment is the more reliable end-game position. To tell yourself, with an optimism that experience still cannot quite quell, that it will be better, different, next time.

It isn't, of course. Often it's worse. Painfully, gut-wrenchingly worse. As John Cleese's character in "Clockwise" mournfully conceded 30-odd years ago, it's not the despair that kills you. It's the hope. The hope that springs resurgent, anew, every August, despite the inner knowledge that, in fact, the next nine months are only sure to confirm what you know deep inside yourself to be true.

No wonder, then, that I blame one man for me becoming the person I am. David Cecil Lipton. He's now happily retired in the Florida sun, the miseries of an English winter, of actually watching his team, long forgotten. Lucky sod. He's the fellow who burdened me with the weight I have carried for 45 years, the shadow that follows me every step of the way.

Had my father been an Arsenal fan, I would have been four and a half when "we" won the Double under Bertie Mee. Yes, I'd have had to put up with Terry Neill and Don Howe, with losing two finals in five days in 1980. With "1-0 to the Arsenal", as George Graham drilled that back four and Alan Smith and then Ian Wright bagged goals at the other end. Boring but successful. To be honest though, I think I'd have put up with that in exchange for Arsene Wenger. For Dennis Bergkamp and Thierry Henry, Patrick Vieira and Emmanuel Petit, Robert Pires and Freddie Ljungberg. For a side that won with thrilling grace and beauty. And the chance to spend most of my life laughing at Spurs, mocking their failures, revelling in the discomfort, celebrating St Totteringham's Day every year.

My father, though, denied me that.

Of course, it was easy for him. He was born in 1946, was

a teenager when Bill Nicholson's side were the finest team in football. And, as a North London Jew, saw the club as part of his birthright .We were also living in Walthamstow, three miles round the North Circular Road (which, in those far off days, was a breeze to drive on at any stage).To be fair, the Spurs team he introduced me to weren't bad either. The two Martins, Chivers and Peters. Alan Gilzean and his bald pate. Jimmy Neighbour, Mike England, a (very) young Steve Perryman, Cyril Knowles at left-back, and, of course, Pat Jennings in goal. All directed by Bill Nick, a mythic figure even then.

Memory plays tricks but that first game I remember was a 4-3 win over Stoke. Thanks to Soccerbase, I now know it was played on October 7 1972. I can't remember anything other than the score. But I know I was hooked. Completely and utterly. Hooked on football. And hooked, crucially, on newspapers. As soon as the Daily Mirror came through the letterbox - and I'm not making this up, we were old fashioned, London working class, Mirror readers - it was mine. I read from the back, desperate, even then, for a scrap of news about Spurs.

You know how it is as a kid. When you see the England team with none of your team's players and can't understand how any other players are better than the ones at your club. I was that kid. That Spurs side were the UEFA Cup holders and six months later I was at Wembley to see Ralph Coates come off the bench in place of John Pratt - there is always a target for the boo boys at White Hart Lane and Pratt was the victim of choice in that team - and dribble his shot past Norwich keeper Kevin Keelan for the only goal.

It was the start of a life-long affair, even if, by the time I was 10, I flirted with Orient - a 20-minute walk down Church

Road - when my father wasn't around to take me to Tottenham. But for years it was the same routine. An hour before kick-off, my father would tell me we were off. It was always me and him. Never any of my younger brothers (although I was captured, with Trevor's grey sheepskin a pair with my camel-coloured one, going mental behind the goal at the Paxton Road end in 1986 when Chris Waddle's dribble round the entire Oxford defence in an FA Cup tie was disallowed for offside).

Into the car. Normally a different car every few weeks - for some reason I never quite understood at the time, my dad always seemed to be turning up with a new one, including at various times a Jensen Interceptor and a Lotus Esprit, perhaps the least sensible vehicle ever for a family of six. Then, about 10 minutes before kick-off, arriving near the ground.

Jose Mourinho always talked about "the game before the game". We had our own version. The start was the car slowing down and my dad winding down the window and blagging his way past the police line, telling the same story of us going to see his mother who lived on that estate, how she was ill and I needed to see her before I went to bed. In truth, I can now reveal, Mabel Cohen (nee Finkelstein) was living, as she had been for the previous 20 years, in Johannesburg, utterly oblivious of her other life in Tottenham.

Incredibly, dad's story was bought every time. No wonder he spent his life in direct selling. He was remarkably convincing, even when he was telling a blatant lie. Including the one I always got five minutes from the final whistle, that we had to leave to beat the traffic. I wouldn't like to think how many late goals I missed.

For any young fan, there is a moment of epiphany. That,

probably, comes with your first night match. In the 70s, the lights inside any stadium concourse were weak, subtle, subdued. And that was nothing to do with the aftermath of the Three Day Week. But there was something about that memory, of walking up through the dark patch between the concourse and the seats and suddenly seeing first the blaze of the floodlights and then the sheer vibrancy of the green below.

Even today, having travelled round the world time and again to watch games, having seen four World Cup Finals, various Champions League Finals, huge England games, I still get that same buzz when I see the pitch, under lights, for the first time. It will never go away. If only I'd known, in fact, that at six it was pretty much as good as it was ever going to get, despite those occasional oases amid the desert, I wonder what I'd have said to him? Maybe "no thanks". Or "do we have to?"

But I doubt it.

Being a Tottenham fan may be far more trouble than it is worth but I am not angry at my father. Indeed, I am profoundly grateful. Without his guiding hand steering me to N17, his influence, his direction, I might have become a very different person. Supporting Spurs may not be a choice any sane man would make. Why on earth would anybody in their right mind choose to be a follower of perennial under-achievers, a side that, as Alan Hansen points out with staggering regularity, you can rely on to let you down?

You wouldn't. You simply wouldn't. Indeed, it requires a singularity of mind, a degree of sheer bloody-mindedness, to remain loyal when everything that is supposed to drive support is yelling at you to seek another mistress.

But maybe, as has been said in other contexts, you do not

choose your team; your team chooses you. Temperamentally, as someone who tells himself it will never be as black as you fear, although probably not as white as you hope, it is fitting.

If you can cope with what being a Spurs supporter throws at you, then you're pretty much equipped to cope with everything life has in store. Forget Kipling's talk of triumph and disaster being imposters. Both are real, genuine. If you're a true football fan, though, not one of those who follow the glory trail, it is disaster, disappointment, frustration that is the constant force.

Actually, for me, it was never that bad. I can claim credit for Spurs' survival from relegation in 1975.

Not that Terry Neill knew it, but the truth is that Tottenham's fate was determined not in N17 but a month before the end of the season, in a terraced house in Farmilo Road, E17. The pitch was our front room. My father - who might have been a decent goalkeeper if he had been a six footer, rather than carrying the gene which means I still aspire to five feet six inches - told me it was all on the next penalty. If I scored, he insisted, Spurs would stay up. If I missed, they would be relegated. Looking back, it was a pretty big burden to place on an eight-year-old. All or nothing. Relegation? Unthinkable, inconceivable.

You will now know that my penalty pinged off the inside of the post despite my dad guessing the right way. When Spurs confirmed their safety by beating Leeds 4-2 I was not surprised. I'd already sealed the deal. They were just signing it off. Two years later, not even a repeat of that pact was enough to deny the inevitable. Even though I scored again, I knew dad wasn't trying to save it. We had both reached the stage when there was only one end-game. Then again, when you lose 8-2 at Derby, it's only going to go one way.

If you can get your head round relegation and promotion by the age of 11 or 12, you are grounded. You realise that life doesn't always turn out the way you want but that there is the opportunity for renewal, resurrection, return. And so, when Keith Burkinshaw brought Spurs back, before he left nodding sadly at what he was quitting and mournfully stating "there used to be a football club over there", I had new heroes in white.

My heroes. Not the ones I had to borrow from my dad. But the ones I could first share with him, then take on as my own. Ossie Ardiles, of course, and Ricky Villa - proving we even signed the best foreign players. And Glenn Hoddle. In my young mind, for a decade, the greatest player on the planet. He had to be. He was a genius. He scored stunning goals. He played 60-yard passes other midfielders could not dream of, without even looking. And he'd come from just up the road in Harlow - we'd moved out to Essex, a dormitory town called Wickford, near Basildon, by then. More crucially he played for Spurs, was the onfield general of the back to back FA Cup Final wins in 1981 and 1982.

That was actually the golden age as far as I was concerned. Probably because I'd started going on my own. Leaving Wickford market - where I worked on my uncle's clothes stall - to catch the 1305 to Liverpool Street, then out to Seven Sisters on the Tube, walking the half-hour down Tottenham High Road, getting there with 10 minutes to spare (old, paternal, habits die hard). It was my team, my time. A few mates but the terrace crack was great. Learning new ways of abusing opposition fans. Singing the songs. Watching not just Hoddle, Ardiles and Villa but Tony Galvin, Chris Hughton, Graham Roberts, Garth Crooks and Steve Archibald.

Spurs being Spurs, though, they could never do it the easy way. They had to put you through the wringer first. Those two FA Cup triumphs both came in replays, watched not in the flesh - money, for a few years, was too tight to mention and my dad had transmuted into an armchair fan - but on television. So Villa's astonishing goal against City was put in the context of how they had been so close to losing in the initial tie, before Hoddle's free-kick looped past Joe Corrigan off Tommy Hutchison's shoulder. My contribution was changing my sitting position from the "unlucky" one I'd adopted for the first hour.

And the Hoddle penalty that squeaked them past QPR 12 months later was bathed in the glow of their inability to get more than one past Peter Hucker at the first time of asking.

Even retaining the Cup felt like a consolation prize. At the turn of the year, a Treble was on, dangling tantalisingly in front of the eyes, as it was to be again in 1987. They even went one up against Liverpool in the League Cup Final, before capitulating in extra-time. And you don't need telling where those title hopes went.

I was learning about disappointment, about things not panning out.

Probably I should have known that from my politics. There weren't too many Labour sympathisers in Essex in 1982. After the Falklands Invasion, nobody at Bromfords Comprehensive really wanted to know that Thatcher should have done what Callaghan did in 1976 and just sent out a warship to scare the Argentinians off. But I didn't care about popularity. I had a cause. I was prepared to stand up for it.

I also knew that it was only football. That I did it for the game, for the excitement of the football. Not for any of the crap that went with it.

Given that I've never exactly been physically imposing, the idea of football being merely a pretext for a tear-up was something I simply never understood. My match-day routine was now set. After the game, whatever happened, it was a milkshake and a burger from MacDonalds. Coming back from one game, we were cornered by a lad who asked: "Are you coming for the scrap?" His anger at our lack of interest was palpable. But it was about the football. And the crushing disappointment, although in the midst of that, there was more coming of age.

April 1985. Tottenham v Everton. The Everton we'd put four past on the opening day of the season, a game that had been postponed by snow and ice a couple of months earlier when we were flying. Despite losing at home to United a few weeks before, this was the big one. Win this and it would happen. Champions. At last. I was in the sixth form but had a free lesson last period and so left early. I knew it would be rammed but still wanted my perch on The Shelf, the raised standing area that gave you a terrific view.

History records what happened. How Mark Bowen, playing because Hughton was ruled out, got caught in possession for the opener, how Andy Gray latched onto a weak header from Paul Miller, how Roberts scored a stunner but then Neville Southall made the save of the season from Mark Falco's header. How the vast majority of the 48,000 inside were left devastated. But there was a final, defining image, one that I never allowed myself to forget.

At the whistle, as the Shelf began to empty, amid the crushing disappointment, stood a father and son. Dad, wearing his Spurs scarf, was the embodiment of despair. His nine-year-old son, an Everton shirt proudly worn underneath his coat, beaming with the sheen that football brings. You had to smile, to recognise that it's not just about how you handle winning. It's as much, if not more, about how you handle losing.

As stands for football, so stands for life itself. The moments when you are carried away with the joy, the pleasure, when you tell yourself that this is the breakthrough. Then the cold dose of harsh reality. And when you are a Tottenham fan, when you know with clarity those two states of being, you are more attuned to seeing it in others.

If there was a group of fans who truly did not envy Manchester City on May 13 2012, it was surely those who were witnessing their own side's Champions League near-miss. When those City fans started walking out of the Etihad, tears streaming down their faces, as they believed their championship party had turned into a title wake, the Tottenham supporters watching at home knew full well what they were going through. Even though you grow, change, mature, in my case learn to develop a professional sense of dispassion, where you feel bound to be more critical of your own team to head off the charge of bias, those vestigial emotions remain part of your core. The nagging sense that things will always find a way of going wrong at some point - so you have to relish the here and now before it disappears.

Take 1987. David Pleat's Tottenham. Hoddle, in his final year, was in his pomp. Ardiles had returned to the club after his Falklands-enforced exile. Waddle was astonishing. Clive Allen scored 49 goals. The 4-5-1 formation was all about possession, thrilling and brilliant, the best football in the country. But still they managed to lose the League Cup semi-final to Arsenal, despite scoring the first goal in all three games - including the second leg AND replay at White Hart Lane.

And didn't even all wear the same shirts at the FA Cup Final, when they conspired to lose to Coventry, the final whistle seeing me start a United Nations peace-keeping mission to prevent Trevor - he of the grey sheepie - launching a first strike against the notion of West Midlands independence. Oh, and Spurs finished third. And lost Hoddle to Monaco that summer. And the manager for decidedly non-footballing reasons within a few months. No matter how good things are, they will end in disappointment. It's just the way things go. The way life goes.

So it went on. Terry Venables signed Paul Gascoigne but sold Waddle the same week.

Gazza was, well, Gazza. Astonishing, unstoppable, his 1990 World Cup tears capturing the nation, making women who had not watched football for a decade or more want to mother him. The following season he took Spurs to the FA Cup Final virtually single-handedly, though just the day before they were to take on Nottingham Forest, it emerged he was being sold to keep the club solvent - only Tottenham could lose money by buying a sportswear company.

They didn't even get the cash as Gascoigne clattered into Gary Charles in the first few minutes, a reckless, hare-brained lunge from which, in truth, he never really recovered, the next year spent in plaster and limbo before eventually joining Lazio.

Again, hope dashed, the sheer certainty of Tottenham's self-implosive ability a bizarre comfort as I went on a professional journey to the wilds of West Yorkshire, where I spent six out of seven years from 1989.

As I was finding out about myself, working out my values, I could watch on as Spurs demonstrated those enduring truths about the club. Take 1994. Alan Sugar - who had evicted Venables - shocked the world by signing Jurgen Klinsmann and Romanian World Cup stars Ilie Dumitrescu and defender Gheorghe Popescu. Ardiles is by now the manager and Spurs have the "Famous Five" - the two new signings plus Teddy Sheringham, Darren Anderton and Nick Barmby - beginning the season with a terrific 4-3 win at Sheffield Wednesday, crowned by Klinsmann's celebratory dive. My first Premier League game for the Press Association.

This time, it is a different Spurs, we were promised. Of course it wasn't.

Before Christmas Ardiles was a dead duck, with Gerry Francis coming in, taking them to an FA Cup semi-final against Everton at Elland Road, Manchester United the likely Wembley opponents once the nailed-on win was recorded. Somehow, the Merseyside fans were handed both ends, with Tottenham getting one side and on the pitch, with no fit full-backs, they were defenestrated by Daniel Amokachi, in his one decent performance for the Toffees, whose manager Joe Royle entered the press conference room, raised glass in hand, to chirrup: "Here's to the Dream Final, lads!"

My own career was progressing. By 1996, I was back in London, covering - yep, you've guessed it. Hardly a labour of love, mind, more hard labour. That desire to avoid bias saw me giving Francis a tough time - one colleague revealed he had been asked if they wouldn't send me again - before a question I asked of Christian Gross at his unveiling, inquiring whether he understood the history of the club, provoked the balding Swiss to produce his Underground ticket - he had come by Tube - and announce: "Here is the ticket; the ticket to my dreams."

More like a nightmare, with Gross sacked 24 hours after Sol Campbell's damning assessment of him during an England press conference, which left me spending the day outside the club's Chigwell training ground, the only light relief coming late afternoon, when Pleat, now back as Director of Football, wound his window down as he drove out to shout: "Lipton - you're supposed to be a Tottenham fan!"

I am, so I know what it feels like. And even when it got better, it got worse, teaching me that you can never take anything for granted in life, that it is supposed to let you down. Take 2006. After 37 games, Spurs faced West Ham on the final day of the season, a team with nothing to play for, knowing that a win would not only mean they finished above Arsenal, but took fourth.

What followed? Lasagne-gate. Whether it was food poisoning or just a virus running round the dressing room will never be known for certain but Martin Jol woke on the morning of the game to discover half his team could barely walk, let alone run, with the Premier League refusing Tottenham's entreaties for the game to be put back. The fact that the League's top brass were at Arsenal, for the final game at Highbury before the Gunners moved to their new home, only added to the conspiracy theories. Spurs, who lost 2-1, had invented a new way of committing suicide.

Exit, soon afterwards, Jol. Enter Juande Ramos, winning the Carling Cup - at the expense of Chelsea - within a few months, before disappearing in a puff of smoke, leaving the same side bottom of the league, staring relegation in the face.

Harry Redknapp rescued the cause, inspired the dressing room, turned the club's fortune's around. Yet even in 2009, triumph - okay, relative triumph - only came on the back of debacle.

The FA Cup semi-final. Opponents: Portsmouth, the worst club in the Premier League. Bankrupt. Heading for the dogs and the wall. Managed by my friend, the much-maligned - and unfairly so - Avram Grant. For 120 minutes, Spurs laid siege to the Portsmouth goal. And lost 2-0. The season had to combust. Typical Spurs. Fourth place surely thrown away. Except, within six days, they had beaten both Arsenal and champions-to-be Chelsea, securing fourth with a game to spare when they saw off rivals money-laden rivals Manchester City.

For one year, the good times rolled. Spurs in the Champions League. All right, they nearly messed it up, going three down to Young Boys Berne inside half an hour before dragging it back to 3-2 and putting four past the Swiss side at home. What followed was beyond drama for a Tottenham fan, a peek into what it must feel like to be a fan of the teams that expect to win in Europe.

Two trips to the San Siro, the first seeing them four down at the break against holders Inter and nearly pulling off the mother of all comebacks, as Gareth Bale warmed up for roasting Maicon at Gas Mark five back at the Lane by scorching past the Brazilian to claim a hat-trick. Then back to take on AC Milan, the second most successful side in the history of the European Cup. Winning 1-0 there was "Glory, glory Tottenham Hotspur" territory, a night when professional detachment briefly parted company with the fan inside. Well, you would, wouldn't you?

After a nail-biting night in N17, when every second

threatened to bring a Milan goal but somehow they held on, the quarter-finals, Real Madrid, the Bernebeu, Jose Mourinho. Expectation, hope, wonderment, met cold reality. In the minutes before kick-off, Aaron Lennon - supposed to stretch them down the right when Bale did the business on the left - cried off, forcing a late change. Before you knew it, a goal down - Emmanuel Adebayor of all people - and a man down, as Peter Crouch made two needless lunges and saw red. And after hope, cataclysm. Three more shipped in the final spell, insult added to injury when goalkeeper Heurelho Gomes demonstrated his talent for elementary blunders from virtual back-passes as the home game was lost as well. To cap it all, a late-season collapse saw them finish fifth again - so near yet so far.

But just when you think you've seen it all, done it all, you're proven wrong. In many ways, the 2011-12 season encapsulated why supporting Tottenham is a curse, not a blessing. A campaign that started in bleakness and despair, with Chelsea seemingly set to sign Croatian playmaker Luka Modric, the first game of the season called off because of the Tottenham riots, back to back thumpings by the two Manchester giants leaving them bottom of the league.

Then the fightback. Chairman Daniel Levy winning the war of wills and refusing to sell Modric. The arrivals of Adebayor, on loan from City, and Scott Parker bringing a sea-change. A run of wins, propelling Spurs to third at Christmas, knowing a home win over soon to be doomed Wolves would take them top, all against the background of the bid to vacate N17 for the Olympic Stadium, shedloads of cash wasted when the club realised, far too late, that they had been lured into a loaded, fixed contest they could never win, just to give the Mayor of London political cover.

Beat Wolves and go joint top on points. Easy. Unless it's Spurs, who somehow managed to drop two points. January was overtaken by the looming trial of Redknapp over allegations of tax fraud, the manager missing the goalless draw at Anfield because his post-courtroom flight from City Airport was delayed by a technical fault. Redknapp was cleared, after 13 days in court. Relief all round. Spurs could get on with their season.

But even while he was eating his celebratory dinner, five hours later, England manager Fabio Capello was quitting, leaving Redknapp seemingly the only contender for the job, as the Football Association began a soft-shoe shuffle. For weeks it went on. Spurs undermined, Redknapp distracted, the players losing focus. Even when the title was gone - it was never really a serious option - there was still a 10-point gap over fourth placed Arsenal, with Tottenham going two up inside half an hour at the Emirates.

By half-time, they were level. By the end they were bedraggled and defeated, the 10 points frittered away, dropping to fifth, staring at sixth, suffering the worst FA Cup semi-final decision of all time against Chelsea at Wembley to add insult to injury.

Suddenly, after the FA decided Redknapp was not, after all, the man they wanted - why couldn't they have done that a month earlier, if Roy Hodgson was always the first choice? - a response.

Wins over Blackburn and Bolton, conspiring with Arsenal drawing at home with Norwich, meaning wins at Aston Villa and Fulham would guarantee third. Time for another implosion. Only a draw at Villa Park, meaning that a final day win over Fulham meant fourth again. Fourth. Champions League football in any other season for a decade.

Millions flowing into the coffers. Modric and Bale staying, for sure. Other players desperate to come.

Except it doesn't work like that. Not for Spurs. Most of North London became Bavarians for a night. If Bayern Munich beat Chelsea in the Champions league Final, fourth would be enough. Imagine what it was like to be a well-known Spurs fan in the Allianz Arena. How every missed Bayern chance made you realise what was at stake for the one participant not actually in Munich. When Didier Drogba steered home the penalty that made Chelsea champions of Europe, Tottenham had lost almost as much as the Germans - they, after all, get another go at it next time. Within a month, Redknapp was gone too, replaced by Andre Villas Boas, sacked – by Chelsea, of course, one last twist – in March. Bonkers.

That is what is like to be a Spurs fan. To have riches, delight, achievement waved in front of your eyes. Then taken away. You have to learn to accept that things do not pan out as you would hope, that sometimes it all goes wrong, that life is not a bed of roses. But that you can retrench, rebound, come again. Seek the next challenge. Get on with it. Just like life. Great moments. And also disappointment, sometimes despair. Feelings of joy and loss.

I'm a Spurs fan. It's what I do. Thanks dad!

## Chapter 10

# Stanley Victor Superstar

## Iain Macintosh

You don't support Southend United for the glamour. Actually, after almost 25 years as a supporter myself, I'm not entirely certain what you *do* support them for. Football has changed dramatically over the last fifty years, but Southend have always been true to their roots, steadfastly rubbish regardless of shifting circumstance. Sure, we've had our moments. The League Cup win over Manchester United and the back-to-back promotions of the Webb and Tilson eras, but it's always been against our nature. Success for us, you see, is like watching a dog walk on its hind legs; it's great fun, but it's never long before the dog falls over. You just don't get world class footballers at Southend. Except for this one time in 1992…

The story of Stan Collymore at Southend always reminds me of a comic strip in an old Roy of the Rovers' annual from the early 80s. Struggling non-league side Durrell's Palace arrive for training one morning and find a confused Scandinavian youth waiting at the gates. Unable to say anything other than his name, 'Kingo Laff,' and the in-no-way-patronising-line, "This Palace, ja? Me footballer," he is quickly given a kit and invited to practice with them. 'Kingo,' it turns out, is an absolute world beater and he is quickly signed up and thrown into the first team for the game on Saturday. He plays a blinder and scores a hat-trick, but the celebrations are curtailed when a representative of another 'Palace', professional, well-financed and absolutely livid, arrives to reveal that 'Kingo Laff' is actually Ken Golath, a Swedish international who signed for them last week and got lost on the London Underground. Durrell's Palace are forced to let him go and reflect on the hard truth that he was always far, far too good for them.

Younger readers may not appreciate Collymore as a footballer and will know him more for his regular appearances on Channel Five and his erudite analysis on TalkSport. Older readers may not appreciate him either, but for entirely different reasons. Collymore's reputation was tarnished by public scandal, notably the assault on TV presenter Ulrika Jonsson and the revelation that he had been caught 'dogging' in a car-park. An exceptional player in his early 20s, the peak years of his career were ruined by his struggles with depression, a battle he continues to fight today. Collymore achieved more in his career than most: he played for Liverpool, his beloved Aston Villa and represented his country three times, but he never fulfilled his true potential. Anyone who saw him between 1992 and 1996 will know that he had everything he needed to be one of the best players of his generation. And for a time, a very short time, he was ours.

Collymore had come through the youth ranks at Walsall and Wolverhampton Wanderers, but it wasn't until he dropped down to non-league Stafford Rangers that he began to make a name for himself. Steve Coppell quickly signed him for Crystal Palace, a team very much on the rise, but the move didn't work out. "I was getting nowhere," Collymore told me. "I was behind Mark Bright and Ian Wright, so I couldn't get in the team and when I was getting on the pitch, I was pushed out wide. It wasn't working. One day, the boss told me that he had an offer from Southend and that was that. I didn't even have a chance to say goodbye. The next thing I knew, I had a bag with my boots in and I was off. Round the M25, on to the A127 and into Essex. I was shitting myself."

As well he might be. It was late November and Southend had won just two matches all campaign. Only in their second ever season as 'full members' of the Football League, a quick return to the third division looked inevitable. Manager Colin Murphy was struggling with the pressure of replacing club legend David Webb and, to make matters worse, the fans were openly rebelling against the owner Vic Jobson, a man whose PR masterstrokes included telling them to support someone else if they weren't happy. But their fortunes were about to change.

"Bobby Houghton, the manager who took Malmo to the European Cup Final, was Murphy's assistant," recalls Collymore. "I'll always remember him talking to me when I first arrived. He said, 'You've got everything, Stan. I'm convinced that you're going to have a fantastic career.' Then the manager sat me down, sketching out maps of where he wanted me to play, marking my runs. He wanted me to play as an out and out striker. It was perfect. Immediately, I knew I could be successful."

And he was. To the surprise of the Southend fans, most of whom had never heard of him when he signed, Collymore hit a brace on his debut in a quite unexpected 3-1 victory over Notts County. No-one was entirely sure what had happened. Who was this gigantic striker? Where had he come from? Why had no-one else tried to sign him? On the popular Southend United forum, Shrimperzone, they're still baffled as to how he ended up at Roots Hall.

"Stan didn't seem to have any weaknesses at all," Southend supporter 'Benji99' recalled. "He was quick, he could pass, he could shoot with unbelievable power and he was virtually impossible to knock off the ball."

"Sad as it is to say," mused 'Angell Delight', "I'll never see a Blues player with that much talent again in my lifetime."

Even from the stands, seeing Collymore run with the ball was like being a foot solider watching a tank crest a hilltop and open up the throttle, thundering towards you. You were in awe of his size, in awe of the firepower, but most of all you were in awe of his speed. Quite what the opposing defenders made of him is anyone's guess.

While he wasn't in the same bracket as pre-injury Ronaldo (the old one), they were very alike. Both men were foreboding physical presences, both were blessed with supernatural close control and both were deadly from anywhere inside the final third. In my lifetime, very few players could match the all-round brilliance of Ronaldo, but Collymore really, really could have come close. More than that, he energised a depressed supporter base, giving them hope on the pitch, even as they struggled off it.

"I can remember the look in Collymore's eyes after he scored, screaming at the celebrating Southend United fans," said supporter Kevin Hogg. "He seemed to actually want to get in the North Bank but at the time there were fences with grease smeared over them."

But even his arrival wasn't enough to save Murphy's job. Southend won another six games, but none of them were consecutive. For every step they took forward, they took another one back and by the end of March, facing increasing pressure on his own position, Chairman Jobson swung the axe.

"I felt for Murphy," said Collymore. "He had given me my chance, he'd filled me with confidence, but it just wasn't working. Some of his ideas were a little too left-field. When we needed to be lifted or drilled, he had us out on the training field doing stuff like cricket catching practice. The new manager was very different."

The new manager was Barry Fry, ebullient, outspoken and…well…crackers.

"We met Barry at a service station, where he'd been dropped off by his wife," said Collymore. "He got on the coach and introduced himself. It didn't take long for him to make his mark. Before his first game, at Sunderland, he just came in, rolled his sleeves up, told us to enjoy the match and go for it. 'If they score four,' I remember him shouting, 'we'll fucking score FIVE!'" It worked. Sunderland scored two, but Southend fucking scored four. Four days later, West Ham came to Roots Hall and left with their tails between their legs.

"Collymore got it on the right," grinned Fry when we discussed the game, "beat three people with his strength and his pace, whipped in a cross and Brett Angell stabbed it in. All of a sudden, from being down and out when I joined on the Thursday night, we've won two games on the bounce and we've got a chance."

A draw at Watford followed before a must-win home clash with Bristol Rovers. "Stan picks up the ball on the halfway line," said Southend supporter 'Billericay Blue'. "He's got his back to goal and a defender tight to him. The guy next to me says, 'He's gonna score here.' With a quick twist, he rolls around the defender, takes the ball on, beats another man and then absolutely smacks the ball into the top corner from 30 yards. The guy next to me just grinned. 'Told ya!'

Southend had won again, but back to back defeats at Barnsley and Leicester quickly followed. A win at Grimsby gave Southend a lifeline that they threw back by losing to Cambridge and suddenly everything came down to the last game. The challenge was simple. Beat Luton Town at Roots Hall and survive.

"Before the game," recalls Fry, "I sat the players down and spoke to them. 'You lads have been amazing' I said. 'You picked yourselves up from an impossible position, you were certs for relegation and you've got yourselves here where you can win and stay up. It's all in your hands. You've come so far. For fuck's sake, don't fuck it up now."

Being of still tender years and living in what then seemed like 'distant' Chelmsford, my hopes of attending Southend games depended on my shift-working father having the right period of time off. This was not one of those weeks. Fortunately, a girl at school, the only other person I knew in Chelmsford who supported Southend, asked if I wanted to come along with her and her dad. To this day, I have no idea if she had ulterior motives for this invitation (I suspect not given that I was an Iron Maiden-loving, Monty Python-obsessed nerd) or if her father thought I might be using football as an excuse to put the moves on his daughter (again unlikely, given that just speaking to a girl at that age would either give me the shakes or full tumescence). Both parties would doubtless have been reassured by my refusal to discuss anything, anything at all that day, apart from the game.

Roots Hall was a sell out, the fans filled the terraces of the North Bank, a rickety, corrugated iron-covered lair of sweaty Essex man. We were in the North-West corner, standing on tiptoe, shifting our weight ceaselessly to find a vantage point between the heads or the shoulders of other, taller supporters. We started so well. Andy Sussex smashed home an extraordinary opening goal, lashing home an absolute thunderbastard from outside the penalty area. Brett Angell added another to apparently make the game safe. But Luton came back and snatched one just before the break. To this day, I maintain that we should have been spared a nervous second half.

Collymore put his head down like a charging bull and roared across the halfway line. He bundled one defender out of the way, left another screaming for mercy in his slipstream, drew the goalkeeper and unleashed a photon torpedo of a shot into the bottom corner. Our musky corner of Roots Hall exploded in delight, bodies smashing together in a jubilant melee, one man slipping down the steps and tumbling into the maelstrom, grinning all the way. It was some time before we realised it had been chalked off for an offence I can only guess at.

Nevertheless, Southend held on and safety was secured. Fry ran a lap of honour in his tracksuit, waving his cloth cap in the air. Collymore was stripped to his pants and hoisted up on the shoulders of the supporters, who rushed onto the pitch.

"I remember going into school on the Monday," said 'Drastic', "One of my classmates proudly proclaimed that he'd touched Stan while he was being chaired round the pitch, like he'd been at the sermon on the mount and grabbed at Jesus Christ."

"He was practically naked," said 'Kent Shrimper'. "He leant down to me and I gave him my lucky Southend hat. He'd given me so many gifts over that short period and that was mine in return."

Collymore still describes that day as one of the best of his life, and one of his finest achievements in football. And, of course, that was the last time he played for Southend. That summer, having scored 15 goals and successfully spear-headed the great escape, he moved to Nottingham Forest in a deal that would eventually earn the club almost £4m.

"I wonder sometimes what that team could have done, had it stayed together," he told me. "Barry was very shrewd. He had an amazing eye for a player and those few games really showed what he could do in a short space of time. There was a balance to that team and there were some exceptional players like Chris Powell and Keith Jones, as well as honest, proper players like Andy Sussex and Dave Martin. There were people there who had been rejected, who had been dropped, who knew what it was to have to fight just to have a career at all. There were no airs and graces at Southend.

"That was as happy as I've ever been in football. I had good times at other clubs, more high profile clubs, but nothing compared to driving into training in my old Vaux-hall, washing my own kit, looking after my own boots and having a crack with the lads, people I actually liked. Everyone enjoyed their football. There was no bullshit, no agents, no hangers on and no cult of celebrity, the stuff I got wrapped up in later on. And the support! It was incredible.

"In my darker days, when I was really struggling with depression, I used to go on Shrimperzone every now and then. I was out of work, I couldn't get back into broadcast-ing, but I could go there and chat to people who remembered me and identified with me. It helped. I don't regret leaving Southend. I try not to have regrets. There were times in my life when I've looked back, but you have to look forward. The move to Forest worked out well. I scored goals, we were promoted, we finished third in the Premier League. Maybe I should have waited longer before I moved to Liverpool. Maybe I wasn't ready for that kind of life. One more season at Forest and I think I would have been better suited to it. But if Southend ever needed me in the future, if there was a role I could play that could enhance the club, well, I'd do anything to help them."

Southend struggled on in the second flight, hanging on for four more seasons before succumbing to consecutive relegations and stabilising in the basement division. A dog cannot walk on its hind legs forever. And yet the memories remain.

"He was blatantly too good for us," admits supporter 'Yorkshire Blue'. "Defenders couldn't live with him. He'd take anyone on, and he could beat them all. For pace, for skill, for strength, for size, he was superior to anyone else in the division."

Collymore and Southend were perfect for each other. A footballer of immense quality was given a springboard to the big time and an unfashionable club survived to fight another day against far larger, far richer opponents. But Collymore's effect was more profound than that. At the start of all of this, I told a bit of a fib. I *do* know why I support Southend. I know why anyone who supports their local team, no matter how much of a shambles they are, does it. It's for memories like this.

I didn't always support the Shrimpers. Like most children brought up in the Home Counties in the 1980s, I grew up supporting Liverpool because they were pretty much the only team that was ever on television in those days. Supporting a football team means different things to different people, and I wouldn't seek to judge others, but I never found the spiritual connection with the Merseysiders that I found the first time my father took me to Southend. On that freezing January day in 1991, amidst the acrid stench of urine and fried onions, something clicked in my soul.

If you support a Premier League team, you must surely grow frustrated at the lack of ownership, the lack of identity. What must it be like as a Liverpool fan to listen to a phone-in and hear a plummy-voiced dissenter critiquing *your* club, giving away their own ignorance of *your* team within sixty seconds? What must it be like for a Manchester United fan, a 20 year season ticket holding veteran, to sit quietly while a foreign blogger who has never heard of Ralph Milne calls for Sir Alex Ferguson's head on a plate? That kind of thing never happens when you're a Southend fan.

Living in South Shields and working as a football journalist, my trips to Roots Hall are now few and far between. Of the small group of Southend fans who inhabit this earth, I am probably the worst of all them, but somewhere, deep inside, it still feels like my club. The football is mediocre, success is relative and thin on the ground, but when the golden moments come they belong only to you and those who have ever stood with you. The win against Manchester United, the win against West Ham, the promotions and the play-offs. And Collymore. Even for just that short time, Collymore was ours. Our super striker, our world class forward in waiting, our 'Kingo Laff'. And that, right there, is why you support Southend United.

*Chapter 11*

# We Will Never Die

## Luke Moore

It remains the most Dickensian place I've ever seen. Despite being born there, growing up just a short hop across the harbour and visiting it more times than I could even begin to remember, Portsmouth is a place of tremendous interest and passion for me. It is an area of sharp contrasts, from the burgeoning creative spirit of the student population along Albert Road in the now fashionable Southsea district to the historic dockyard containing HMS Victory, Nelson's flagship in the Battle of Trafalgar, this reasonably small 'northern city in the south' contains more nooks, crannies and rum old characters than any scene in Oliver Twist. Indeed, the author of that and many other classic works of fiction was born in Landport, smack bang in the middle of Portsea Island, which itself is entirely contained within the city.

Among the spectrum of attitudes, places of interest and experiences lies what is undoubtedly the beating heart of the city. Located in Fratton, just a five minute walk from Fratton station, on Frogmore Road sits Fratton Park, home of Portsmouth Football Club. Since 1898, the only football club in this conurbation of terraced Victorian housing, windswept seafront apartments and spit-and-sawdust public houses has been the lifeblood of social activity and the focal point of the community.

I can still remember with fondness the first time I walked up Frogmore Road and saw the mock-Tudor exterior of the entrance between the South Stand and the Fratton End. Men and their sons walked purposefully hand-in-hand towards the theatre of drama and conflict, munching on mystery meat burgers or pies, their faces wide-eyed with anticipation and fervour. This was their time. The shifts at the docks or in the factory were over for another week and ahead of them was an afternoon of recreation, camaraderie and male-bonding.

It was the 15th of February 1992 when I first crossed the threshold into the stadium that would play a huge part not just in my social and recreational life, but my life in general. I was aged eleven. My Uncle Les, himself a lifelong fan and season ticket holder at the club, took me to see the FA Cup Fifth Round clash with Middlesbrough which finished 1-1. Guy Whittingham put Pompey ahead before Alan Kernaghan equalised from a Gary Parkinson free kick and forced a replay back in the north east. I remember it all.

The result isn't the thing that sticks in the recesses of the young mind, however. It was the noise, the endless, soaring noise that seemed to ascend up and out of the stadium and disappear over the horizon. That, and the fact that just about every person in that place was there for the same thing. It didn't seem to matter where you were from, what your politics were, what pub you drank in. You were Pompey. That was the only question that needed answering. That first experience stayed with me a lot longer than I expected it to, and I barely slept that night trying to remember everything

I'd experienced, terrified that it would disappear into the darkest, unreachable corners of my memory before I'd fully savoured it.

Portsmouth would go on to beat Middlesbrough 4-2 in the replay, an astounding result purely because Portsmouth's away form that season was largely dreadful despite finishing ninth. What's more, Middlesbrough would go on to finish second in the table and lose only two games at home all season in the league.

It would come to pass that Portsmouth would lose on penalties in the FA Cup Semi Final replay at Villa Park to Liverpool after a scoreless draw. Before that we were nine minutes away from reaching the final after Darren Anderton put us ahead in the 11th minute of extra time, only to see Ronnie Whelan equalise just five minutes later by tapping in a John Barnes free kick that had hit the inside of the post and bounced agonisingly along the goal line.

The reason I mention all this in such great detail is because it was absolutely pivotal in my gestation as a Portsmouth fan for two reasons: Firstly, it gave me a huge amount of excitement. I could anchor in my mind a vivid, almost tangible set of reasons why I wanted to return to that place: the roar of the crowd, the songs, the back-and-forth between the Fratton End and the travelling support at the distant Milton End across the other side of the pitch behind the far goal.

Secondly, the way that Cup run gripped the city and surrounding area made it feel like it was literally the only newsworthy thing happening at the time. I have no memory of coverage of the Bosnian War or the Los Angeles riots, two world events that happened in the same month, but I can picture walking down Gosport High Street ahead of the semi-final with Liverpool and seeing the local newspaper office's window plastered with Play Up Pompey front pages. It just seemed so *important*. Sure, Tottenham Hotspur had Paul Gascoigne and Gary Lineker and Liverpool had John Barnes and Ian Rush, but that didn't say anything to me about my life. They may as well have been Martians. Portsmouth FC was something of which I could be a part.

The following season was a bittersweet one as the boys in blue managed to miss out on promotion to the fledgling Premier League by virtue of scoring one goal less than West Ham. Guy Whittingham scored 42 league goals that season and 48 in all competitions, a bar set so high that for years afterwards I was unnecessarily harsh on subsequent forwards, who failed miserably to live up to the standard set. I spent the majority of the home games that season perched on one of the barriers in the terracing in the Fratton End and was always half-ecstatic, half-terrified whenever we scored due to the amount of large men around me threatening to crush me without even noticing they'd done so.

Soon, my life started to revolve around playing football and attending Fratton Park whenever I could. My Uncle had a pretty established routine on match days which involved his mates and absolutely not a lanky, pretty awkward 13-year-old boy (although he'd have happily continued to take me if I asked) so I rapidly set about putting a bunch of friends together with which to attend games. Over the years, we'd get the bus down to the harbour, hop on the ferry across to the Portsmouth side and then go two stops on the train to Fratton. A bus, ferry and train seemed a pretty small price to pay to get to see the boys.

I would badger my Mum and Dad for ten pounds every time I wanted to go, knowing that the price of admission was £7 and the spare £3 would cover my travel. There were very special occasions where the local newspaper would run a 'Kids for a Quid' deal, and that would involve me cutting the entire page out of the paper before my Mum saw it, so she would have no idea about the reduced admission and would therefore still give me the full tenner. The spare money would of course be spent on a burger and enough sweets to sink whichever battleship was docked in the harbour at the time.

At this time in my life I had no real grasp of what a football club's business was like off the pitch. My interest pretty much started and ended with the players and the manager. As it turned out, Portsmouth had been through some financial strife in the 1970s and 80s which involved a drop all the way down to the old Fourth Division. In late 1976, the club had narrowly avoided bankruptcy by selling a lot of the playing staff, and in 1988 they narrowly avoided further misery by selling to a new owner. They were chilling portents of what was to come.

Throughout this mid to late 90s period I was given regular reminders of what the club meant to the city. It was often joked that one should avoid the pubs and clubs of Guildhall and Southsea on a Saturday night if Pompey had been defeated, the atmosphere seeming more heated and on-edge. That may sound trite, but consider this: Portsmouth is largely situated on an island, which in itself breeds a certain siege mentality. That, coupled with the fact that what was once a hugely important part of the United Kingdom has now found its main employment sectors and strategic relevance severely restricted by changing priorities among the armed services and shipping industries, meant there were fewer and fewer focal points to identify as the city's *raison d'etre*. The residents of Portsmouth are a largely proud people. If you remove the very cornerstones of their pride, they will look to other masts to nail their colours, if you'll excuse the pun. It stands to reason this will manifest itself in the form of something that is also common to all, the only professional football club situated in the city.

As time moved on, the club eventually found itself in the hands of Milan Mandaric. This was via a short stint in administration after a largely disastrous spell under Terry Venables who, in that used-car salesman manner which he appears to hold so dear, purchased the club for a solitary pound of the Queen's sterling. He populated it with several Australian players (he was fresh from a stint as Australian national team manager), steered us to the bottom of the league and got us losing a steady £150,000 a month despite selling Deon Burton and Lee Bradbury for a combined £5m. His company Vencorp pocketed a cool £300,000 'performance bonus' before he departed.

By the time all this had happened I certainly was very aware of what was going on off the pitch, and became almost permanently angry and frustrated with Venables. This all came to a head some years later when I abused him live on my university radio station and had to issue an instant, grovelling apology. Mandaric was treated largely as the saviour of the club. It's funny how you attribute certain weather to the mood of the time. In my memory, games around this period always seemed to be played on a perfectly sunny afternoon with no hint of that cruel wind that could occasionally rip off the Solent and seem to cut right through your chest.

This mini-era also coincided with a masterstroke on Mandaric's part: the signing of Robert Prosinecki. It was a

PR triumph. The Croatian was accepted by three generations of my family to be the greatest player to pull on a Pompey shirt, and the solitary season he plied his trade on the south coast harvested a bank of memories one would be unlikely to forget in a hurry. Finally, we had a superstar to call our own, and despite him being regularly let down by his teammates' comparative lack of ability and his own inability to track back, sprint or stop smoking in his spare time, Prosinecki was the standout player in the entire league regardless of Pompey conspiring to finish a lowly 17th in the division.

How the fans loved him. We all took him in as one of our own and his readiness to entertain us, sometimes at the cost of making a more beneficial decision for the team, was greatly appreciated. It had been a long time since Fratton Park had seen an entertainer in this mould, and we graciously lapped up every second of his playing time.

I once saw him leaning nonchalantly against the wall of the stadium waiting for a lift long after a game. Just about all the fans save me had gone home. He had a knapsack-style bag over his shoulder and was smoking a cigarette down to the butt. Shortly, a battered old car pulled up with an Eastern European man driving and Prosinecki looked around, flicked his cigarette away, chucked his bag onto the back seat and got in before the car spluttered off. He looked more like a drifter hitching a lift than a world-class playmaker, and it was this unassuming style and attitude that endeared him to the fans. I was and remain delighted to have 'shared' a moment of my own with the great man.

If Mandaric's cheery disposition, charming nature, ability to attract former World Cup semi-finalists and apparent bottomless pit of cash seemed to almost guarantee success for the club, his love of the press and readiness to hire and fire managers seemingly on a whim (I have a friend who can put across a stunningly persuasive argument that Mandaric has, on occasion, fired managers simply to attract attention from the national media) appeared to hold us back. Still, in the coming years Portsmouth fans like me were to feel very lucky indeed as our club was largely immune from the collapse of ITV Digital, something that sent a number of Football League clubs spiralling into an abyss of debt as the promised money from the broadcaster failed to materialise. It was beneath this storm of uncertainty that Portsmouth, by then under the stewardship of Harry Redknapp and his assistant Jim Smith (architect of Portsmouth's aforementioned agonisingly close run to within a whisker of the 1992 FA Cup Final), finally broke into what's commonly known among bombastic broadcasters and more thoughtless football fans as 'The Promised Land' of the Premier League.

I've often thought this a bit of a misconception of what it actually is to be a football fan. Even the most ardent supporter would surely concede that not every club can win the Premier League and, probably more importantly in the case of Portsmouth, not every club can obtain and then subsequently sustain Premier League status. Some clubs and their respective fanbases are simply not big enough. This fact was to make itself horrifyingly apparent on the south coast in the coming years.

Besides, football fandom isn't and shouldn't be about the endless quest for a positive result. That's for the players. Being a fan is of course about supporting your team and wanting them to do well, but it's also about experiences, relationships formed over common (and indeed uncommon) ground and escapism from the grind of daily life. As a Pompey fan I am clearly in no position to comment extensively, but winning every single week would undoubtedly quickly become humourless. As Kipling once said, victory and defeat are both impostors. They rarely stick around for too long. To me, what matters is the journey and the experience.

Around this time it was assumed that, despite reports of him losing several millions of pounds in the post-September 11th business environment, Mandaric was still comfortably bankrolling the club and the increasing amount of high-earning personnel it employed. For my part, I knew that players such as Paul Merson, Tim Sherwood, Gianluca Festa and many others weren't stepping down to the second tier purely for the seaview even if others were ignorant to it (sometimes wilfully so). But I comforted myself with two 'facts': One, Mandaric was rich, vastly rich in a way that I would probably never be, and two, as Mr Redknapp was fond of implying, these players wanted to work with him due to his reputation and achievements in the game thus far. It wasn't just about money.

So, in April 2003, my beloved Portsmouth were promoted to what was then known as the Premiership. It was the first time we'd tested our mettle in the top tier since 1988 and the city was abloom with positivity and happiness. Svetoslav Todorov had secured the promotion with a striker's goal to beat Burnley 1-0 and celebrated by jumping straight into the Fratton End to enjoy the moment with the supporters. The link between the club and its fans hadn't felt so strong since Alan Ball's men in the late 80s, a squad that famously all lived within the city's limits and were regularly seen socialising with fans at one of Portsmouth many watering holes.

Elsewhere, the relatively newly-opened Gunwharf Quays centre was doing great business situated in the old dilapidated ruin where military ships would once store their guns when in dry dock on the west side of the harbour. Regeneration seemed to be occurring all over the city; that relic of horrendous 1960s brutalism The Tricorn Centre, once voted the fourth ugliest building in the UK by a survey of over 500 designers, was finally earmarked for demolition. New apartments and commercial buildings were popping up all around the area. Another example of how the success of the football club is intrinsically linked to the city itself.

Redknapp embarked immediately on a huge recruitment drive for players of Premiership quality. Ex-England internationals Steve Stone and Teddy Sheringham, current Czech international Patrik Berger, Russian international Alexey Smertin and hotly-tipped Nigerian forward Yakubu were drafted in. Admittedly the majority of these players were brought in for free (with the exception of Yakubu who cost a hefty £4m), but the wages were again setting alarm bells off, at least for me and my peers. Again, we consoled ourselves with the knowledge that, despite only having a 20,000 capacity stadium, we now had the Sky/Premiership cash cow to rely on, so, along with most of the rest of the supporters we trusted the Mandaric, Redknapp and by now Peter Storrie (drafted in as Chief Executive on the advice of his friend and longtime collaborator Harry Redknapp) axis implicitly. Why wouldn't we? According to them, Pompey had never had it so good. Mandaric and Sky were stumping up the cash, the experienced Storrie was negotiating the deals and agreeing the wages, and Our 'Arry was coaching the side. Dream team.

Around this time I returned from a stint living overseas in New Zealand where information about Portsmouth was pretty sparse even in the internet age. During my time there

I would stay up until 3am local time pretty regularly to watch them on television when the chance arose and tried to obtain consistent updates from friends and family back home. It was at this time that I fully realised Portsmouth's reputation around the world as a noble, well-known club. Every person I'd met that liked football had heard of Pompey and not just because of their recent promotion to the Premiership. The fans' reputation preceded them and it was down to their passion, ability to generate almost unbelievable levels of noise in comparison to their relatively small number and their pride in wearing the colours wherever they went, not just in the form of a club shirt but indeed often tattooed into the skin itself.

However, after a time it became abundantly clear that the Mandaric money was running out. Despite the lucrative financial support offered by Sky's deal with the Premier League, Portsmouth were obviously spending way beyond their means and the only option was to cut spending dramatically, something that, from my memory, hardly seemed to have been considered and would have been tantamount to public suicide anyway given the messages previously extolled by the ownership, or offload the club to another, more wealthy backer.

With the aid of so-called super-agent Pini Zahavi, Mandaric sought to offload the club to Alexandre 'Sacha' Gaydamak, son of the notorious Arkadi. Despite continuous doubts over Gaydamak Jr's ability and means to own and run a football club, (expressed most notably by the always-excellent David Conn of the Guardian newspaper who highlighted a failed business and questioned his opaque background) the FA didn't even need to pass him 'fit and proper'. That exercise in self-declaring box ticking merely applied to directors and not owners. The deal was done for £15m, writing off Mandaric's personal exposure and he at first stayed on as joint owner before fading into the background and disappearing off the scene altogether.

By this time, as a supporter, it was becoming increasingly concerning. Even if the new owner had the money he claimed, we were all yet to see proof of it. Despite Portsmouth fans welcoming him to the club with open arms, as they always did, Redknapp and Storrie were signing more and more players on bigger and bigger wages. Around this time a good friend of mine was working at the local newspaper, and reports of alleged shady dealings around the club were becoming more commonplace. Towards the end of his tenure, Mandaric banned the paper, one of the biggest local newspapers in the country, from the stadium and the training ground.

Looking back, it was the beginning of the end. Enough has been written about the players who moved to the south coast and the wages they were on. It is trite to delve into that here. The salient points were becoming clear and heartbreaking: Gaydamak wasn't interested in the club, and when reports emerged after he'd gone that rather than put any money of his own into Portsmouth he'd merely secured more loans against the value of it and the Sky income, it was hardly surprising.

The bottom fell out of my and every other Portsmouth fan's world. We would be the ones to suffer. There was no help from the Football Association, no sympathy from the Premier League and Pompey fans like me were faced with the real prospect of no club left to support. The promotion to the Premier League, the FA Cup win in 2008, the appearance in the Europa League, was that all worth it in return for an ancient, 114 year-old institution to bite the dust? Of course it wasn't. We were to suffer further indignity before heading into the abyss of administration yet again. Every Portsmouth fan found themselves connected, by association, to a football club and company that stiffed on payments to many local businesses (forcing some of them to fold) and, as usual, charities such as St. John's Ambulance.

It was a disgrace too far. The Portsmouth Supporters' Trust was set up, specifically to try and take back at least a stake in the club and obtain a position on any future board to ensure that no catastrophic decisions of this magnitude would happen again. At time of writing it may still be too late to save it, but Portsmouth fans as well as being a proud bunch are also knowledgeable, interested people who recognise their naivety and misplaced trust. We want to safeguard the club against future indiscipline and embarrassment.

Meanwhile, in the city itself the recession is biting hard. In yet another mirroring of the football club's travails, Portsmouth is experiencing the same economic downturn as many other working class, salt-of-the-earth type cities, yet there is currently no escapism for football fans as they spend the majority of their spare time wondering if they'll still have a club to support next season.

It still beggars belief that, at one stage at the beginning of 2012, Storrie had the brass neck to suggest he'd be open to returning to Portsmouth. He had been the Chief Executive of a football club with a stadium capacity of just 20,000 that managed to run up an estimated debt of over £110m. The fact that there has not been an adequate investigation to date on the management's conduct during this period is a sad, festering indictment on the way football is run in this country. Not just because it happened to affect my club but because it could affect many other clubs in the future. How many Portsmouths must there be before something is done? We can look to the rather glib argument of 'free market economics' and the dog-eat-dog world of capitalism and competition. We're told that these football clubs in the 21st century are businesses and their balance sheets must add up. But as Simon Kuper argues superbly in his book 'Why England Lose: And Other Curious Phenomena Explained', the way football clubs are run is more reminiscent of a charity than a business; they have money ploughed into them with little to no hope of a financial return, and they offer a genuine service to the local area. They should be protected as such. When Storrie, Mandaric, Redknapp and Gaydamak undermined the club with their farcical decision making, they didn't just destroy the fabric of a football club, they threatened to destroy the fabric of a city and a people whose relationship with each other depends on it.

When I think about the effect that the recent financial plight of the club I support has had on me as a football fan, there are many facets to the disappointment and upset that I and my fellow fans experienced. The worst, most cutting aspect of the entire foul jamboree for me is undoubtedly the reaction a Portsmouth fan can now expect to receive when he or she imparts that they support Pompey. I can vividly remember owning a sort of abstract football currency by just mentioning who I supported pretty much anywhere in the UK and sometimes even the world over. The questioner would always, without fail, respond to my answer with something along the lines of 'Portsmouth eh? That's a proper club, that.' or 'What an atmosphere at your place, brilliant!'

Now, it is somewhat different. It is almost depressingly close to pity. The first thing the questioner will do is profess sympathy. As I mentioned earlier, Portsmouth is a proud place, and the last thing the fans of the club want is to be felt sorry for because of what some arrogant, smug, clueless buffoons did at the very top of their club. But sadly that is now invariably what they're dished up.

I hope there is a bright future for Portsmouth FC. It is something that is woven into the very consciousness of the area and has provided me with many unforgettable memories. What's more, the city needs a football club. And more importantly, it deserves one. Whether that is in its current guise or an AFC Wimbledon-style phoenix from the ashes manifestation, I am more certain than ever that the spirit of the club will continue. It cannot be broken, and the proof is heard in the voices of the fans. Where they once sung many different songs in addition to the world-famous Pompey chimes, a new, more defiant chant regularly rings out from the guts of the North, South and Fratton ends, the simple yet effective 'We will never die!'.

And, after what we've been through, you'd be a fool to doubt us.

*Chapter 12*

# Every Club Should Have Two

## Ian Ridley

Everybody has a story worth telling, of a life lived with its hopes and dreams, dashed and fulfilled; of grand turning points and mundane moments, successes and failures. Jean Lucas doesn't believe hers is much of a tale when I advance my theory to her. Not like Bob's. But I think it is. Though supporting cast rather than leading lady, she played her own huge part in the life of the football club that took over my own life.

She is well prepared when I arrive. She has some old club programmes out, a magazine article about him, and the cosy council house is immaculately clean and tidy, as expected. She is, after all, a woman of a working-class generation with standards, at odds from many of the modern families among whom she resides on the clearly recession-affected Little-moor estate in one of the Dorset seaside town of Wey-mouth's tougher suburbs.

She is not expecting me to say, however, that I want to talk about her as much as her late husband, Bob. "Get away," she says. "I was always happy to be in the background, to do the gardening and look after the kids."

Jean's life, though, was always so touchingly intertwined with Bob's, for the 59 years of their marriage that was shared with Weymouth Football Club, which he served with such dedication and distinction as goalkeeper, physiotherapist and president. In the end, so popular was he indeed, that they renamed the Wessex Stadium the Bob Lucas Stadium.

I couldn't know him when he kept goal in the club's most famous game in 1950, against Manchester United in the third round of the FA Cup - Old Trafford's first Cup tie since finally being rebuilt after the War - and he was man of the match in keeping the score down to 4-0. I was five years away from being born.

I then got to know him noddingly, though, through the 30 years of him being physio of the club I have supported since childhood. Finally, I grew to know him intimately when he became club president in 2002 and I became chairman of the club a year later. Rarely has a relationship so enriched my life.

Such was Bob's genial, supportive nature, his sheer pleasantness - and his role at the now empty heart of my footballing life - that I begin to fill up whenever I think about him in any depth. I have had heroes in football; Jimmy Greaves as a player, Jimmy Armfield as a man. No character in the game has ever had me both smiling and crying at his memory like Bob does. Did. I still struggle to get used to that past tense.

I couldn't help weeping the night I saw Jean at the first Weymouth game following Bob's death from prostate cancer in August of 2010 at the age of 85 and rushed over to hug her. Now we are both in danger of shedding a tear again as we remember fondly his life while sitting here in his old living room containing modest mementoes of his time at the club we both loved: a picture of him kneeling on the pitch, a cigarette lighter from the Football Association as recognition of his service as a physio for them; a plaque to mark his testimonial at Weymouth against Bristol City in 1998.

Bob Lucas was born on January 6th, 1925 in Bethnal Green, East London. Before him, his mother had lost three daughters to infant death, such was the severity of capital life in those days. At the age of 12, Bob was delivering newspapers in the morning and, after school, beer and spirits house-to-house from a barrow for an off-licence. By 13, he had left school to help feed the family and got a job in a printing works. It paid him 7 shillings and 6 pence. After giving seven bob to Mum, it left him with a tanner, the cost of the boys' enclosure at Tottenham Hotspur and Millwall.

When War broke out, the Lucas clan moved to Maidenhead after the family house was damaged in the Blitz and, his talent quickly spotted, he became Maidenhead United's first team goalkeeper at the age of 16. Back in London in a new house a few months later, he was spotted playing for Golders Green and recruited for mighty Crystal Palace.

Active service as a radio operator in the Royal Navy intervened, though, and he spent three years in the Mediterranean, Atlantic and Far East before rejoining Palace in 1946. In his two years with them, he played four Football League games but wanted to get a job and play part-time, knowing he could earn more. The fear of financial insecurity, given his background, would never leave him.

He joined Tonbridge in Kent, where some Palace team-mates had gone to form a new club. There, a contact of the then Weymouth manager Paddy Gallacher saw Bob and recommended him. The club then helped him find a job with a printing company in the resort.

In 1949, Weymouth were just joining the highly regarded Southern League - as members of which Tottenham had won the FA Cup in 1901 before being accepted into the Football League - and needed a higher calibre of player. Bob fitted the bill. He made his home debut against traditional, fierce rivals from just across the Somerset border, Yeovil Town, in front of 10,497 - still Weymouth's attendance record - at the club's charming old Recreation Ground by the harbour before the concrete Wessex Stadium was completed in 1987.

He also made an impression that August, during his first week in Weymouth, on a pretty 17-year-old girl working in Harry Cole's sports shop in the town centre, where he had gone to buy new boots. Jean Wheeler also made an impression on Bob. Soon they were stepping out.

"I was a quiet girl and was surprised he showed me attention," says Jean, her smiling face recalling happy days. "He was my first boyfriend, the first man to show me any attention. He was quite a catch. Everyone in the town looked up to him. I came from a wooden bungalow in Wyke Regis. My family had no money."

They married in March 1951, the wedding a big occasion in Weymouth. "I remember the pictures being on display in a photographer's shop in the town," Jean recalls. "There was a couple looking at them who didn't know Bob and I were behind them. I remember her saying, 'Fancy him marrying her.'

Was it not hurtful? "We just had a laugh about it." It says much about the nature of both of them. A year before the wedding came that FA Cup tie at Manchester United. The local paper, the *Dorset Evening Echo*, carried a picture of Bob phoning her from the hotel the night before the game. "He didn't," she confides. "We didn't have a phone. It was just for the paper."

She didn't even get to the game, even though she was a Weymouth supporter, having been taken to the old 'Rec' by her father, who also ran, unusually for the times, a women's team in the town to which the family had come from Devizes in Wiltshire when she was four, Dad having found work at the old Whitehead's factory that manufactured torpedoes for the Navy.

Harry Cole, a club director, wanted her to stay behind and mind the sports shop while he went. She found out the score, and about Bob's outstanding performance, from the 'football final' edition that the *Echo* brought out by 6pm on a Saturday night in those days. Some years later, as a kid in the 1960s, I would queue for it myself outside the paper shop, waiting for the van. Now some kids on a Saturday night seem to be waiting for the man.

Soon after getting married, printing work in Weymouth dried up for Bob after two years with the club - during which he once spent three weeks in hospital with a head injury after diving at an opponent's feet - and he and Jean moved back to London to live with Bob's mum at Mile End, where daughter Linda was born. Having found a job again with a printer off Fleet Street, Bob began playing for Ramsgate on the Kent coast. At the age of 28, he punctured a lung, however. Devastatingly, his playing career was over.

The smog of early 1950's London, before the Clean Air Act, was damaging Bob's breathing so they all moved back to Weymouth for the sea air. Bob became a bus driver for 10 years and watched plenty of local football as a scout for his contacts around London. Tragedy then struck the family when their second child, Bobby, died of cancer aged just four years and 10 months old.

"It was a very sad time," says Jean, the pain hanging in the air. At the time, she was nursing young Bobby and Bob, who had suffered a recurrence of lung trouble. Bob and Jean were heartbroken but football offered solace. Having become personally familiar with footballers' injuries, Bob decided to train as a physio. Nearby Dorchester Town took him on and, once fully qualified, he also worked for the Football Association, who were impressed by his knowledge of new scientific techniques. He always was more than just a sponge man.

Not a manager, though. Dorchester put him in caretaker charge for a short while but he detested it. He could not really be firm with players, let alone ruthless. He had to watch from 'over the hill' in the county town when Weymouth won the Southern League title in 1965 under Frank O'Farrell, who would go on to manage Manchester United, and then retained it the year of England winning the World Cup.

Then, in 1972, Weymouth took on a young player-manager by the name of Graham Williams, a Welsh international left back who lifted the FA Cup for West Bromwich Albion in 1968. He came to this very council house that Bob and Jean had moved into in 1957 and asked Bob back to the club. Bob accepted readily.

After 74 appearances as a player, Bob would now go on to make a remarkable 1,948 "appearances" as a physio over the next 30 years, turning down offers of jobs in similar capacities at Bournemouth and Torquay United. He would see all the club's 'greats' come and go; would treat them all.

In the 1970's, there was Jeff Astle of WBA and England at the end of his career; Graham Carr, father of comedian Alan and now Newcastle United's chief scout, who would also later manage the club.

In the 80's came the Alliance Premier League - now the Conference - and promising kids like Andy Townsend and Steve Claridge. Graham Roberts was sold to Tottenham for £35,000. The 90s were less successful, times for such as Darren Campbell, the Olympic sprinter who had a spell with the club before making the right choice of career, and local heroes like David Laws and Anniello Iannone.

In the end, by 2002 when he retired at the age of 77, Bob was on just £20 a week as physio, having taken a cut from £40 when the chairman asked him to help out as the club had financial problems. It was no wonder he never wanted to buy the council house they were offered after Michael and Leslie became their third and fourth children. "He would never get into debt," Jean explained. "That wasn't Bob. We always rented."

My acquaintance with Bob throughout those 30 years was mainly through my father, who had worked with him on the buses, and whenever I was back in my home town to see Dad, we would go to games, speak to Bob afterwards in the bar. Such is non-League football, where you can talk to anyone. We would bitch and moan, at the team and the board of directors. Bob would smile non-committally.

In the gossipy world of football, his discretion was what would surprise and impress me most when I took over as chairman in 2003, having offered my services and contacts to the club when they were at a low ebb in the Southern League. If he had nothing good to say about someone, he would say nothing.

When I first arrived, Bob came to see me. Characteristi-
cally humble, he asked if I wanted him to stay on as
president. "I never take my position for granted," he said.
Of course I wanted him to stay on. Asking him to go would
have been like ignoring the wisdom and demeanour of the
Dalai Lama. It wasn't just about anything he might have had
to say. Often Bob only spoke when spoken to, even if when
it did come it was always incisive. It was simply that the air
of serenity and sense might rub off.

Weymouth, believe it or not, are a ridiculously intro-
verted and political football club and I quickly became aware
of it. A traditional non-League power - though further down
the hierarchy these days with all the ex-Football League clubs
populating the Conference - they will attract crowds of 1,500
if the team is doing well, as they did in my first season there
when I appointed Steve Claridge as player-manager and he
scored more than 30 goals as we finished runners-up in the
Southern League to Crawley Town to qualify for the new
Conference South. In that, a couple of years later, there
would even be 5,022 for a title decider against St Albans City.

Anything less than top-class non-League football - with
the aspiration of the Football League always in the background - would provoke fierce debate and criticism in pub,
club and on rabid message board. The town was isolated
geographically with few entertainments outside of the
summer holiday season, and thus the club was at the centre
of so many of the 55,000 population's lives. The demands
were so great, that even Claridge, veteran of Premier League
and many intense outfits like Birmingham City and Millwall,
said he had rarely come across a club with such high
expectations.

Before my time were a group of local businessmen with

their hearts in the right place but unable to turn a tide of decline. Once the playing fortunes had been turned round by Claridge, a local hotelier by the name of Martyn Harrison decided he fancied a piece of the action and after he took control, I departed. Harrison lost £3 million over two years in taking Weymouth to the verge of the Football League before pulling the plug and becoming ill in the process. He would pass away in 2012.

After him, came, briefly, a Bournemouth music promoter called Mel Bush, then a property developer named Malcolm Curtis, who shifted all the land around the stadium - some 10 acres - into the ownership of a development company, leaving the club land-locked and owning only its ground and no longer the adjacent training area or car park.

In 2008, at the request of two local businessmen who did a deal for control with Curtis (after one ludicrous episode when a potential buyer who turned out to be a cleaner from Torquay tried to acquire the club with a cheque for £300,000 that had Tipp-Ex marks on it), I returned as chairman for six months but was unable to solve the problems created by the new £750,000 worth of debt built up after Harrison. Then a man named George Rolls made Weymouth a staging post between his chairmanships of Cambridge United and Kettering Town, taking the club into administration.

Through it all, Bob had his private thoughts and feelings about many of the characters and charlatans who came and went - and he would see some 35 managers and 16 chairmen in his 40 years of service, in the last decade of which more than 500 games as President took his involvement in first-team matches to well in excess of an astonishing 2,500.

There would be a glance here, a raised eyebrow there - a nod and a wink - but verbally he would always keep his counsel. He knew who were the good guys and who the bad, but he would also support the incumbent, always support the club. There might be those who would see it as a sign of weakness, of a fiddling while Rome burned all around him as he declined to comment on some of those who had started the arson when his words would have carried much weight. Loyalty was his watchword, however. If he ever made a comment to me about a player, or an issue around the club that needed attention, it would be constructive and telling.

It meant that I, and probably all my predecessors, could confide in him with confidence, knowing I would not be judged badly nor my inner thoughts relayed to supporters or local press. It meant trust, a commodity that had become discredited at Weymouth and so short in modern football.

Above all, I saw Bob as the beacon of Weymouth FC's honesty and integrity, as a symbol of what we should all aspire to. Amid the frequent chaos, bitter politics and twisted economics of the club, he represented probity and reminded us, me, of the goodness of men and the game to keep me fighting a good fight. At times, some of the club's characters disgusted me. Bob reminded me of the importance of principles, and the club, above personalities.

I remember the day he told me he had been diagnosed with prostate cancer. I myself had been forced to leave Weymouth due to treatment for the same variety of the disease but they had caught mine early.

"I've left it a bit late," he told me, by contrast. "I've been daft really. I thought getting up three or four times in the night was just old man's trouble. Still," he added, "most people spend their life worrying that they are going to get cancer. I don't have to worry any more, do I?"

And Bob was a worrier. From a young age, family deaths,

financial worries and a perennially troubled football club close to his heart, all contributed to it. "Yes he was," says Jean, when I remind her. "He was always fussing around the kids, telling them to be careful. And I still hear his voice today when I am crossing the road."

The cancer responded to chemotherapy and radiotherapy only to prolong his life but not to cure him. He still attended home games over the last year of his life but couldn't travel away, partly through tiredness and partly through embarrassment at needing toilet facilities so often. "He was such a clean man. Such a clean man," says Jean. And a proud one.

Towards the end, he underwent blood transfusions at Dorset County Hospital in Dorchester. While there, the unpopular George Rolls came to tell him that he was renaming the stadium the Bob Lucas, to which Bob replied, typically, that he shouldn't do that. It was some redemption for Rolls and fitting tribute for a man who would not last much longer. The transfusions were no longer working. Bob went home.

The end came on the night of August 12th, 2010. "I had just done some washing," Jean recalls. "I went upstairs and he had gone to sleep. To be honest, I was really pleased for him. He had gone peacefully, without any pain."

I felt humble in Jean's company, inadequate when I contemplated their collective acceptance of life's cruelties and the club's insensitivities.

That first game after his death, the night I wept as I hugged her, I ran into an old club official who had once carried out an edict from a crass chief executive that she was no longer allowed into boardroom or directors' box on match days. I lost my temper, expressing my contempt for him and his old boss.

There was no such bitterness from Jean or Bob, hurt as they were by it. Both bore the trials of the football club, and the tribulations it caused them, with stoicism. My doubt that I would be so forgiving was one reason why I did not attend the funeral. I did not want to encounter men who had been unkind to Bob, goaded into speaking out at the sight of them, and so potentially mar an occasion that would become so big that Jean had to hire the Ocean Ballroom of the town's Pavilion Theatre to accommodate all the well-wishers.

"I was going to ask you to speak at the funeral," says Jean now, and for a moment I feel sad, guilty even, that I hadn't attended. Then I felt grateful to be a writer given a privileged opportunity to spill the contents of his heart. Jean's gratitude is at having spent such a contented married life with Bob and shared his passion for a game and a club that may have beset them with angst but also gave focus and meaning to their lives.

I press her. Come on, I say, no-one is that good, no couple that happy. Surely he got angry, surely you argued?

"Well, there were times when I might have done some-thing he didn't agree with, or the other way round," she says. "Then it would go quiet for a while. In the end, he would say something like, 'What do you want for tea?' We never got too upset about anything really."

Apart from the football club. "I still think of Bob up there looking down on another crisis at the club and saying, 'not again.' He used to say 'that club made me more ill than the cancer.' "

Jean was still looking down on the football these days from her seat in the main stand - first-team, reserves and the women's team - as she approached her 80th birthday. A local taxi firm was generously taking her to games for nothing.

And like everyone else, she looked beyond current Southern League travails and hoped for better days for the club now that it was back in the ownership of Trustees - one of which she had been asked to become - rather than one man.

She was getting used to being on her own, she said, as she had done at times during Bob's life. "I was a bit of a football widow," she says. "Bob was working, then away with football at weekends. Well, you know what it's like."

Apart from weekly trips to the stadium that bears her husband's name, she kept his memory alive by repeating the walks along the seafront that Bob loved so dearly, always feeling himself lucky to have lived in Weymouth. She made a point of getting out every day, she added, even if it was just to go and get a copy of the *Echo*.

Jeans offers me a cup of tea and as she goes to the kitchen to make it, I take the chance to use the upstairs toilet. There on the landing is a framed picture of myself and Steve Claridge - who called him "the nicest man in the world" - with Bob in the middle, our arms around him. I remembered the occasion. It was the night we went top of the Southern League. I felt flattered, moved. Nowhere else in the house was there a picture of another chairman or manager.

"He always liked Steve, ever since he came to the club as a young player," says Jean when I remark on it. "And," she adds quietly. "He did think you were a good chairman." Praise from the understated is always praise indeed.

Those in football often joke that the game takes years off your life. Actually, as the 85 of Bob Lucas's show, for many it may well put years on life. You hope as the carrier of his torch, the same can be said of Jean Lucas. Over five decades, she enabled Bob to become the conscience and figurehead of the club. Now the club needed her presence as reminder, not least in how to be effective in working happily together.

The pair certainly enriched my life and enhanced Weymouth Football Club as they rose above its in-fighting to illustrate what is good in life, all that is good in the game - and could be again, as James Earl Jones said in Field of Dreams. Every club should have such a couple.

## Chapter 13

# Sgt Wilko's Barmy Army

## Janine Self

My name is Janine Self and I am a fraud. There. Said it. So put away your pen, Peeved of Pudsey, switch off your laptop, Bolshy of Beeston, and don't be a text pest, Cheerless of Chapeltown. I'm cutting you off at the pass.

Slice me open and the search for LUFC DNA would be a futile one. Have a rootle round the old pine chest in my spare room, however, and there might be a special-edition T-shirt proudly proclaiming "us" the champions of England – unworn, squirreled away next to a teddy bear of white-yellow-blue hue also bought in 1992. And, yes, I even believed ooh-aah Eric Cantona when he told me he loved me. Proper fan? Glory hunter, more like.

For a start, I'm not from Leeds nor, in fact, Yorkshire. Born in Germany, brought up all over the world, a tumbleweed child of the British forces who grew up to become a tumbleweed journalist. If geography is a realistic indicator of club worship, I should be a Borussia Moenchengladbach supporter. I nearly was once, for one game only, and it turned out to be a memorable occasion on two counts – my first live match and the first time that a clenched fist was brandished in my direction.

I can still remember feeling the downdraft as the punch fell a millimetre short of my chin. Apparently the sight of a schoolgirl loitering in the car park, waiting for friends and family to catch up, was seen as an overt act of aggression to the Liverpool fan who ordered his driver pal to a screaming stop next to me, wound down the window and, to the accompaniment of rapid-fire expletives, tried to whack me.

He missed. Oh, and he thought I was German, so that's all right, then. They were a bit upset too, the poor mites, as Liverpool had just lost the first leg of the European Cup semi-final 2-1. To recap, the defending champions of Europe, managed by Bob Paisley, captained by the delightful Emlyn Hughes [a man I was privileged to get to know a few years later], and containing legend-in-the-making Kenny Dalglish, thought they had snatched a draw with an 89th minute goal from sub David Johnson.

Sixty seconds later Rainer Bonhof – now there was a midfielder who could pack a punch (with his shooting ability rather than his fists) – scored the winner. Up to the point when I almost had my block knocked off, my feelings for Liverpool had been sympathetic. I was officially in love with Dalglish's predecessor, Kevin Keegan, anyhow. The outrageous perm, the unique Scunthorpian German accent when he was interviewed on the goals highlights show, pumping thighs in shorts so short the stitching must have been in a permanent state of high alert. Hamburg's new darling couldn't half play, too, and at that point my rookieness as a follower of football meant I was in blissful ignorance of his Charity Shield dust-up with dear, sweet Billy Bremner in 1974. By the time I'd caught up, it was too late. I liked Mighty Mouse.

So, 1978 was a watershed in many ways, although my Dad

continued to refuse to buy me a Rothmans Football Year-book. Fine for my brother, not suitable for a young gel. That breakthrough came the following year. I still have the yellowing tome (price £3.25), foreword by Rothmans of Pall Mall. Page 247 is the Leeds United page; particularly well-thumbed and fraying evidence as to my loyalties. In green ink, I have carefully written the name of Jimmy Adamson, next to that of namesake Armfield, by now ex-manager. On the player page, in the same ghastly green, I have scribbled "sold" against David Stewart, Paul Reaney, Frank Gray, Tony Currie and John Hawley. That page should be tear-stained – Gray and Currie were absolutely gorgeous.

This was my disembodied view of Leeds. From another country, via the pages of Shoot and Rothmans and really, honestly, only a fan because aforementioned brother sup-ported them too and it seemed like a good idea at the time. There might have been more than a stamp of the foot when Joe Jordan and Gordon McQueen were sold to Manchester United but it would be an exaggeration to suggest that my emotional barometer was calibrated by the fluctuating fortunes of LUFC. I am a fraud, after all; but not completely, not in 1989-90 when, for one season, I was Leeds.

It is December 15th 1988. I am sitting in the foyer at Elland Road, ever-so-slightly twitchy about the prospect of interviewing Howard Wilkinson, a manager whom I had already met on many occasions when we both worked in Sheffield. He still frightened me to death, though. Persuading him to do a sit-down exclusive was something which had gone down well with the sports desk of The Post, a newly-launched national paper which lasted all of six weeks before gurgling into oblivion.

Sgt Wilko. A tabloid headline writer's dream not to

mention a terrace chant made in heaven. And, boy, were the
fans chanting his name. Wilkinson replaced Bremner with
Leeds second from bottom in the old Second Division and,
at the point of this meeting, had just led the team to a
record-breaking unbeaten League record of 10 games. The
November manager of the month was waiting in his office.
Memories fade but there is still a clear image of a large, shiny
polished wooden desk and a huge studded leather sofa.
Bookshelves down one wall supported video after video.
The Goons, Spike Milligan, Sgt Bilko. Sgt Wilko likes Sgt
Bilko: could this get any better for a tabloid hack?

As it happened, Wilkinson was a charming interviewee.
He barked occasionally but happily confided that his idea of
relaxing involved a glass of red, a large cigar and some
off-the-wall humour. His task at Leeds was huge; to stamp
a new identity on a club seemingly unable to move on from
the Don Revie legacy.  Bremner, who turned out to be
neither dear nor sweet incidentally but still makes an iconic
statue, had followed Eddie Gray, who followed Allan Clarke
… get the picture. Wilko's job was made harder by the fact
he had been manager at Sheffield Wednesday and his tactical
reputation was of the long-ball variety. He embraced the
challenge. By hook or by crook, here was someone who
intended to yank Yorkshire's fallen giants back onto their
feet. In the event, this was a season too soon and Leeds,
having been threatened with relegation, finished mid-table.
Meanwhile I got my exclusive and lost my job.

By August 1989, I was taking a year out and living in
Anglesey, North Wales, approximately 165 miles from Elland
Road. For the first – and only - time in my working life, I
had no requirement to be anywhere on a Saturday; the world
was my oyster and Leeds United became my pearl. That

summer was a scorcher, if memory serves, and the Saturday drive took me through meandering country lanes lined by drystone walls, across the Britannia Bridge which spanned the sparkling, glistening Menai Straits. The dramatic Snowdonia skyline provided a backdrop to a vista that could stand picture postcard to picture postcard comparison with the lakes of northern Italy or the Oleander-lined Med.

Shame about the A55. Back in those days much of what is now a pacey dual carriageway was a pain-in-the-butt single road which went from slow to crawl round Conwy back to slow again. This, I feel, is irrefutable proof that my newly-discovered credentials of "BEING A FOOTBALL FAN" were bona fide. As I sped, ha-ha, eastwards, dozens of caravans and 4x4s towing boats queued westwards. They were heading to the seaside, I was going to junction one of the M621. And I was excited. Excited about the drive, about buying my programme and then finding somewhere to have a coffee after trying and failing to shoehorn myself into The Old Peacock pub. Did Leeds fans, sorry "we", really use The Peacocks as a nickname? Leeds, United, Whites, as far as I was concerned.

Back to that shivery feeling, butterflies even. The upside about being a journalist is that sometimes you meet your heroes. The downside about being a journalist is that sometimes you meet your heroes. The view as a fan is wonderfully simplistic, rose-tinted even, and my specs were firmly in place. The arrival of Gordon Strachan, Carl Shutt and Chris Fairclough at the fag-end of the previous campaign had hinted of glorious revolutions to come. Welcome Jim Beglin from Liverpool, a defender of undoubted calibre before a terrible leg break, goodbye John Sheridan, that wonderfully languid midfield playmaker who went to Nottingham Forest. Mel Sterland, a whopping £600,000 from Glasgow Rangers, arrived, so reuniting Wilko with his flying fullback from Sheffield Wednesday. David Batty was one of our own already while excited whispers about the emergence of Gary Speed were gaining volume.

There was one name which caused a few swift blinks through those rose-tinted spectacles. Vincent Peter Jones, Esquire, scourge of Wimbledon, the man who put the crazy into the Crazy Gang. Following his £650,000 transfer, Leeds legend Johnny Giles had declared: "Don Revie would not have let him through the door." A few years on, I adapted Vinnie Jones's brilliant autobiography for The Sun and part of the deal involved an interview at his house. The guy was an absolute sweetie-pie just as I suspected when I watched him, every home match, head down to the corner between the West Stand and the Kop where he stood and chatted and signed autographs and had his photo taken with disabled fans.

*"I thought there was a good player, a good bloke, trying to get out. If Vinnie was a friend, you'd got a friend. He was well liked among the staff and not just the football staff; his courtesy, his generosity, he was full of pleasant surprises. I'd be in my office at 3.30 in the afternoon and he'd turn up with a big bag of cakes for everyone."...the words of Howard Wilkinson.*

It is March 30th 2012. I am in a leafy suburb in Sheffield, the sun is streaming down and Wilkinson has just finished his daily run in unseasonably warm temperatures. He has come to the front door in his dressing gown. My fault. I'm early. A quick time-out and he joins me, dressed casually in Ralph Lauren pink shirt, jeans and loafers, and looking remarkably unchanged. I stopped being frightened of him years ago, incidentally. The 20th anniversary of Leeds's title and the aftermath of Speed's tragic death have been at the forefront of Wilkinson's thoughts but he readily accepts my request for company down a different memory lane.

To help, he heads back upstairs, to his study, and emerges with a bound copy of Leeds match programmes from that promotion campaign. An *aide memoire*, as he puts it, not that he needs much reminding. Strachan is the starting point. Wee Gordon, Scottish, ginger, feisty but with more guile and imagination than wee Billy Bremner, who was also Scottish, ginger and feisty. Strachan played all 46 League games that season and finished top scorer on 16 goals. I was one of the 21,694 when he scored a hat-trick in the 4-0 thrashing of Swindon at the end of September, probably watching from the West Stand.

The first few times I visited Elland Road, when I nipped the 40 miles from Sheffield where I lived and worked, I proudly stood on the Kop so that I could shout and sing and cheer. Except I couldn't see a bloody thing and I was never wholly convinced about the benefits of paddling in a sea of pee either. For me, it was the West Stand usually, although I do recall being over the other side when West Ham came and lost 3-2 in March. Looking at the attendance of 32,536 I wonder now whether those were the only seats left. Strachan scored that day too while Lee Chapman grabbed a couple. Chappy, 12 goals in 21 matches following his arrival in January, and a major reason why we were all marching along together so nicely at the top of the table. There was another memory from that Hammers game, Liam Brady was saluted by us nasty Leeds fans on his farewell appearance at Elland Road shortly before he retired.

But we are getting ahead of ourselves. Rewind to the previous summer and to the mindset of Wilkinson, who was

under no illusion that promotion had to be delivered. Give
or take, this turned out to be his team. In goal the safest pair
of gloves around in Mervyn Day, right back Sterland, left
back Mike Whitlow, plucked from non-League Witton a year
earlier. The central defenders were Peter Haddock and
Fairclough. Haddock was skinny, long ferret-like face, and
who, at first glance, appeared vulnerable to being knocked
off his stride. It was an easy mistake for strikers to make.
Alongside him Fairclough, who defied the notion that a
central defender had to be a big, bruising, broken-nosed
bloke. He had the looks of a movie star, pretty boy but
certainly not made of celluloid. Strachan, moaning, snapping,
urging on one wing, John Hendrie on the other but sometimes up front. Hendrie, lightning fast and with a quirky
running action which made him look like he was slicing air,
was the only player I could claim to know, by virtue of a
couple of interviews when he was at Bradford. We have kept
in touch.

To central midfield where Batty and Jones frightened the
rest of the Second Division to death. I loved Norah. In the
event, so did Wilkinson until the final few games when Chris
Kamara, recently signed from Stoke, replaced him. A perfect
footballer who liked to train, go home and play with his
motorbikes. That's how Wilkinson described Batty. Someone
with a dark side but who never let it cast a permanent
shadow. As Wilko put it: "Nobody would have not wanted
Bremner and would allow for his occasional misdemeanour
and Batty was one of those. Sometimes he was a nightmare
defensively because he did things wrong and they came out
right. He'd go chasing the ball and as a coach you'd be
shouting 'stay with your man, stay with your man' but David
would go for the ball. And get it."

Up front, Ian Baird, Bobby Davison, Chapman or Imre Varadi with support from Shutt. Speed finished the season a versatile regular and Beglin deposed Whitlow. Varadi was one of many ex-Wednesdayites at Elland Road and is remembered with particular fondness by the press regulars at Hillsborough. The Imre Varadi Trust Fund. Never heard of it? Not surprised. Varadi was a striker, whose shooting could be somewhat, er, wayward. To spice up interest the journos introduced a sweepstake competition based on the individual advertising hoardings round the pitch; 50p in the pot and winner-take-all. So while the fans groaned in unison at a Varadi miss, up in the press box wild cheering could be heard as the ball smacked into Hallam Haulage, est 1925, two down from the corner flag.

That's the difference you see. Journalists are cynics, world-weary, seen-it-all, done-it-all, know-it-all. Fans pretend to be all the above...until the match kicks off. One-eyed and passionate? You betcha. Sgt Wilko was going to give us all something to shout about, once he had disentangled the legacy/curse of the Revie era, with a little help from a player whose diet included porridge, seaweed and bananas.

"I wouldn't say it was harder to cope with the Revie history than I thought but it was more deeply rooted than anyone could ever have imagined," admitted Wilkinson. "But now I look back and see the likes of Sir Alex Ferguson at Manchester United and it's hardly a surprise. The one thing that people like Sir Alex, Shankly, Wenger, Revie have in common is their ability to create their own culture. They turn a building into an institution. But if there's no continuity plan, no succession plan, then it starts to flake. Like a building it starts to get tired even if the foundations are still there. Instead of becoming an incentive, it became a crutch.

People become prisoners of that experience and you have to change it and change it quickly."

Step forward Strachan, surplus to requirements at Old Trafford and on the verge of moving to Sheffield Wednesday. Wilkinson chuckles as he recalls that Ferguson upped the price when he realised Leeds were also in the hunt. In the great reckoning, £200,000 still had to be a bargain considering the influence the Scot was to have on the dressing room.

"Gordon was the start. Quite soon after I arrived, I realised that if they were going to change quickly I needed to get a significant person on the playing staff, who mirrored my values, my beliefs. He was that person. He became a reflection of the way I wanted to do things and he helped in attracting players."

Signing Strachan could have been seen as a no-brainer. Forking out for Jones was a bold, imaginative move with a seal of approval from Sheffield United manager Dave "Harry" Bassett, a good friend of Wilkinson, who was to become one of his main rivals in the promotion race. Vinnie's stay only lasted a season and that is now a matter of regret to Wilkinson. Me too. With my fan's hat on, bobbly and woolly rather than flat cap, he was fab. Yin to Batty's Yang.

"I was talking to Harry about playing for Leeds, a one-team town, handling the pressure of that and the Revie era. I needed people on the pitch who could deal with it and one of the names I mentioned was Vinnie because...I don't know why! I'd never met him - but I had an intuition," recalled Wilkinson. "There was a culture at Wimbledon and he bought into that culture, he embodied that culture but I felt there was more. Harry reaffirmed my thoughts. Vinnie was a better player than he thought he was and he fulfilled every expectation and more. Looking back, it was a mistake to sell him. If he'd stayed, and continued what I like to think was an education, I think he would have been a manager."

Football's loss has been Hollywood's gain. Mind you, screen stardom would have been the furthest thing on Jones's mind, that steamy August. The big kick-off has to be one of the most hackneyed phrases around but it doesn't half sum up the occasion. To a supporter, the morning of the first day of the season is similar to opening a diary on January 1. A clean white page, no smudges, nothing to spoil the sense of anticipation, like, say, a dentist's appointment. Everyone was starting level. Then the whistle blew and Leeds lost 5-2 at Newcastle. Micky Quinn got four of them on his debut. Yup, Micky Quinn, who liked a pie and became a horse trainer.

For goodness sake. Actually, given my status as proper fan, would it be appropriate to swear here? My ticket for Blackburn, home, one week later was booked and paid for. We'd only gone and lost the first &^%*ing game. THIS WAS NOT SUPPOSED TO HAPPEN. Wilkinson out. Strachan out. Everyeffingbody out. Back in the real world, the manager of Leeds United insists he remained remarkably composed, although may I point out the benefit of hindsight?

"That defeat at Newcastle wasn't all bad. It gave the players a kick up the arse. That game gave me the opportunity...well, let's just say I marked one or two cards in my head after that. I knew that some of those players were not going to be long term for us."

By the time I bowled up for Blackburn, Leeds had beaten Middlesbrough 2-1 at home in midweek, the start of an amazing run which saw my boys lose only once at Elland Road all season. The sole defeat came at the end of April, 2-1 against Barnsley, now described as a bad day at the office by Wilkinson and expunged totally from my memory banks. Selective recall is another wonderful fan thing. Back to August and Blackburn, a forgettable draw except that Wilkinson has the programme in front of him. He remembered: "I bumped into the chairman, Bill Fox. He turned to me and said 'All that money and you still can't win a football match'. I remember saying to him 'Come back at Christmas and see where we are then'."

Top, Mr Fox. Tip-top, in fact. Following the unscheduled debacle at St James's Park, Leeds went on a 15-match unbeaten run which included ten wins. There was a blip in November when the lads lost 4-3 at Leicester and 2-1 at West Brom but most of the time it was onwards and upwards. After beating Middlesbrough 2-0 at Ayresome Park in early December, Leeds headed the table and were never deposed. My 330-mile round trip to Elland Road had become a pilgrimage of pleasure. There could only be one ending, a happy one. The warmth of summer had long gone; hot soup and frozen fingers were the order of the day. But I was still basking in a golden glow. I was convinced but was Wilkinson? A quick reference to the bound programmes and he is off.

*"I think there is a point, a game... when everything falls into place even if you haven't won. With Leeds it took a while. Sunderland, at home. That was the one. There's a big rivalry and we murdered them. After that, I knew."*

Leeds beat Sunderland 2-0 in October [stats and facts are courtesy of Rothmans, 1990-91]. With all due respect to the gaffer, I didn't know. Not then. Not when we thrashed the Blades 4-0 in April in front of the biggest gate of the day in England, 32,697 desperate souls dreaming of the big time. I didn't even know on May 4th 1990, the night before the last day of the season. Leeds, Sheffield United, Newcastle. Perm any two from three. Wilkinson's – my - pace-setters were at Bournemouth, the Geordie boys had a tricky north-east derby day at Middlesbrough while the Blades faced Leicester at Filbert Street. All those miles, all that emotion, and all I could do was plug myself into the radio for a Bank Holiday bonanza of nerve-jangling, stomach-churning, nail-biting agony. No-one mentioned this in the Idiot's Guide to Being a Football Fan. No-one. Thankfully I only knew half the story [another perk of fan over journo] or I would have been in an even worse state. Over to you, Mr Wilkinson:

"That weekend at Bournemouth was huge. We were going down on the Thursday and that morning, in order not to get injuries, we were playing baseball. Vinnie hit a ball and slung the bat behind him and it hit Andy Williams on the face and broke his cheekbone. A total accident. That was the first thing. Then Bobby Davison did his hamstring. We trained Friday morning down in Bournemouth and he came to me and said 'gaffer, I'm not right'. You what? I said 'Don't tell anybody else. If you're not playing, I'll have to play Shutty and I don't want to tell him he's playing until five to three at the earliest and I'd prefer to leave it to five past three. If you can, go out and do the warm-up, one minute after the ball has kicked off you can come off.' What I didn't know until about two years ago was that he told Kamara on the Friday night. Strachan got to know as well.

"Then, in the hotel on the Saturday morning, the copper comes, a chief inspector. He told me there was a slight amendment to arrangements. 'If you want to be at the ground for twenty to two, we are going to have to leave here at 12.15 instead of 1.15,' he said.

'Are you joking?' was my reply. His response: 'We think there are in excess of 15,000 Leeds fans in Bournemouth at the moment and most of them are round the ground now. As only 3,000 can get in, I'm assuming there will be 12,000 outside. So we will be going at snail's pace.' Last game of the season, it looks like we have to win, Carl Shutt is going to have to play but doesn't know it and now we have the prospect of the players sitting on the coach for an hour and a quarter. I say no.

"He started to make all sorts of noises about how he couldn't be responsible for us getting to the ground in time. I told him to get us as near as possible, which was about 400 yards, and I'd take responsibility. The lads would get off and walk. If we'd set off that early and sat on the bus, the players would start thinking and the last thing I wanted for them was to start thinking. I'd rather take the risk of them walking through the crowd because it wasn't going to be a hostile one. So that's what we did and the crowd just parted. In we walked and by the time we got into the dressing room, there was a physical closeness. It was not what they expected but it was a positive difference. It was a case of 'fucking hell, what are we doing here?' but in a good way."

What they were doing was winning a football match. Chapman scored the only goal of the game while the United of Sheffield beat Leicester 5-2 and the United of Newcastle lost 4-1 to Boro. Leeds were up on 85 points, champions ahead of Bassett's mob on goal difference. As for Wilkinson, he was knackered. While everyone else partied, he headed off to a weekend in the New Forest with wife Sam and some close friends and did not catch the team bus back to Yorkshire. Hopefully red wine and the fattest, longest Cuban cigar in the world was involved.

As for me, I was ecstatic. I was a proper football fan. I was Leeds.

## Chapter 14

# The Liverpool Way

## Rory Smith

On the morning of May 26, 2005, the day after the night before, the shutters on Liverpool's club shop remained firmly down. There was nobody around to open them, after all. In line with tradition, all of the team's employees had been taken to Istanbul, to the European Cup final, as reward for their work. The thousands of fans in the city for that evening's victory parade, jubilation clouding economic senses, would not be able to buy a commemorative t-shirt to wear, a new scarf to twirl, a mug, a trinket, a key-ring, any memento at all of that most momentous of days.

All over the world, new converts were no doubt flocking to declare their suddenly-discovered love for Liverpool in the only way that really matters: financially. The club's website – unveiled as recently as 2000 and the youngest in the Premier League, so unconvinced had Liverpool been in accepting that this new-fangled internet might catch on – was heaving under the strain. A series of complex and largely unnecessary outsourcing arrangements which meant the website was unable to assess how many kits it had in stock, though, meant that most of those desperate and delighted to put a healthy portion of their hard-earned money on red that day would, most likely, have been told that no shirts were available. Liverpool had discontinued the Reebok kit that had been worn in Istanbul; the new, adidas version was not yet available.

That is the parable of May 26, the day that should, in Liverpool's commercial department at least, live in infamy. Few clubs will ever have been presented with such an easy, such a lucrative windfall. It is hard to imagine any club, in an era when football has as much to do with profits and sales and revenue streams as it does headers and corners and offside traps, to spurn it quite so spectacularly. No other club would have worn it as a badge of honour. Liverpool, almost, did, a sign of their disdain for the way the game had gone, for what football asks of you now. May 26, 2005 is Liverpool in microcosm; it stands for all that has held the club back. It illustrates Anfield's struggle to accept the 21st century.

\* \* \*

Liverpool is the only city in the world where acceptance of belonging is judged by the colour of your bin. If the wheelie which stands on the edge of your drive is Liverpool City Council purple, you're in. If it is Sefton grey, as it is in Bootle, you're out. You are not, technically, from Liverpool. To some, the hard-liners, you're not even Scouse.

This creates a problem for outsiders, even ones who have developed an immense attachment to the city, in turns thrusting and insular, bold and withdrawn, through first developing an attachment to the football club of the same name. By the bin logic, Jamie Carragher, who would place well in the inevitable BBC Three documentary *World's Scousest*

*Scouser*, may not actually be eligible. Carragher has the quick wit, the roguish edge and the inability to say the word chicken on which Liverpudlians pride themselves. But he's from Bootle. Grey bin. Not a Scouser.

But then Liverpool has not, it will tell you, ever really cared much what outsiders think (there is an irony, of course, in declaring so publicly and so volubly your apathy to the opinion of others, in that it is broadcast because you care that other people know you don't care about them). All outsiders can be safely grouped together under one, umbrella term: wool. And what wools think, as everyone will tell you, does not matter.

Wool, it is thought, developed as an epithet for those workers who came to Liverpool's docks from the hinterlands of the city, stretching from Kirkby to St Helens and perhaps as far as Warrington, to carry bales of wool to and from the tall ships docked in the world's largest port in the 19th and early 20th centuries. The white fluff on their shoulders made them, from a distance, look like they had woolly backs; elided, it provided a common identity for the casual labourers who ventured to the Mersey every day. *Woollyback*, eventually, easily, became wool; the tag stuck.

As the world has grown smaller, so the territories of the wool have grown: I grew up in Yorkshire, but count; Mancunians are excepted, as Milltowners or much worse, but the term can be applied to anyone not from the immediate vicinity of the Mersey basin. From the Midlands? Wool. From London? Southerner, cockney, wool. Scots are wools, Australians are wools. From Japan? Wool. Cameroon? Wool. It is stretching the point, but Liverpool may not be a bad place for extra-terrestrial visitors to land. "Alpha Centauri? Wool, are you?"

This should not be construed as an assault on Liverpool's exclusivity, its insularity. It is the warmest of northern cities, of English cities, because it is not really an English city; only by accident of geography is it located in the north. It is Catholic; it has more in common, they say, with Dublin than London, but there is a dash of Barcelona, or Madrid, or Buenos Aires in there, too, in attitude if not in weather. Wool is not a term of abuse; it is just an identifier. It is not that they are not welcome, but they certainly do not belong.

\* \* \*

That is how the 21st century has been treated by one of Liverpool's most important cultural institutions: its eponymous football club. The 21st century, at least in terms of football, is very much a wool. It is not abused or mocked or attacked, but it does not belong. Not here.

Liverpool, club now, not city, is often accused of harking back to its past; of not wanting to forget, of not wanting to move on. In some cases – as in the enduring campaign for justice over the Hillsborough disaster – it is the most positive, most heartening of traits, something that should be lauded for its sheer doggedness, its unbridled determination.

But in others, such yearning proves pernicious. It is a drug, the past. It releases its addicts from an uncomfortable present, one which they do not have the heart or the stomach or the nerves to face, with the promise of bliss in its purest form. It offers relief from pain, reassurance from doubt, certainty from unknowing. It separates its users, its victims, from the here and the now, it creates its own, distorted reality, and in doing so prevents them from confronting the underlying causes of their addiction.

There is nothing wrong, of course, with a football club – or a country, or a political party, or a pop singer or a faded actress or whatever it might be – celebrating and commemorating the greatest moments in its history. That is natural, understandable, right. Liverpool have more than most: the 18 league championships, the five European Cups, the countless pots and trinkets and nights under the blazing floodlights in which the Kop seemed a seething, breathing beast, one that would not be slayed. All of those moments that have gilded the years since 1892. Anfield should be proud of all that it has achieved, all that it has seen. It should sing of the days it will remember all its collective life, the vignettes of greatness that infuse Liverpool's history.

There comes a point, though, where the past, obsequy to the past, becomes a barrier to the present. Empires fall; they tend to do so when they have grown obsessed with venerating their own greatness, when they forego the need to adapt and improve and mutate and grow because they look back at what has gone before and gorge themselves on the sweet, but unfulfilling, taste of self-satisfaction.

\* \* \*

How best to illustrate Liverpool's failure to accept entry into the 21st century, beyond the parable of May 26, 2005? The totem of the stadium, perhaps: old, ramshackle, crumbing Anfield, due to be replaced 10 years ago now, its necessary but heart-wrenching demise only delayed by council bureaucracy, administrative ineptitude, the global financial crisis and a pair of snake-oil salesmen in cowboy boots and walking shoes, promising the earth and mortgaging the silver.

It stands at odds with many of the space-age super-domes that house the Premier League, Anfield. It is not just the paucity of corporate boxes or concession stands or the lack of leg room or the restricted view seats. Even Goodison Park, another relic of another age, has a big screen. Liverpool did not even have a scoreboard until 2003. By that stage, it was akin to accepting the need to own a portable music player but buying a Walkman instead of an iPod. Even so, it was greeted as a "break with tradition," presumably in the same way as the invention of the motor car was a "break with tradition" from riding around on horses or being carried in a sedan chair.

There are other, more personal, examples, ones drawn from five years of dealing with the club on a professional level - the press room with no mobile phone signal; the director of communications with an encrypted, and rarely dispensed, email address – but the complaints of the football media tend to fall on stony ground, and entirely understandably so.

Best to stick with the broad brush strokes: the commercial department that is dwarfed in scale and achievement by that at Manchester United, just 35 miles down the M62 but a world away in so many ways; the failure to exploit the power of Liverpool's brand – certainly until recently – by expanding the sponsorship base across the world, giving airlines and tyre manufacturers and all the rest of capitalism's broad menagerie the chance to be associated with one of England's few remaining blue-chip brands.

All add up to a picture of a club not just left behind by the modern world, but almost wilfully standing apart from it. There is a mantra that can be wheeled out on these occasions, on pretty much any occasion, whenever something stands at odds with what is expected of the club, whenever talk of change, unsettling, discomfiting change, rears its head. "That is not," they say, they cry, "the Liverpool Way."

\* \* \*

As with any philosophy, the Liverpool Way is a personal, private thing, something that changes from day to day and person to person. That is the danger with any unwritten constitution; it is open to interpretation and to mutation in equal measure.

To some it exists solely on the pitch, an approach to football that dictates the primacy of attacking, attractive football, or a relentless pressing game, or a brutally effective winning mentality. To others it applies in greater measure away from it, demanding a degree of privacy in the business of the game.

In all cases, though, it is defined more by what it is not than what it is. It is mentioned only in the negative, when something is adjudged to jar with what went before. Nothing is ever praised for being fitting to the Liverpool Way; only when something is not is the subject raised. Briefing the media? Not the Liverpool Way. Sacking a manager? Booing a player? Zonal marking? Not the Liverpool Way. The pursuit of wealth so as to strengthen the club and to strengthen the team, the recognition of the internationalism of the game and the need for expansion and exploitation of the brand? Having a scoreboard? Not the Liverpool Way.

Whatever the Liverpool Way, whatever it was meant to be, has been lost in the mists of time, confused and confounded by each incremental alteration. What it is now, in all cases and in all interpretations, is an albatross. It anchors Liverpool to its past; not in the sense that it grounds the club, keeping it in touch with its traditions, but in the sense that it does not brook escape, and growth, and development. The Liverpool Way is a prison.

Its jailers are the phalanx of former players who clog our airwaves and fill our newspapers and bestow their wisdom in glorious technicolour from our television screens, railing against their latest batch of heirs. This is the natural price of success, that all must be judged by what went before, but to an unhealthy degree. Gerard Houllier and Rafael Benitez both produced teams which enjoyed considerable success, by the standards of most clubs; the former won three trophies – the three lesser trophies, true, but three trophies nonetheless – in one season, after a decade in which the taste of glory merely fleeted by Liverpudlian lips – and stood accused, still, of not doing it in the right way; the latter won the European Cup, returning that famous trophy to Anfield after a 21-year wait, and yet his legacy is tarnished to some because his style was not the style the club's highest-profile alumni had decreed fitting.

And their willing accomplices are the fans, all too ready to indulge themselves in wallowing in what went before, whether it is on the pitch or off it, all too happy to compare and contrast and insist that what they see before them is not right, simply because it is not the same. The past is seen as a panacea: when Roy Hodgson's disastrous reign led the club into the miasma of mid-table, the roar from the Kop was that Kenny Dalglish would guide them from the wilderness; when the Scot proved out of his depth, when his second tenure failed to match the lofty heights of his first, there was a more muted cry to return Benitez, the irony – of course –

being that the Spaniard had been hoist from his position, a year after finishing a narrow second to Manchester United, for not being a valid guard of Liverpool's traditions. The past, as ever, provided the solution.

Liverpool exist in a game that, for better or worse, functions according to free market principles. There are thousands of footballers in the world, and the task facing every club is to acquire as many of the best of them as they can. All English clubs restrict their economic reach with their yearning for English players, but Liverpool go one step further, insisting there must be a Scouse heartbeat to their team, for that is the Liverpool Way (though it is not, as all the Scots and Irish and Welsh that litter the club's history prove). It is the purple bin rule applied in microcosm. You are one of us, or you are not.

It is the same off the pitch, where the 21st century and the version of the game that exists within it, has been ruled not to possess a purple bin. As distasteful as it is, the money men have taken charge of football. The game has become a business. Liverpool have not simply been slow to accept that unpalatable truth, they have done all they could to resist it. From the kings of Europe to King Canute, holding back the remorseless, relentless tide: that is the Liverpool Way.

* * *

There is one aspect of Liverpool which is devoutly, devotedly modern. Forged in the white heat of battle to rid Anfield of Tom Hicks and George Gillett, the rapacious speculators who hoodwinked Rick Parry, the then chief executive, and David Moores, the fan who became the owner who became a desperate vendor, into selling them the club in 2007,

Liverpool has a supporter base more 21st century than any other club in the world.

All clubs have internet forums, where supporters of sufficient technical savvy come together to discuss the issues that concern them most, and all clubs have a presence on the abundance of social media which glue our increasingly fragmented society together, defining us, offering a window into how disparate we have become: where once there might have been conversation or correspondence, now relationships have been broken down into brief messages, answered or ignored on your own schedule; friendship is now based upon an occasional snapshot into someone's most recent photo-worthy activity; social worth is judged minute-by-minute, kudos won with a witticism, scorn attracted with a different perspective. It is the playground, writ large, played out at whirligig speed. Round and round and round we go, the planet spinning ever faster, universes and celebrities created and destroyed in a day.

Whether Liverpool have a greater presence on Twitter than any other club is a spurious debate, rather like those surveys commissioned by Manchester United or Chelsea or Real Madrid to "prove" they have the most supporters in the world. A personal favourite was one carried out by Flamengo, which concluded that the Rio de Janeiro side is the most loved in the world, followed by Vasco da Gama and Club America, denizens of the Estadio Azteca in Mexico City. "This is because while Manchester United count millions in China," the conclusion, paraphrased, ran, "we have not counted these figures, as they clearly are not proper supporters."

What Liverpool do have, certainly in personal experience, is the most voluble support-base among Twitter's millions of users. Manchester United, Chelsea, Arsenal, Manchester City and Tottenham are well-represented, too, but no group can match the same pitch of fury or crowing or fear or delight as Liverpool.

This is often taken as a sign that Liverpool supporters are touchy, or defensive, or arrogant, or rather too opinionated for their own good. It is popular perception that Liverpool dominate social media because their fans will not hear a word against their club; perhaps this is true, but it is, liké any phenomenon, worthy of an attempt to comprehend why that might be.

The battle to rid Liverpool of Hicks and Gillett lasted for almost three years; almost to the day. The first salvo was fired when a group of supporters, correctly understanding that the Americans might be about to do away with the troublesome Benitez, constantly chiding them and prodding them for greater investment in the team and greater alacrity in transfer dealings, organised a march down Walton Breck Road to Anfield's directors' entrance to show their support for the Spaniard. "You're the custodians," ran one banner. "It's our club. Rafa stays."

That march led indirectly to Sons of Shankly and Spirit of Shankly, the supporter unions, who co-ordinated many of the protests against Hicks and Gillett, and to the splinter factions, Save Liverpool and Kop Faithful and the others. They harassed and harried and harangued the Americans until that October day when Ian Ayre, Christian Purslow and Martin Broughton, the three English members of the indebted club's five-man board, staged their midnight putsch, selling an asset owned – on borrowed money – by Hicks and Gillett to John Henry's New England Sports Ventures, later renamed Fenway Sports Group.

All such organisation took time; much of it was, as is the way of things, orchestrated on the forums. From there, it was a natural step to Twitter, to Facebook, to all of the others, to publicise the message. Liverpool's fan-base, or a portion of it, grew tech-savvy. Hicks was pictured outside Deutsche Bank in New York: the photo spread around the world, instantaneously, on Twitter. Email campaigns to alert potential investors as to the unpopularity of the Americans' regime were masterminded on chat sites.

But it also created energy; in this instance, one of the fundamental laws of physics was overturned. Liverpool are an isolated system, and yet the total amount of energy has not remained constant. The battle to get rid of Hicks and Gillett, to throw off the carcinogenic shackles they had placed on the club, mobilised the fan-base.

That was shown even while the two cowboys were still in place, as supporters divided into factions based on whether they supported Benitez or not, or whether they liked a certain player or not. And it is even more true now, when every criticism of Liverpool is treated as a deep-seated personal assault, when the cudgels are taken up at the first available opportunity to protect the name of the club. That energy seeps from Twitter, from websites, from podcasts and from blogs. The fans' attitude may remain linked, inextricably, to the past, but their passion is broadcast in the most modern of means.

* * *

Here, then, the circle joins. A fan-base with endless, bound-less energy, once directed at a mutual enemy but now earthed wherever a threat is identified, real or imagined. It is used to protect and cherish a club that is anchored to its past, held back by what it once was. Any attempt at change is met with howling derision so deafening, so impassioned, that progress is agonisingly slow.

It is scarcely possible to discuss Liverpool without reference to their long wait for a league championship. At the time of writing, it is 22 years since Anfield last hailed the best team in England. There have been close shaves and near misses – 1997, 2002, 2009 are the pick of the three – and there have been trophies and glories to dull the pain; Istanbul, of course, was quite the tonic. But that the length of time that Liverpool have not been what they are meant to be is so relevant is instructive. Liverpool are defined by the past, and conditioned to thinking that anything less than a return is but a pale imitation. The past is an addiction. It enslaves the club, smothers the stadium, and dulls the senses.

Change will come. Change must come. The club must begin to think not of how long it has been since the league title was procured but how long it is until it is regained. The Liverpool Way, in all of its various guises and disparate interpretations, must become less of an absolutism, a means of excluding and dismissing. It must become a positive again. The positives that surround the club, on and off the pitch, must be welcomed as part of an update of the Liverpool Way. The club's guiding philosophy must be open to reinvention, accessible to change. Liverpool need a Year Zero, to gouge a line in the sand and declare that history, as Francis Fukuyama, not a likely bedfellow, observed, is dead; that life begins again here. It is only then that the present can begin, and the future follow in its wake. It is 12 years too late already, but Liverpool must begin their 21st century.

## Chapter 15

# The Tony Soprano of Old Trafford

## Rob Smyth

On 8 December 1999, at 8.23pm, I fell in love with another man. Roy Keane probably wouldn't care much for this revelation, but then I'm pretty sure I wasn't alone. The context was a long-forgotten match between Manchester United and Valencia in the long-forgotten second group stage of the Champions League. Long forgotten, that is, by everybody except those besotted with Roy Keane.

For the preceding five months, there was a serious danger that Keane, aged 28 and at the peak of his not inconsiderable powers, would leave United. His contract was due to expire in the summer of 2000, and United were unwilling to break their rigid wage structure to give Keane the £50,000 a week he wanted. Moves to Juventus and Bayern Munich were frequently discussed in the press; the Bosman rule meant that, as of 1 January 2000, Keane could discuss terms with foreign clubs. All that scaremongering about the Millennium Bug had nothing on the millennial angst felt around Old Trafford. The word 'unthinkable' does not begin to do justice to the thought of that United side without Keane. Impasses are usually tedious; this was terrifying.

Then, on the afternoon of United's match against Valencia, the club announced that Keane had signed a new contract. It was a match United had to win; they had lost the first group game away to Fiorentina, largely because of a rare and hideous error from Keane. A fortnight later he righted that wrong, slamming in a joyously emphatic opening goal from the edge of the area. Keane had already made far greater contributions for United, most famously away to Juventus in the previous season's semi-final, but the combination of the goal and the earlier defenestration of the desperate thought of a world without him made it a nigh-on perfect moment. The sort that makes you realise that, even when you grow old and doddery, and when you wouldn't recognise your other teenage heroes if they were stood in front of you holding a walking stick, you will still love Roy Keane.

There is something about Keane that inspires such extreme devotion – and also wonder. At the 2012 Soccer Aid event, superstars like Robbie Williams and Will Ferrell were clearly in awe of Keane. Most fans of big English clubs other than United hate him, of course, and in that respect Keane is an uber-Marmite figure: those who love him would generally be willing to go to the ends of the earth for any unspecified Keane-related purpose. As a player, he was of his time by not being of his time: he captured the pre-millennium angst of the outsider who cannot understand the world of which he is part. In doing so he brought to mind a number of pop-culture characters of a similar disposition. Two in particular: Tyler Durden in Fight Club and Tony Soprano in The Sopranos. Like Keane, both raged, raged against the dying of society's light. There are other similarities. The intense adoration Keane receives evokes that of Tyler Durden, while his obtuse charisma, anti-heroism and scattergun frustration is shared by Tony Soprano. Keane, like Soprano, was raging for a better world and a better him. He has always been an incredibly complex man, a compelling fusion of instinctive intelligence and pathological desire.

Keane, like Tony Soprano, is a mass of often uncomfortable contradictions. Thank goodness for that. The most interesting people in life are invariably flawed, and Keane has been the most interesting person in British football for the last few decades – an outsider even down to his Diadora boots, never mind the candour that is so rare in modern football. What kind of hero would you prefer? Prom kings are for dreamers and liars. Having Roy Keane as a hero allows a vicarious ride through life in all its miserable glory.

For all his success – Keane won seven Premier Leagues, four FA Cups and, although he'd tell you otherwise, one European Cup at Manchester United – football has often been brutally unkind to him. He was booted out mercilessly by a club and manager to whom he had given his soul and body. He missed out on his only European Cup final because of suspension. A year later, when he seemed to be on a personal mission to win the trophy – he scored six Champions League goals that season, almost half his career total of 14, and played with almost demented purpose – he then scored an own goal and missed an open goal in the quarter-final defeat to Real Madrid. Having got Ireland to the World Cup in 2002 with arguably the greatest football of his career, he missed out on the tournament because of his infamous row with Mick McCarthy. Keane always defined himself and his teams by global competition; you only have to see his boyish excitement as he stood pitchside for ITV ahead of Milan v Barcelona to realise that. Despite playing some awe-inspiring football for Ireland and for United in Europe, he played just in just one major tournament and no European finals.

If this tells us of the essentially cruel nature of football, they will not necessarily be our abiding memories of Keane. We will remember him as somebody who personified leadership, who controlled games with forensic intelligence, who was a grossly underrated passer and who, on occasion, put the fear of God into both opponents and teammates. That was a consequence of an intractable obsession with excellence. Keane combined a higher state of concentration and an inhuman perfectionism to consistently reach a level of performance beyond almost anyone else – even if that level of performance regularly did not satisfy the critic within. He was not interested in glory. Glory was something that came if you did your job properly. That, nor heroism, interested him. "You can be a hero – whatever that is," he sniffed in his autobiography.

Players of Keane's type are regularly described as 'winners', and with good reason. Keane did not so much have a will to win as a *need* to win. "If I was putting Roy Keane out there to represent Manchester United on a one against one, we'd win the Derby, the National, the Boat Race and anything else," Sir Alex Ferguson once said. "It's an incredible thing he's got."

It was not just winning that interested Keane, however. He was equally concerned with excellence and personal pride; winning was usually the result of the exhibition of those qualities. It was not necessarily a deal-breaker. In his autobiography he talks about the performance that first caught the attention of Nottingham Forest scouts. His team were 4-0 down with a few minutes to go. Everybody else had waved the white flag, but Keane kept doing the right things: demanding possession, moving the ball on crisply, putting out fires when the opposition had the ball. The qualities were in evidence at Forest, too: in 1992-93, the first season of the Premier League, Keane fought a lone, heroic and ultimately doomed battle to keep Forest in the Premier League.

Keane detested mediocrity, and sometimes that need for excellence proved overwhelming. It is no coincidence that his infamous foul on Alf-Inge Haaland in 2001 came immediately after Manchester City had equalised at Old Trafford. United were already champions, but they had surrendered feebly in Europe to Bayern Munich earlier in the week and Keane was convinced they were in the comfort zone. When City – a poor side who would be relegated – equalised, it all bubbled over. Prawn sandwiches, mediocrity, couldn't even beat City at home, comfort zone, Haaland in possession. "Alfie was taking the piss". Bang. Haaland was toppled like a folding deckchair and Keane was the villain again.

It might simply have been the case of him waiting for the right moment to hit Haaland, but it seems a bit of a coincidence: this was the 266th minute on the field together since Keane's return. That was one of Keane's low points. Another was his furious harassment of the referee Andy D'Urso, who had given a penalty against United at Old Trafford (insert your own joke here). Keane admitted he was "out of order" but that didn't reduce the opprobrium.

A month earlier, he had imposed himself physically in a more palatable manner. In their first game after returning from a trip to Brazil for the World Club Championship, a sluggish United were trailing 1-0 at home to Arsenal on a Monday night. With the crowd and team subdued, a rabid

Keane changed the entire mood of the match by charging round challenging everything that moved and much that didn't in an exhilarating five-minute period. United woke up, eventually drew the game and went on to win the title by 18 points.

Keane was always a master of the tone-setting challenge. His most famous came for Ireland, a legendary foul on Marc Overmars in the first minute of the decisive World Cup qualifier between Ireland and Holland in September 2001. Ireland won 1-0 and qualified ahead of a star-studded Dutch side. Keane had never been more of a one-man team than during that campaign. A less famous but equally rousing tackle came against Galatasaray in 1994, again in the first minute, when Keane gave Tugay a ten-yard start to a loose ball and still got there at the same time. It roused the Old Trafford crowd and a team of youngsters, with United going on to win 4-0.

Such challenges linger in the mind, for richer and poorer. Keane's detractors say he was little more than a thug who went round booting people at a time when the game's laws had not evolved sufficiently. This is such offensive poppy-cock that it barely merits mention. The primary weapons in Keane's arsenal, by a distance, were his energy, positional sense and game intelligence. Never was this more evident than during a magnificent performance in the 1996 FA Cup final against Liverpool. The game is remembered for Eric Cantona's masterful late winner, which clinched the Double for United and completed his fairytale; justly so, yet that goal was infinitesimal in the grand scheme. In this game, as much as any others, Keane's footballing philosophy emphatically came to pass.

This particular devil has always been obsessed with detail,

and the minutiae of football matches. "They say God is in the detail; in football that's true," he said in his autobiography. "Sometimes games are won by a magical goal - that's what people remember. But the essence of the game is more mundane. Detail. Wearing down the opposition. Winning the psychological battles - man on man - from the moment the ref blows the whistle for the first time." Keane called it the Law of Cumulation. "First tackle, first pass, first touch, everything counts. A lot of little things add up to the thing that matters: breaking the opposition's hearts - but first their minds, their collective mind."

Keane learned all this from Brian Clough. "If you weren't doing your stuff, Clough would spot it. A seemingly innocuous mistake that resulted in a goal conceded three or four minutes later, a tackle missed, or a failure to make the right run, or pass, would be correctly identified as the cause of the goal. It was no use pointing the finger at someone else - which is second nature to most players. He knew; you knew he knew. Every football match consists of a thousand little things which, added together, amount to the final score. The game is full of bluffers, banging on about 'rolling your sleeves up', 'having the right attitude' and 'taking some pride in the shirt'. Brian Clough dealt in facts, specific incidents, and invariably he got it right."

Liverpool were a dangerous, free-flowing side who created umpteen chances in the two league games against United that season: a 2-2 draw at Old Trafford and a 2-0 win at Anfield that could have been 8-0 but for Peter Schmeichel. Keane did not play at Anfield, but he grudgingly respected Liverpool's abundant attacking talent: Robbie Fowler, Jamie Redknapp and Steve McManaman all played the most progressive football of their career under Roy Evans. The unpredictable brilliance of Stan Collymore was also worthy of respect. Keane's fear of Liverpool's capabilities was accompanied by loathing. In short, he couldn't stand them. The notion of the Spice Boys was anathema. Lee Sharpe tells a story of him and an "absolutely smashed" Keane bumping into the Liverpool players in a bar one Saturday night. Keane went through them one by one, dismissing their England B caps, England under-21 caps and League Cup winners' medals. The gist, frequently expressed, was simple: "What the hell have you done in the game?"

Then they turned up at Wembley in cream Armani suits. The FA Cup final had been turned into fancy dress day, a jolly boys' outing. You can only imagine the unremitting contempt on Keane's face as he looked those sartorial monstrosities up and down. With help from his trusted lieutenant Nicky Butt, Keane shut Liverpool down with remorselessness, concentration and intelligence. They had barely a chance all game. It was one of the great defensive-midfield performances. It meant the game, as hyped as any FA Cup final in the modern era, was a stinker, but are you going to tell Roy Keane that was a bad thing?

There is a good argument that this was Keane's finest performance. It is moot. When his individual performances are considered, all discussions and streams of consciousness lead to the Stadio delle Alpi on 21 April 1999, the night that defined Keane's career in all its bittersweet beauty. The memory makes thousands of grown men - the sort who wouldn't flinch at a funeral – go moist at the eye. You'll know the story by now: Keane dragging United back into the match from 2-0 down, then receiving a booking that would rule him out of the final. "I felt it was an honour to be associated with such a player," said Sir Alex Ferguson. "It was the most emphatic display of selflessness I have seen on a football field."

The nature of Keane's performance is often misunderstood. He didn't break into a snarl all night. Even his booking was an awkward attempt to win a loose ball rather than a full-blooded tackle. Throughout the game he was in a zone of serenity and formidable certainty; at 2-0 down, when everyone else was bracing to accept the inevitable, Keane looked the beast in the eye and made it blink. He got United going with relentless, hypnotic passing and a mood of controlled urgency that slowly overwhelmed Juventus. The usual superlatives are hopelessly inadequate to describe his performance.

Clough had taught Keane the value of looking after the football, and of passing progressively. In many ways, Clough is a more relevant reference point for Keane's managerial career than Ferguson. There is the inscrutability, the wild and unfathomable mood changes, the bitter and bitterly sad fallout with his closest friend in football - and the unconditional love for the only tool of the trade that matters, the football. Clough once chinned Keane for playing a backpass, and it was from him that Keane learned to detest the aimless, brainless pass. By the end of his career, a strength had arguably become a weakness: Keane became so obsessed with not giving the ball away that many felt he was slowing down United's attacking play.

In Turin, six years earlier, there was speed and decisiveness in his passing. He was the star of a breathtaking team performance that is surely the greatest by an English side in Europe. United hit the woodwork twice; the otherwise magnificent Andy Cole missed a sitter; and Ciro Ferrara of Juventus should have been sent off for a professional foul after 20 minutes. Context is everything, and for any team – never mind an English team - to do this to an Italian side in the European Cup was impossible. No Italian side had lost a European Cup knockout game at home for 20 years. There had been an Italian side in each of the previous seven European Cup finals. In the next three seasons, despite the increased number of teams, they would provide just one quarter-finalist. The manner of Juventus's defeat thrust Serie A into a prolonged period of introspection. It is not entirely hyperbolic to say that Roy Keane's will broke an entire institution. His appraisal of his performance was a little less grandiose. "I was content," said Keane, "that I had justified my existence."

Keane did not do it on his own, of course, but there is no way United could have produced such a performance without him on the field. Even though they went on to win the final, most acknowledge that they were extremely fortunate to do so. Keane's absence was painfully obvious. This was the case for much of his United career. World-class players were frequently not the same in his absence. When they turned round and saw Keane, they knew everything would be okay. When he wasn't there, all bets were off. United suffered a number of unthinkable defeats in his absence. A 1-0 loss at home to Middlesbrough and a draw at to-be-relegated Derby probably cost them the 2001-02 title; a young team collapsed desperately in the second half of the 1997-98 season when Keane was injured; the Derby humiliations of 2002-03 and 2003-04 both came in his absence, as did 5-0 defeats at Newcastle (1996-97) and Chelsea (1999-2000). The notorious 6-3 defeat at Southampton in 1996-97 was mainly the result of Keane being sent off at 1-0. Keane also missed the miserable 4-1 thrashing at

Middlesbrough, a game that sealed his fate at Old Trafford. Had he been on the field there would probably have been no thrashing, and no video nasty for Keane to review with such scalding honesty as to effectively get himself the sack.

Keane's leadership was not just apparent during games. For a Manchester United fan, there has been no greater primal thrill in the past decade than seeing Keane take on Patrick Vieira in the Highbury tunnel in February 2005. Vieira had attempted to intimidate Gary Neville in the warm-up; Keane decided that Vieira should "pick on someone your own size" - even though Neville is actually taller than Keane. A startled Vieira was informed that "I'll see you out there". Utter that phrase to any hardcore Manchester United fan, anywhere in the world, and watch a smile break out. Although Vieira scored the opening goal, a Keane-inspired United won 4-2. Such moments resonate ever more in view of the leaderlessness of the current United side – there is no way in the world a team with Roy Keane in it would have blown an eight-point lead – and the emasculation of football. Forget goalscorers and playmakers; fans have traditionally related to hard men more than any other type of player.

So have managers. For almost all of his United career, Keane was his master's voice on and off the field. When United won the Premier League by beating Spurs 2-1 in the final game of the 1998-99 season – the first part of the Treble – Ferguson gallivanted straight onto the Old Trafford field to embrace Keane, who had played while half fit and ensured United got over the line. He ignored everyone else. At that moment, Keane was Ferguson's world entire.

All of this makes their fallout so much sadder. When Keane became dispensable on the field, Ferguson cut him loose with chilling ruthlessness. On some level, Keane must have known it would happen. When Jaap Stam was surprisingly sold in 2001, Keane reflected that players were "pieces of meat" and that it was "just business". On some macabre level, part of him probably welcomed it to be this way.

Keane's leadership suggested he might make an outstanding manager. Hindsight tells us this was never going to be the case. Not in the 21st century, with player power so rife and mediocrity so tolerated. There were times when Keane was at the limit in a Manchester United dressing room full of exceptional talents and proper professionals. He had no chance in a football world full of snides, phonies, cheats, bluffers and duffers.

It is commonly said that Clough could not manage in the modern game – as if this is somehow a good thing – and with Keane modelling his management on Clough, the same rules apply. Modern football is too pampered for somebody who has such rage in him, and too dishonest for somebody with a bullshit detector that never stops zinging. Keane would rather punch someone in the face than stab them in the back – and then tell them precisely why he's just punched them. This might be his biggest problem. Not all great leaders are great politicians. Keane does not want to play that game, and couldn't if he tried. But almost all great modern managers are great politicians.

The upshot is that we now have Keane as a pundit. This fits the Keane contradiction; he once said it was a job he would never consider. At times he makes for blistering television, better than the match itself, although there is a suspicion that he states the obvious a little too much for a man whose interviews as a player were bursting with pithy insight. His enduring rant about prawn sandwiches is the most obvious example, while Niall Quinn described Keane's ostensibly foul-mouthed verbal defenestration of Mick McCarthy in Saipan as "the most articulate, the most surgical slaughtering I have ever heard". Saipan really should be in the dictionary as a verb.

Keane's snakelick appraisals also create a rich black comedy. Phil Taylor recalls the time he was shown round Old Trafford shortly after losing his Darts world title. A flunky introduced him to Keane as the "world champion". Keane looked Taylor up and down and spat "ex-world champion". Keane is also the man who said "Dogs aren't like humans – dogs don't talk shit" and reportedly replied to a text message that said "This is Gary Neville's new number" with "So what?"

You suspect Keane enjoys the absurdity of his extreme nature. It is not always obvious, but he does a decent line in self-deprecation. When ITV's Adrian Chiles asked Keane whether Joe Hart had "any weaknesses, any demons", Keane replied "We all have demons" and burst out laughing.

Nobody else could turn walking a dog into a comedy sketch and an intimidatory gesture, as Keane did with Triggs over the years. When he was at Nottingham Forest, he reportedly painted the walls and ceilings of his flat black. The only furniture was a mattress with no bed, and piles of football magazines. All this contributes to the picture of an incredibly complex man: brilliant, flawed, eloquent, kind, savage, charming, erratic, intelligent, shy, fearless. A real human being, and a real hero.

## Chapter 16

# Egg and Chips For Two

## David Walker

Considering it was to prove one of the most momentous meetings in the history of Leeds United, it didn't get off to the best of starts. Leslie Silver, the Leeds chairman who had just sacked the legendary Billy Bremner, was hunting for a new manager.

Two names had emerged as the front-runners for the Elland Road vacancy. They were Arthur Cox, then the manager of Derby County, and Sheffield Wednesday's Howard Wilkinson. Both had their supporters among the Leeds directors. The year was 1988. Leeds had been out of the top flight of English football for six years. Both Cox and Wilkinson were experts at winning promotion and were working in the old First Division. In terms of club status, moving to Elland Road would be a step down for them. In fact, at this juncture Leeds were second from bottom of the old Second Division. Three of Don Revie's old boys had been given the chance to manage the club. All had failed. Life at Leeds was bleak.

Chairman Silver had a personal inclination to recruit Wilkinson. As a trusted friend of Leeds and Howard he asked me to arrange a secret meeting between the parties.

We met at the office of Leslie's paint factory on the outskirts of Leeds. Those who know Wilkinson will not be surprised by the depth of research he had done. He knew all about the Leeds chairman's personal wealth and commitment to the club. He had assessed Silver's fellow directors and their stakes, the day-to-day running of the club, attendance figures, wage bill, and a host of administrative detail. And that was all before he got to individual assessments of the playing staff and the signings he'd want to make. Thorough was Howard's middle name.

But Howard wasn't sure of the way to Leslie's factory, which was situated in a not so popular part of the city. We arranged to meet at the Hartshead Moor services on the M62. From there I was to lead Howard into Batley for his critical meeting.

Except there was one huge problem, an issue that could have wrecked Howard's hopes of landing the Leeds job before he'd even had chance to say hello to the Elland Road chairman and ensured Arthur Cox landed a lucrative deal. To our eternal discredit, Team Wilko couldn't find each other in the service station. And these were the days before mobile phones. Well, Howard had one in his car. I didn't have one in my Daily Mail company Vauxhall Cavalier.

He was hanging around the petrol pump area at which he thought we were meeting. I mooched around the petrol pump area I thought was our rendezvous. The clock was ticking and a multi-millionaire who owned Leeds United was in danger of being stood up. I couldn't believe Howard could have screwed up something so important. We were close to the point of real embarrassment when I scrabbled around to find enough ten pence pieces to fund a call from a phone box. To my eternal relief I was in the right place; Howard had made a mistake.

We became friends reunited and raced to the tryst. It was four o'clock - well just after, because we were late - on an autumn afternoon when Silver met Wilkinson for the first time. I left them to their talks knowing I'd get an update later from one of the interested parties - hopefully both.

Silver tells the tale lyrically about sitting in his office mesmerised by Wilkinson's sales pitch as he outlined his blueprint for Leeds United's future. The sun set, the street lights began to twinkle and Howard explained the three routes to glory. Silver bought into route one - the quick route that carried a hefty price.

Leslie was estimated to have committed at least £2million of his own wealth in backing the Wilkinson plan. For the previous five years Wilkinson had worked within the tight financial restraints of Sheffield Wednesday. Suddenly he had a chairman telling him to sign Gordon Strachan from Manchester United, bring in proven top flight stars and get Leeds back into the big-time. In retrospect, Wilkinson and Silver circa 1988 were made for each other. With the added support of Bill Fotherby, the club's managing director, they formed an alliance that transformed a struggling Second Division team into the last champions of England when the Football League had 92 clubs. That was in 1992, less than four years after the meeting that almost never happened.

Silver remains a charming man. In those days he bore the air of a successful, wealthy businessman but exuded an avuncular approach that allowed him to be sensitive to the feelings of the fans as well as the boardroom. His wealth may have been immense but he remained firmly grounded. He was convinced he'd got the right man when he signed up Wilkinson. History was to prove him right. Indeed, it is often overlooked that Wilkinson was the last Englishman to guide his team to top flight glory in England.

A few years later Leslie wanted to have a chat with me to discuss football issues and sports politics. The telephone call came from his personal PA inviting me for lunch with the chairman in the Elland Road boardroom. It was lunch for two at 1 pm.

Having remembered the lessons of a previous late arrival at a meeting with Leslie I turned up ten minutes early. I was shown to the boardroom and saw the huge oak table had been set for us. Leslie arrived and told me that he'd asked the club chef to provide his favourite meal for us. The waitress offered wine, the chef arrived with our plates covered by glimmering cloches and "voila", Leslie's favourite meal was revealed.

Egg and chips. I think I managed to disguise my amazement/ astonishment/ disappointment. (Delete as applicable.) But my host was typically open. "You know David, I get sick and tired of attending all those fancy formal lunches and dinners. It's great to be working down here, eating my favourite meal."

During that particular lunch I looked around the Leeds boardroom and imagined other meetings which had happened before Leslie was a director. Manny Cussins, the then chairman, and his colleagues, first hired and, 44 days later, fired Brian Clough in that room. Leslie admitted how hard the club had found replacing Don Revie. Perhaps they never did. Wilkinson came the closest. But Leeds had been transformed from those days in the Sixties when Revie had dragged an unfashionable northern club into the big-time. How times were different then.

When Leeds drew Standard Liege in the UEFA Cup in 1968 a Leeds director announced: "I'm really looking forward to this trip. I've never been to Standard." By 2000 I had answered the call to join the Leeds board and my first two foreign sorties were to Munich and Barcelona. I was appointed United's director of PR and Corporate Affairs. In the wake of two fans being killed in Istanbul and with what was to become known as the Bowyer-Woodgate trial on the horizon, it was a daunting challenge. And yet there is something bewitching about Leeds United.

There are no half measures. In a sense Leeds fans wouldn't want it any other way. But around the Millennium Leeds was the fastest growing commercial centre in Britain. It remains the biggest city with only one football club. That creates a one-eyed view of the sporting world. There's no local derby to be won. It's simply Leeds against the rest of the world.

Back in Wilkinson's era scientists did tests at football grounds to establish the loudest fans. Leeds won that accolade. On a day of deafening passion Elland Road could be a bear pit. I totally accept you either love it or loathe it. Where Leeds are concerned nobody sits on the fence. I promise you I've seen players - Leeds and opponents - relish playing in front of those crazy fans. I've seen others - home and away - crumble under the weight of expectation, vitriol and critical complaint. The best Leeds players down the years have had nerves of steel. Anything less and they were found out.

The long-serving club president until his death last year was Lord Harewood. He and Lady Harewood were not just token aristocratic, fair-weather followers. They were Leeds through and through. Lord Harewood, then 77, insisted:

"David, please call me George and my wife is Patricia." And with that request started a friendship that sparked some memorable moments of fun and frivolity.

My wife and I used to sit next to the Harewoods in the Leeds directors box. One day a rhythmic clap and chant erupted around the ground, starting at the Kop end. Leeds fans around the packed stadium laughed loudly then joined in. George turned to Patricia to ask what was making them laugh. So Patricia turned to me and asked the same question. I was in a quandary.

The words being chanted were "Danny Mills is f**king brilliant." Now Danny hadn't enjoyed the most auspicious of starts since his transfer from Charlton but that day he turned a corner and became a firm fans' favourite. But you can understand my problem. How do you tell the Queen's first cousin the real reason for the crowd's amusement? In the end I decided the best course of action was the truth. I turned to Patricia and said: "They're chanting: 'Danny Mills is f**king brilliant." With that she turned to her husband and passed on the message, which appeared to make the club president smile.

Imagine my amazement at our next home game when the Harewoods arrived, spotted me in the boardroom and with a broad grin George wagged a finger in my direction and said: "Now, now David, you didn't need to be so coy. I found out what the fans were really chanting." I was intrigued and had to ask what he thought I'd told them. Patricia stepped in: "David, don't worry I've heard the F-word before. You didn't need to change the chant to Danny Mills is looking brilliant!"

George Harewood had been President of the FA in the Sixties and had genuine knowledge of football. He also came from an aristocratic line that he rarely flaunted in our company but proved priceless during our Champions League campaign in the 2000-01 season.

George and Patricia joined our treks around Europe - and we were drawn against some pretty good opponents and visited some fantastic cities. We beat Munich 1860 in the play-off preliminary round. It was on that trip that George Harewood entertained us with stories highlighting his ineptitude as an army officer that led to him and his men being incarcerated in Colditz Castle as prisoners of war. From there we ventured to places like Barcelona, Rome, Istanbul, Milan and Valencia.

It was our Champions League games against Barcelona that brought out the wickedly impish side in Lord Harewood. On our visit to the Nou Camp the brutally frank message from the Catalan hierarchy was that we were wasting our time. There was an arrogance and air of presumption that was quite distasteful. The fact that Leeds' first game in the Champions League ended in a 4-0 defeat at the Nou Camp suggested Barca's president and directors might be right. But their air of superiority really annoyed us. We had qualified to play them in the Champions League. We were there on merit and the best two teams from the group would qualify for the next stage. Barcelona were convinced they would go through with AC Milan while Leeds and Besiktas could squabble over third place and a UEFA Cup berth.

In the speeches at the formal pre-match dinner they pressed home the point that it was nice to see us but we were no more than a minor irritant on their path to Champions League glory. The sneers hit home with us all - especially our president. A couple of weeks before the Catalans were due to visit Elland Road, George asked if he could stage the pre-match dinner for Barcelona and UEFA officials at his home, Harewood House.

Now Harewood House was built from 1759 to 1771 for the first Baron Harewood. It's listed as one of the Treasure Houses of England. If you want to play at name dropping in architecture this place has the lot. The house was designed by the architects John Carr and Robert Adam. Much of the furniture is by Thomas Chippendale and Lancelot "Capability" Brown designed the grounds. So it was a real pleasure to be wined and dined by the Harewoods at their home. And to use the Yorkshire vernacular, even the Barcelona officials were gob-smacked when they saw the place. But the best had yet to come.

During the speeches Barca reiterated their belief that we were a nice, friendly little club, the sort they had to sweep aside on their way to glory. Even the UEFA officials present winced at the presumption of it all. And then George Harewood struck. He stood up and graciously welcomed our guests from Catalonia. He emphasised our honour in playing such a fine team, a sporting institution that prides itself on being "more than a club". He was warm, erudite and sincere. He then began a tour of the magnificent dining room, delivering a potted history of his noble ancestors depicted in the massive oil paintings hanging on the walls.

As George jabbed a finger at his great, great, great grandfather, it turned out that his relative had led the English fleet to victory over Spain in a famous sea battle. And then he turned to another stern looking relative. He'd been a military man, too, and had been in the army, leading his troops to many triumphs including a particularly famous one over, yes you've guessed it, the Spanish. The roll call of the good Lord's brave predecessors, who'd all defeated the

Spanish foe, seemed endless. You'd have thought Lord Harewood had hand-picked the oil paintings that hung on the panelled walls of his dining room that night.

He finished with a lovely line that as well as being proud of his family he was also proud of his football club, Leeds United. And he promised that we would give Barcelona a game the next night at Elland Road. The fact is that we drew the game 1-1 but we did have the last laugh. In the final qualifying group game Leeds headed to the San Siro knowing a draw would see us reach the second group stages and eliminate Barcelona. Yes that very same Barcelona who were going to sweep us and the rest of Europe aside.

AC Milan officials met us before the trip and explained the security issues around the game and suggested we'd have 3,000 fans following us. The estimate was based on the numbers other English teams had taken for that kind of game. We pointed out that the Leeds fans were a bit different, that taking on Milan in a crucial game would see our fans turn out in force. "Yes, we know but you'll still only have around 3,000 with you," said their security officer. Leeds had over 6,000 fans for the night when Dominic Matteo's near-post header clinched the club's passage into the next round and Barca's elimination. After the game, the Leeds fans inside the stadium called for the players to join them in their party. Matteo and his mates happily obliged and one of the finest spontaneous sing-songs involving fans, players and officials erupted. It was a special night - and a long one back at the team's Lake Como hideaway.

That group of Leeds players were bright, committed and willing to listen to this gnarled old hack about the ways of the media, the way to present themselves in public and the fundamental requirements of representing the club both to the media and at fan and charity events. In fact, some of them really blossomed at the extra-curricular activities.

It was Wilkinson, aware of the club's badly tarnished reputation, who ensured that Leeds United were the first club to insert a clause in the players' contracts that they had to commit time each week to represent the club at charity, educational and media events. Howard would not tolerate any debate about this. It was in every player's specific terms of employment. Leeds United players would give their time to the community and good causes.

The club had a thriving section for disabled fans. This was the Leeds United Disabled Organisation or LUDO. We would support their events and each season they would stage their own Player of the Year gala dinner. This would be staged in the main banqueting suite at Elland Road after a home game. We didn't need a three-line whip to get all the players to attend. We did have a quiet chat with the organisers to confirm that after 10pm the players could quietly drift away. I recall leaving at midnight and getting a call of thanks from the organisers the next day. Apparently Mark Viduka and Jason Wilcox had stayed until chucking out time at 1 am, chatting with the disabled fans, having pictures taken and ensuring that every Leeds fan had enjoyed a great evening. It was heartening to hear. They were both a credit to their profession and families.

The results within the Leeds United education programme were astonishing. Inner city youngsters who had no interest in learning at their schools were suddenly motivated by lessons at the Elland Road learning centre. Numeracy and literacy results over a period of weeks showed how inspired these youngsters had been. At the end of each term we'd stage presentation evenings for the pupils. Mums and Dads who had never attended a formal parents' evening at school suddenly turned out to see Alan Smith hand over a certificate of progress to their son or daughter. And given he was from the tough streets of south Leeds nobody could dispute Smithy's status as a home grown hero. He was adored back then.

Of course there were times when the players were reluctant to fulfil requests and requirements. One memory stands out here. In that season when we'd progressed beyond Barcelona in the Champions League we actually reached the semi-finals. We drew our home game with Valencia 0-0 and then got blown away in the Mestalla 3-0. Alan Smith became so frustrated he lunged into a wild, late tackle and was red carded. He was in tears in the dressing-room when I arrived to commiserate with the troops but also to point out that there was media mixed zone where they were expected to walk through and conduct interviews.

There was a collective groan at my request. Manager David O'Leary knew he had to attend a press conference. The players wished they could skulk away into the night to lick their wounds. At that point Brian Kidd, the first team coach, stepped in. He said: "Lads, you've really enjoyed the run to the semis and you've conducted yourselves brilliantly along the way. Now tonight's the test. We've lost. So we go out of here with our heads held high and see the campaign through properly. If the Press want to talk to you then you talk, sensibly and civilly."

Seasoned journalists in attendance that night admitted their respect for the defeated Leeds players who behaved impeccably as they walked out to their coach. Every single player - and there were a couple on whom we couldn't always rely - followed Kiddo's guidelines. We were beaten but we showed a style and class that spoke volumes for the individuals concerned and the club.

Of course not everything in the Leeds United garden was rosy at this point. The bond scheme funds, used to bring in the top quality players, could only be justified in the long term by regular Champions League qualification. We were invited to join the UEFA Club Forum with Manchester United, Liverpool, Arsenal and Chelsea after five consecutive years of European combat. But we only managed that one year in the blue ribbon competition. The investment gamble backfired. It may only have been down to one point and one Premier League place but that gap became a financial chasm.

Peter Ridsdale was the chairman who delivered his own epitaph with the words: "We lived the dream." Fans from all over the country, who voted him football's best chairman in 2001, were taunting him just two years later. Leeds fans felt betrayed by one of their own. Rival fans were delighted to see the collapse of Leeds and heaped scorn on the beleaguered Elland Road supremo.

Ridsdale's resignation as Leeds chairman led to the arrival of Professor John McKenzie as his successor. McKenzie used to walk around the Elland Road offices, producing slips of paper from his pocket that he'd scrutinise and explain reflected the share holding he had in the club via family trust funds. We all took him at face value. But McKenzie's credibility gradually began to unravel, too. First came the revelation that the man who presented himself as a professor of economics was actually a professor of re-organisation. In fact, he was a self-appointed professor. He had taken on an academic role as rector at the John Moores University in Liverpool, reorganised the college and handed himself a professorship. He had not fulfilled the usual academic requirements of delivering papers in a new field that justify such recognition.

At Leeds he went on the attack, ridiculing the "climate of indulgence" he had inherited and revealing the monthly cost of hiring the goldfish in the chairman's office. His interview gave people more reasons to pour scorn on the club - and I sensed all was not right. Within the infamous goldfish interview he also cited the number of company cars we had. I couldn't believe his claim and made a call to the person responsible for company car leasing and purchases. My suspicions were right. The new chairman's estimate was almost 100 per cent above the real figure.

Then we discovered that from having a dry directors' suite of offices McKenzie had asked his PA to ensure there was chilled Chablis in a fridge. He also requested freshly-cut flowers on any day he was in his office. And he wanted special personal stationery headed: "From the Chairman's Office." I decided to raise this hypocrisy with him. The man who had attacked a culture of indulgence seemed very keen to indulge himself. In fairness to John he performed a speedy U-turn and cancelled the wine and floral orders.

But he did see through the order of his own company car. It was a Porsche Cayenne. And it was somewhat astonishing to discover that while he had the largest vehicle in the Porsche range it was too wide to get onto the drive at his home in Baildon. McKenzie soldiered on. I resigned and left the club at the start of the 2003-04 season. John wrote a charming letter asking me to stay on the board and deal with PR and football issues. By this time he'd made a spectacular impression at a Premier League meeting by falling asleep. He might have got away with that if his head hadn't crashed forward and thumped against the table ensuring all eyes were on the new man from Leeds.

I realised it was best to move on. I was bitterly disappointed to see Leeds relegated that season. And there was still a sting in the tail with Professor McKenzie. The man with the family trust funds and bundles of shares had never had to publicly reveal his stake in the club. But at the club's AGM as a director he would have to go public with the details. Unfortunately, a few days before that AGM, McKenzie resigned as chairman, saying he would have to leave the board to launch his own takeover of the club. That was the last I heard of him in connection with Leeds. The takeover never materialised.

So in a fairly short period of time Leeds United had moved from Silver to McKenzie via Ridsdale. It was a roller-coaster ride. You might even say from the sublime to the ridiculous.

*Chapter 17*

# When Torres Chose
# to Walk Alone

## Dan Willis

Fernando Torres strode forward towards the Liverpool fans for the corner kick, as hungry as ever to find the net. More than a dozen replica Liverpool shirts with his name on the back were tossed in his direction, landing at his feet.

But they were not thrown in adulation; they were hurled in anger and disgust. The shirts were followed by a flurry of coins and taunting chants of "Chelsea rent boy", as the Reds supporters vented their fury at their former hero. A banner read: "He who betrays will always walk alone."

This was the Spaniard's Chelsea debut after his shock £50m move from Liverpool in the January transfer window of 2011. A match I attended. But rather than share the anger and resentment of many of the Liverpool fans I was sitting with that day, I felt sadness. Sadness that he had decided to leave, and sadness that a player who had enjoyed such popularity and respect at Liverpool was now being greeted with such disdain and vitriol.

Before Torres signed for Chelsea I'd really been looking forward to the game, but knowing he was now due to play against us left me dreading it. Seeing Torres in a Chelsea kit for his press conference was bad enough, but the prospect of watching him play in the flesh against Liverpool was almost too much to bear. What if he scored?

Approaching Stamford Bridge before kick-off that day, there seemed to be Torres-emblazoned Chelsea shirts everywhere. It was clear their glee at signing him was as pronounced as our disappointment at losing him; a glee best expressed with their adaptation of our beloved Torres song to one about him "growing a brain" to sign for Chelsea.

Despite my apprehension about the match, the mood among the Liverpool fans outside the ground was good-natured. Even the customary long delay to get past the police and stewards didn't seem to dampen spirits. There were all the usual triumphant songs, including the one about Chelsea having no history compared to the mighty Reds.

It was a very different atmosphere inside the ground, however, and it was largely focused on one man: Torres. He got dog's abuse from the Liverpool fans that day. He was booed mercilessly and called a "Chelsea rent boy" whenever he touched the ball. His first effort on goal ballooned wide, much to the delight of the travelling masses.

He didn't react to the Liverpool shirts hurled in his direction. Nor did he flinch when the coins arced their way towards him, or show any emotion when the hateful chants rang around Stamford Bridge. He seemed resigned to his fate for 90 minutes.

Not that he lasted that long. As debuts go, his was one to forget. Jamie Carragher, in his first game back from injury, kept the Spaniard quiet until he was substituted to jeers midway through the second half. No sooner had

Torres taken his place on the Chelsea bench than Raul Meireles (who would later follow Torres to Stamford Bridge) scored what proved to be Liverpool's winner.

Given the huge salaries enjoyed by footballers such as Torres, they get very little sympathy on occasions such as these. I'm sure he was expecting a negative reaction – his comment about Chelsea being a bigger club than Liverpool had clearly touched a nerve – but I bet even he was surprised at just how aggressive the abuse was.

I, too, was shocked. It was heartbreaking to see someone idolised by the fans just a week before turn into such a figure of hate. That's not to say I felt Torres deserved a positive response from the Liverpool fans. Like them, I felt I could never forgive him for leaving us for Chelsea; it's just the reaction of the fans seemed over the top to me.

I stood there silently on the upper tier at Stamford Bridge as those all around me screamed their fury at Torres, wondering how things had ended like this.

I had been tremendously excited at the signing of Torres back in the summer of 2007. There are never any guarantees of success, of course, and his scoring record for Atlético Madrid in the previous couple of seasons hardly suggested he'd be prolific. But he was young, exciting and in demand.

His first season could hardly have gone any better. Torres showed no Premier League teething problems and scored a staggering 33 goals in 46 games (including 24 at Anfield).

Having Torres as Liverpool's No9 was a source of immense pride to me. How good some of his team-mates were was definitely open to question, but there was no disputing Torres' quality. Even fans of Manchester United and Arsenal openly admitted how much they wished he played for them.

The last replica shirt I had owned was as a teenager, with my beloved Kenny Dalglish's No7 stitched into the back. I thought I'd long since grown out of wearing replica shirts, but such was the bond I felt with the Spaniard I soon bought one with the No9 and Torres' name proudly emblazoned on the back.

It didn't take the fans long to come up with a fitting song for our new hero. Some players never get their own song; others rarely have theirs sung. But the Torres song, to the tune of The Animals Went In Two By Two, was sung en masse with such passion, over and over again, that most of the opposing fans must have come to know the words.

In fact, the song was sung so often the fans even came up with another to precede it: We're Going To Bounce In A Minute – which we literally did. The euphoria of being in the stands and singing these songs was spine-tingling. I often wondered how satisfying it must have been for Torres to hear such an outpouring of appreciation from the fans. After all, most of the other players hardly got a look in, such was the focus on Torres.

But he deserved it. It felt like we'd score against anyone, so long as Torres was playing. We might not win, but I expected us to score. His presence seemed to unnerve opposition defenders – he prayed on their weaknesses. His 24 Premier League goals in 2007-08 was a record for a foreign player in their debut season. Little did I know it, but that first season was as good as it would get for Torres at Liverpool.

Torres struggled to reach the same highs in his following two seasons. He still scored some hugely important goals and was a constant menace to the opposition, but the goals came less often. And while the 2008-09 campaign saw

Liverpool mount a serious title challenge for the first time in Premier League history, things started to unravel the following season.

The Reds finished a demoralising seventh in the Premier League, missing out on Champions League football by some way. They were also booted out of the FA Cup and Carling Cup early on and, embarrassingly, failed to make it out of a Champions League group containing Fiorentina, Lyon and Debrecen.

I was convinced Rafa Benitez's decision to sell Xabi Alonso before the start of the 2009-10 campaign had been a key factor in Liverpool's struggles. Alonso was the man who dictated play for the Reds, and without him they lacked the same purpose. He, along with Steven Gerrard, was also a direct source of through-balls for Torres to feed off.

Despite losing some of his potency in front of goal, I remained as staunch a fan of Torres as ever. For a joke, my wife and I started to refer to our unborn baby as Fernando. We had no intention of calling it Fernando at birth – we didn't even know the gender – but it just seemed more personal.

In keeping with this, my brother managed to obtain a personally signed photo of the Spaniard to give us as a Christmas present in 2009, in which Torres congratulated my wife and me on the impending birth of our first child. The photo was of Torres celebrating his first goal for Liverpool, at home to Chelsea. It went straight up in the nursery.

Liverpool's problems worsened as Benitez, after constant bickering with the Liverpool owners at the time, Tom Hicks and George Gillett, left shortly after the 2009-10 season to take over at Inter Milan.

Roy Hodgson took over, but like most of the fans I was underwhelmed. You suspected the players were, too. What followed was a very unsettling summer as endless articles suggested that Torres and Gerrard were now both so disillusioned at Anfield that they might leave. I found myself glued to the internet, poring over reports in search of news that they intended to stay.

But with both players set to be involved in the World Cup that summer, any confirmation over their futures would have to wait. While England were soon sent packing by Germany, Torres was there until the very end as the Spanish triumphed. But having rushed back from a season-ending injury, he was clearly off the pace in South Africa and had a poor tournament. Watching him toil was an unpleasant experience for any Liverpool fan. In truth, Spain won it with very little help from Torres.

After what seemed like an eternity, Gerrard and Torres announced they were staying at Anfield. But while Gerrard's seemed an ultimately straightforward decision, you felt that Torres had needed some convincing. As if it had taken a big effort to commit himself to the club.

I tried to look at it from his perspective. He had won no trophies in three seasons at Liverpool, some of the team's star players had left, and there was no Champions League football to come that season. Plus, being managed by a journeyman such as Hodgson was unlikely to have been his lifelong ambition.

The hangover predictably continued in the 2010-11 season, with Torres unrecognisable from his peak of three seasons before. The goals came less frequently, there wasn't the same hunger about his play, and he seemed to spend more time arguing with referees than scoring goals. His powers looked to be on the wane. The decline had probably begun a year or two previously, but even his movement now looked laboured. There was very little joy about his play, and watching him struggle was painful. Yet, despite this, us Liverpool fans continued to get behind him, to sing his song and offer him support.

I'd felt that for some time that the team had been over-relying on him for goals – just as it did on Gerrard for spirit and creativity. Torres had put every last bit of effort into his performances in those first few seasons: he had chased down every ball, constantly pressurised defenders and made countless darting runs. But now it seemed to me that things were catching up with him, both physically and mentally. Injuries seemed more and more frequent.

Added to this, the team now had less quality and Hodgson had them playing a different style, a style ill-suited to Torres. We'd all enjoyed his sudden bursts of pace on to clever through-balls, but now he was expected to deal with high balls with his back to goal. His contribution lessened. It looked to me as if he was in a daze, while the rest of the players could only huff and puff.

Hodgson's ill-fated reign was soon over and, in January 2011, Dalglish was brought in to lift the Anfield gloom. An immediate return to a more passing style brought some much-needed victories and even a handful of goals for Torres. But while the fans got excited at the notion of a deadly partnership between Torres and the in-bound Luis Suarez, rumours began circulating about serious interest from Chelsea in the Spaniard.

Like most Liverpool fans, I knew Torres had been underperforming for some time. But the hope remained that he'd soon return to the marauding menace of the first season, especially given the upturn in fortunes under Dalglish. The club, no longer hampered by debt, was now looking to the future. Everything pointed towards building, not more picking apart.

Interest from Chelsea was nothing new, of course: they'd followed him closely for years. But what was different about these reports was the fact that he was actually keen to move.

The prospect of Torres leaving had quite an effect on me. I'd always known he'd leave at some point, but now just felt far too soon. He was just 26, and hadn't yet reached his best years. But as news of an offer from Chelsea emerged, the sense of horror and dread began to build. Then came the revelation that Torres had submitted a transfer request. He *wanted* to go.

The panic set in. I desperately hoped the possibility of him leaving would go away. The end of the transfer window was just days away – surely we could get to February before he was sold. Perhaps with some time for reflection, and some further improvement under the new regime, Torres would realise the error of his ways, and come round to the idea that he could achieve his ambitions at Liverpool.

It was not to be. Torres sealed his move to Chelsea for £50m on the final day of the January transfer window in 2011. The dual negotiations for Torres and Andy Carroll, the player Liverpool replaced Torres with from Newcastle for £35m, was a crazy episode, even by deadline day standards. I didn't do a great deal of work that day, as I avidly followed Twitter, Sky Sports News and various live blogs for news of developments.

There were brief moments of hope when it looked like Liverpool were going to be unable to strike a deal with Newcastle for Carroll, meaning Torres' move to Chelsea was off. But despite the price for Carroll reaching a staggering level, the price for Torres increased accordingly. In the end, with Newcastle finally satisfied, Liverpool settled with Chelsea for Torres.

The notion of selling Torres and buying Carroll seemed ludicrous to me: like replacing a Mercedes with a Vauxhall. Yes, the younger Carroll had potential, but I wasn't even sure I wanted him at Liverpool at all, let alone for £35m. He just didn't seem a Liverpool player to me.

Suffice to say, the signed Torres picture in my son's room came straight down.

All the cliches about your favourite player leaving for a rival club are true. Seeing Torres waving to the rapturous Chelsea fans that night, and giving his first interview to the club's official TV channel, felt like seeing your girlfriend going off with someone you disliked at school – and every day you had to watch them show the world how happy they were together.

It was especially hard to take seeing how genuinely pleased he looked to be there; as if the time he'd spent at Liverpool had been a long-suffering hardship and he'd been keen to leave for months.

That he had chosen to leave Liverpool was bad enough, that he had chosen to sign for Chelsea made it 10 times worse. Chelsea and Liverpool had had many run-ins in recent times, especially during their Champions League encounters, and there was considerable bad blood between the fans. Plus, having lived in London for long enough to remember when they had just a handful of supporters, I had my own reasons for disliking this new breed of Chelsea fan, attracted by Roman Abramovich's spending-fuelled success.

After signing, Torres claimed that choosing Chelsea over

Manchester United or Manchester City proved his loyalty to Liverpool. Utter nonsense. Showing loyalty to Liverpool would have meant staying at the club, or at the very least signing for a team outside of the Premier League. How can loyalty involve signing for a club in direct competition with the one you've just left?

But putting aside the antipathy of most Liverpool fans towards Chelsea, and Torres' bizarre interpretation of loyalty, there was something else that puzzled me about this move: that Chelsea weren't enough of a step up from Liverpool.

I'd always imagined that if he did leave us it would be to one of Europe's elite clubs, such as Barcelona or AC Milan. It probably would have been even more painful had he signed for Man Utd instead of Chelsea, but at least I could have understood a move there for footballing reasons, given their standing in the game.

Yes, Chelsea were a team better positioned to challenge for honours than Liverpool. In fact, they'd won the double the season before. They also continued to invest in the team, they had a top coach in Carlo Ancelotti, and they were based in London (often a draw for foreign players). That much I could see.

But they just didn't have the lustre, the global reputation of the top teams. And if Torres had chosen to leave Liverpool, I expected him to sign for one of those. Not Chelsea.

I'd been disappointed by the departures of Alonso and, to a lesser extent, Javier Mascherano. The closest I'd felt to this was when Gerrard very nearly packed his bags for Chelsea all those seasons ago. But Torres represented something different to Gerrard for me. While Gerrard had single-handedly dragged Liverpool to victory in numerous key games and the Reds owed him a great deal, there was something extra special about Torres. The way he played the game, his supreme talent, his work ethic, how he behaved off the field. Perhaps it was because he was foreign. There was never one single reason.

And I knew I wasn't alone. Such was the blow of losing Torres, my Liverpool-supporting friends and I couldn't bring ourselves to even discuss it. It became a taboo subject that, without planning to, we avoided for weeks.

Another possible reason why his departure hurt so badly was, having already seen Alonso and Mascherano go, losing Torres felt like further evidence of our demise. We were supposed to be strengthening, not weakening. Handing over our prize asset to a rival Premier League team seemed foolish, even for £50m.

That said, I understood Torres' determination to win things. Not even the most fervent Liverpool fan could argue that our team was primed to claim more trophies than Chelsea in the coming seasons.

He talked of winning the Champions League on his unveiling in west London. Well, that wasn't something Liverpool were going to do any time soon. Certainly not while they were competing in the Europa League, and with Champions League qualification seemingly so far out of reach.

Torres admitted that he thought the change of ownership would improve fortunes at Liverpool, but he believed he didn't have the time to wait for that to happen. Again, that there was some sense in that.

Dalglish, meanwhile, described player sales as part of the game, adding that the footballers he was most concerned about were the ones who wanted to stay at Liverpool. But

I'm sure privately he was as disappointed about Torres' decision as the rest of us. After all, it was hardly a vote of confidence in his management skills.

But while Dalglish gave off the aura of someone who'd moved on, the fans certainly hadn't. And neither had I.

It took Torres 14 games to score his first goal for Chelsea. I have to confess to finding it mildly amusing to begin with, that Chelsea's £50m striker was proving unable to do the one thing they'd bought him to do. But as the drought went on, not only did I feel sorry for his plight, I felt the need to defend him amid huge ridicule from football fans everywhere.

Maybe he didn't play for Liverpool anymore, but the fact that he had done, and so impressively, meant that he had my support.

That rain-soaked goal against West Ham was to be his one and only strike for the club in 18 appearances that season. It was, quite frankly, a pitiful return. Practically every mention of Torres in the media at that time mentioned two key figures: the £50m Chelsea had paid for him, and the solitary goal he'd scored for them.

Ancelotti was sacked, but first André Villas-Boas, and then Roberto Di Matteo, couldn't kick-start a scoring run in Torres during the 2011-12 season. Astonishingly, he went 24 games without scoring. I would watch him struggle during games and find myself in the odd situation of willing him to score, while at the same time wanting Chelsea to lose.

His difficulties integrating into the team were so obvious that reports emerged that Chelsea wanted to offload him, with one of the possible destinations being Liverpool. This caused much discussion among Liverpool fans and I was surprised to hear that some were actually receptive to the idea.

Despite the pain he caused me when he left, I wasn't one

of those that wanted him back. Not because of the manner in which he left, rather that I genuinely felt that the prolific striker of that first season at Liverpool was gone forever.

The poor run of form had gone on for so long now, for two different teams (three if you include Spain), under six different club managers, each with a different style of play. Surely, if the ability to regularly score goals was still there, one of those managers would have coaxed it out of him.

But while Torres' individual form during the 2011-12 season was seriously substandard, Chelsea's wasn't; certainly not in the final few months when, under caretaker boss Di Matteo, they clinched a Champions League and FA Cup double.

On the face of it, the two cup wins vindicated Torres' decision to move to Chelsea. In that time, Liverpool won just the Carling Cup. The problem with this theory is that he played a peripheral role in their triumphs, such was Di Matteo's confidence in Didier Drogba as his main striker. Torres was a late substitute in Munich, and not among those trusted to take a penalty in the shootout. He didn't even make it off the bench for the FA Cup final against Liverpool.

A paltry 12 goals in 67 matches tells its own story of his contribution during his first season-and-a-half in a Chelsea shirt. And when it comes to telling his grandchildren of how the Champions League and FA Cup medals were won, his will not be a glorious tale.

And tellingly, only hours after the final in Munich, during scenes of great celebration, he gave a very frank interview complaining of his huge disappointment and surprise at not starting the match. He also told of the mental torment he had suffered at Chelsea and how he needed reassurances of his future role in the team.

Those reassurances duly arrived, along with news of Drogba's departure. But whether Torres can take full advantage is debatable. He has shown no signs during his time at Chelsea to suggest he can recapture that early form at Liverpool.

While some Liverpool fans might hope his career never recovers, I'd like to see him once again rampaging through defences and doing what he used to do best: effortlessly scoring goal after goal. But preferably not for Chelsea.

And as for the signed picture of his first goal for Liverpool? I've still got it – but I can't imagine it ever going back up on a wall in my house again.

## Chapter 18

# Malcolm Crosby's Red-and-White Hankie

## Jonathan Wilson

The thing that stands out still is the silences. After every line of every chant, the silence was complete: everybody was joining in, nobody shuffling or muttering, 26,000 people united. We'd heard the legends, of course. We knew about the Roker Roar, the great visceral howl of encouragement for which Roker Park was famous. We knew the stories about how Malcolm Allison was so struck by the atmosphere as Sunderland, then of the Second Division, beat Manchester City in a fifth-round replay in 1973 that he broke into the ground the following morning to check if amplifiers had been installed. We knew all of the history, but this was the first time we'd experienced it, the first time we'd really felt the noise roll off the corrugated roof of the Fulwell End and pour down across the pitch. We'd thought we'd felt it before, but we hadn't, not till then, not till that night when we beat Chelsea to reach the FA Cup semi-final.

My dad refused to go. He was a devout Roker-Ender – "It's where I've always gone," he would say, leaning always on the same barrier on a line from the penalty spot over the left-hand post, having gone for his lucky pre-match piss in the same lucky patch of the urinal he had done since the end of the war – and the Roker End had been given over to Chelsea fans. "I'm not going anywhere else," he said. "It wouldn't feel right." I wonder now whether he was just looking for an excuse not to put himself through the tension.

His lucky pre-match piss hadn't been that lucky, of course; or rather, it had been for six glorious months between December 1972 and May 1973 and never since. Every Sunderland fan remains defined by that success. I was born three years - alright, three years, two months, four days, one hour and twenty-nine minutes - after the final whistle confirmed victory over Leeds and I can recite chunks of the commentary off by heart. I'd find it very hard to take seriously anybody who claimed to be a Sunderland fan and when asked the team for the final didn't respond immediately, "Montgomerymaloneguthriehorswillwatsonpittkerrhughesh alomporterfieldtueart." You didn't break the words up because you'd learned the mantra before you had any idea what it meant: it was just noise that made people happy. Really, of course, you should add in, "and the sub was Davie Young" with the oddly essential coda that he "used to play for Newcastle, you know." So had Ron Guthrie, but nobody ever seemed to say it about him.

I mist up thinking about the game – and I didn't even exist. God knows what it must have been like for fans of my dad's generation, who had witnessed the under-achieving big-spending years of the fifities, presumably with that insistent clock counting up constantly: ten years since they'd won the league, fifteen years since they'd won the league, twenty years since they'd won the league until, in 1958, the first ever relegation. Then the years of Second Division near misses, of more big spending and Brian Clough's injury, of

promotion at last and relegation soon after, of debt and
disillusion and the dread realisation as relegation to Division
Three loomed in 1972 that we really weren't a big club any
more. And then, just as you accepted that, Alan Brown was
sacked.

Brown had overseen two relegations – the first after an
illegal payments scandal of which he almost certainly knew
nothing, and the second after taking over three months from
the end of a doomed season – but he was an ascetic,
puritanical visionary. His sides played open, attacking football as he pioneered training methods such as shadow play
- that is, playing without a ball to develop positional
awareness; mocked at the time but standard now. And just
in case that sounded a bit intellectual or soft, he'd make his
players run in the North Sea if the practice pitch was frozen;
had them practise heading with golf balls, reasoning that if
your technique was right it wouldn't hurt; and got them to
spend their afternoons off helping him build a training base
at Washington, mixing cement and lugging timber about. My
dad rated him the best manager he'd ever seen at Sunderland.

Brown was a clear leader, a man who radiated authority.
When he was succeeded by Bob Stokoe, it surely seemed like
an acceptance of Sunderland's second-rate status. He had
been under pressure at Blackpool and had won nothing but
the Anglo-Italian Cup. He was forty-two, but with his
crooked yellow teeth and thinning brittle hair he looked
much older. He was a former Newcastle centre-half and
openly supported them. It seemed the very opposite of
visionary. And yet, under him, Sunderland climbed from
nineteenth in the Division Two table to sixth. In the Cup
they beat Manchester City when they were eighth in Division
One, Arsenal when they were second and Leeds – Don

Revie's mighty Leeds – in the final, when they were third. This was the underdog story to end all underdog stories, all the more so as Leeds were so loathed; this was romance against cynicism and romance won. As Brian Moore had said in the final minutes of commentary when, in all honesty, he became slightly delirious, "It seemed as though... the experts said... it couldn't happen, except it looks as if it's going to... They came from the North East with hope, and they're going to go back with the Cup... A great result for Sunderland and, with all due deference to Leeds, a great result for football."

When you'd experienced that as a fan, when you'd lived something so impossible, you wonder whether even in that moment of victory, even at that climactic moment when, after fifty-nine minutes of clinging on, the triumph was sealed, there was a tinge of sadness, a knowledge that it could never be that good again.

Underdog victories are doubled-edged. There's a glory to them, of course, a special glory even, but the particularity of that glory comes precisely through the fact that really, in essence, you're crap. Sunderland beating City and Arsenal and Leeds (and Notts County and Reading and Luton) was a romantic tale that gripped the nation because it was so ridiculous, so implausible. And as if to make sure that aspect of glory wasn't tainted by subsequently becoming good, Sunderland kept on being reliably crap for the two decades that followed. Yes, there were Jimmy Adamson's kids, cheated by Jimmy Hill in 1977; yes, there was the five-year relegation battle that followed promotion in 1980 and was ended in 1985, the same year Sunderland lost the Milk Cup final by scoring an own goal and missing a penalty; yes, there was the emphatic promotion from Division Three (but we should never have been there in the first place); and, yes, there was the improbable promotion despite defeat in the play-off final – to another own goal - in 1990 when Swindon were found to have made illegal payments. But crapness underlay it all. Promotions were merely the preludes to relegation; appearances at Wembley merely another opportunity to shoot ourselves in the foot.

The season after promotion in 1990 brought, to nobody's great surprise, relegation. This was a squad that had been lucky to nick sixth in the second division; bringing in Peter Davenport and Kevin Ball to replace Eric Gates and John MacPhail wasn't suddenly going to make them a top-flight team. We played some nice stuff at times, were roundly patronised, chucked away leads all over the place and were relegated amid high drama at Manchester City on the final day. Marco Gabbiadini left and, eventually, was replaced by John Byrne, signed from Brighton after a 4-2 win in which David Rush, a local kid, scored twice. Byrne made his future pretty clear by standing by the Sunderland dug-out after being substituted, chatting to Denis Smith, our manager, while the next day the papers almost as one asked whether, with Rush in such fine form, Sunderland really needed Byrne. As anybody who'd ever seen Rush play in any game apart from that one knew, the answer was a resounding yes. A few years later, in court in Hartlepool on some driving charge, Rush claimed he couldn't take the bus because if he did he'd be mobbed; whether it was an inspired defence or mind-boggling self-delusion was never clear.

The Brighton game came after defeats to Middlesbrough and Grimsby and was followed by a dismal 3-0 defeat at Cambridge. There was a slight upturn with victories over Watford and Ipswich, but then came a run of four defeats in five games. Back-to-back 1-0 wins over Leicester – Don

Goodman scoring on his home debut - and Portsmouth weren't enough to keep the pressure off, and when a defeat at Tranmere on Boxing Day was followed by a 3-0 humbling at Oxford, Smith was sacked – the victim, like so many managers, of having taken a club up too soon, before they were ready.

Sunderland, of course, had no plan. Something had to be done; sacking Smith was something and so they did it, without really thinking of the consequences. While the board looked for a successor, Malcolm Crosby took over as caretaker. He was respected as a coach, but had no manage-rial experience and, frankly, he looked slightly comical, with an enormous nose and a mop of curly hair, like an exagger-ated version of Robin Williams in Toys.

There was an immediate improvement. Goals from Gordon Armstrong and Goodman saw off Barnsley in Crosby's first game, then Port Vale were dismissed 3-0 in the Cup, despite Goodman being cup-tied. He returned the following week to score a hat-trick in a 6-2 win over Millwall and scored again in a 2-1 win at Derby the following week. Crosby's winning streak ended with a 1-1 draw at home to Port Vale at the beginning of February, but the form of January had all but extinguished relegation worries.

When we won 3-2 at Oxford in the fourth round of the Cup – Crosby avenging his former boss Smith's honour – suddenly the focus shifted. Looking back, it's hard to understand why the fifth round of the Cup meant so much then, but 25,000 turned up for West Ham – at a time when 15,000 was about standard for league games. Was it just we were so crap that that felt like glory? Did the Cup mean so much more then? Or was it that Sunderland were so hooked on 1973 that we snatched at any vague hope of replicating it? It was a cold, bright, windy day and the game was quite possibly the worst ever played. Mike Small gave West Ham the lead but, just as we were giving up hope, a ball to the back post bobbled in off a combination of Byrne and Tony Parks.

That meant Byrne had scored in all three Cup games, and he got two more in the replay. I listened to it in my bedroom, playing Kick Off 2 on the Amiga. My dad sat downstairs, refusing to acknowledge there was a game on until it was over, as he always did when he wasn't actually there. He was a master, when we had days out on a Saturday, of getting back to the car at precisely twenty to five (that being when games finished in the days before proper injury-time and 15-minute half-times). I remember being at Heighleygate garden centre at the beginning of April 1985 and, at about quarter past three, bumping into my gran's next-door neighbour, Alan. "They're 1-0 up," he said. "Scored after two minutes." In retrospect, Alan was a little obsessive about when goals were scored; on another occasion I recall him lamenting – I don't remember the opposition - "they only equalised twenty minutes from time," as though a disappointing home draw would somehow have been more acceptable if only Sunderland had equalised earlier. My dad was furious and stomped about in a huff for the next hour and a half. We got back to the car, turned the radio and found we'd lost 4-1. He didn't say it, but you could tell he was thinking, "See; I told you so." Everton went on to win the league while Sunderland won only once more that season and were relegated.

At the time, I didn't understand my dad's insistence on not knowing until it was over, but as I've got older I've started to go down the same route. Not to the same extent but, after smashing a dustpan and brush after we let a 2-0 lead slip against Birmingham on the opening day of the season two years ago, I've found myself arranging to be out when games are on; the agony of a lead is hideous. I used to go out with an Argentine, a Boca Juniors fan, and she would deride my "small-team mentality", the way I'd respond to Sunderland taking the lead by swearing and cursing and counting the minutes till full-time. She was right, of course, but that's the difference between giants like Boca and the rest.

Even then I didn't quite dare listen to the full commentary on local radio, so I had Radio 5 on. Twice they went over to Steve Tongue at Upton Park; twice Davenport had laid in Byrne to score on the break. They went over to him twice more: two Martin Allen goals and it was 2-2. And then they broke off from commentary of Liverpool v Ipswich to go to Steve Tongue for a fifth time. I steeled myself for the worst, but as soon as they switched over you could hear the "Davie, Davie Rush" chant in the background. I assumed he'd been sent off like the daft lad he was, but it turned out Kieron Brady – a wonderful player who we all thought was a lazy genius till he was forced to retire aged 22 with a vascular condition, when we realised he was a genius with an illness - had worked space on the right and whipped in a cross that Rush had converted.

That set up a quarter-final against Chelsea, who were managed by Ian Porterfield, scorer of Sunderland's winner in the 1973 final. Times have changed, but back then I hated Chelsea and so did pretty much every other Sunderland fan. It all stemmed from the 1985 Milk Cup semi-final. We'd been lucky to beat them 2-0 in the home leg, but afterwards their fans had gone on the rampage, smashing up pubs, attacking cars and breaking shop windows. I remember seeing the windows of Fulwell Library boarded up the next day and, presumably having just read something about it, equating it to the sacking of the library at Alexandria. Truly, I thought, these people were barbarians.

The second leg, which we won 3-2, was even worse. There'd been multiple pitch invasions. Fans had attacked our goalkeeper Chris Turner and the forward and former Chelsea player Clive Walker. We'd even scored a goal with half the defence distracted by a police horse chasing somebody across the other side of the penalty area. Afterwards, their fans set up road-blocks in the streets, hauled Sunderland fans off buses through the emergency exits and slashed their faces.

Of course we then shot ourselves in the foot in the final. It wasn't just the Gordon Chisholm own goal and the Walker missed penalty, it was the move leading to the own-goal, the teenager David Corner – in for the suspended Shaun Elliott – trying to shepherd a ball behind and being dispossessed by John Deehan, whose half-cleared cross led to the Mick Channon shot that deflected in off Chisholm's chest (while Deehan stood in an offside position in Chris Turner's eyeline, but we'll let that injustice pass).

Most Sundays, Corner goes for a drink with the friend he shares a taxi business with in Sunderland. At least twice each Sunday afternoon, his friend reckons, somebody will come up to him and say, "Yer should've just put it out, Davie lad."

Corner now works for Durham police. A couple of years ago, he was called to a disturbance in Seaham where a man was going berserk with an ornamental sword. All attempts to reason with him failed until he caught sight of Corner's flaming ginger hair.

"Are yiz... are yiz Davie Corner?" he asked disbelievingly.

Corner confirmed he was. The man dropped the sword and offered his hands to be cuffed. "Yer've not had much luck, son," he said. "So I'll give yer this 'un. But, Davie lad, why didn't yer just put it out?"

I sat in my bedroom again for the quarter-final, with my dad downstairs again, reading the paper as usual. This time I had homework to do, so I kept turning the radio on and off, unable to settle to either. Clive Allen put Chelsea ahead in the first half and it sounded like we were getting a pounding. I pretty much gave up. I turned the radio on again. Still 1-0, still all Chelsea. Radio off. I finished the work and started to play Kick Off 2. I turned the radio on again to hear the last five minutes. The tone was different. There'd obviously just been another goal but it took me a while to realise for whom. Eventually it became clear: Byrne, running onto a Paul Bracewell diagonal, had shaped in a header with his highlights that he insisted weren't highlights. Suddenly, the thought occurred to me that we might actually win the FA Cup.

Such were the security fears for the replay that Chelsea fans were packed into the central section of the Roker End, the two sides being left empty for segregation. Even so, over 26,000 crammed in. "There were twice as many in 73," my dad said, which was true. There'd been even more for the sixth-round replay against Manchester United in 1964. Sunderland, on course to promotion at last under Alan Brown, had drawn 3-3 at Old Trafford, having been 3-1 up when Jim Montgomery suffered concussion late on. Nobody knows how many squeezed in for the replay, but it was something approaching 80,000 with as many as 40,000 milling in the streets outside.

My gran lived about 200 yards from the back of the Roker

End and my dad was still living there at the time. He'd intended to come home from work, have his dinner, and then pop out an hour or so before kick-off as he usually did for evening games, but after two hours of trying to battle his way through the crowds, he gave up, joined the queues and went into the ground still wearing his suit. Four people were killed when a gate collapsed.

That night Nic Sharkey put Sunderland ahead with an overhead kick just before half-time but United levelled just after the hour, Denis Law capitalising on a mishit goal-kick from Montgomery. That took the game into extra-time, which had barely begun when Maurice Setters diverted a Sharkey through-ball past his own keeper. Law hit the bar with time running out and then, with seconds remaining, Bobby Charlton headed in a right-wing cross to take the game to another replay. Emotionally and physically shattered at having twice let United off the hook, Sunderland lost the second replay at Huddersfield 5-1.

That was a side that specialised in near misses. The previous year, they'd looked on course for promotion when Brian Clough had ruptured knee ligaments against Bury on Boxing Day. They'd stuttered badly, not helped by a bad winter that forced a serious of postponements leading to major fixture congestion but had still gone into the final game needing only a draw at home to Chelsea to return to the top flight. Chelsea won 1-0 and were promoted in Sunderland's place. There were many reasons not to trust them.

This time, Sunderland began well. They flew into challenges, unsettling Chelsea, hounding them at every turn. Every tackle brought a roar; every foul a bigger one. We even, every now and again, put together a handful of passes amid the maelstrom and then, midway through the first half, Byrne drove the ball across goal and Davenport - nice, polite Peter Davenport with his neat side-parting, a quietly thoughtful footballer who had no place amid the bloodlust that night - put Sunderland ahead. Had Goodman not been cup-tied he probably wouldn't even have played.

There were moments of anxiety, of course. I remember Tony Norman, a heroically unorthodox goalkeeper who is now a policeman, emerging somehow above a crowd of players and, with a strange stiff-armed action as though he were wearing a plaster-cast, flipping a cross away with his fingertips. At half-time we deserved the lead, but we also knew there was no way we could keep up that pace.

We didn't. As the second half went on we got deeper and deeper. It became a siege, a bombardment in front of the Fulwell End. Norman made save after save, and when he slipped, Andy Townsend hit the post. Shot after shot, cross after cross rained in; an equaliser seemed inevitable but never arrived. It was agonising, but each wasted chance, each block, each save added to the belief: our name was on it; this was our time again. In the year Sunderland was granted city status, in the year the polytechnic became a university, we were going to win the Cup; it was going to be the greatest of all possible years.

Then Dennis Wise scored, lifting the ball cleverly over Norman from close range as the keeper threw himself out to block. Let's get this over with, I thought; let them score again because we're knackered and in extra-time it could get embarrassing. We don't deserve to lose this 4-1, or 5-1.

But even as I was thinking that, Paul Bracewell launched a long diagonal at David Rush. Steve Clarke got there in front of him, although he needn't have bothered; it was only Rush.

Perhaps spooked into thinking Rush could actually play by
the media attention he'd received at West Ham, though,
Clarke put the ball out for a corner. The youthful, fluffy-
haired Brian Atkinson took it, an outswinger. Armstrong
met it with a firm slap. Of course you couldn't hear the slap,
but we'd seen him head balls like that a thousand times
before: he had a vast shiny forehead, as though specially
polished for better contact on headers.

From the stand at the other end, I could see it was looping
over Dave Beasant's dive. They didn't have a man on the
post. The angle was right. The trajectory was right. It was
going in, and yet it wasn't in. Only later, seeing the highlights
on television, did I understand why it had taken so long:
Armstrong was almost 18 yards out. For an age the ball hung,
and then finally the net rippled and Davenport went up and
the paddocks at that end went up and then the whole ground
went up and the unthinkable had happened. Crosby leapt
from the bench, fists clenched awkwardly in front of him,
pelvis thrusting slightly, then seemingly decided a manager
should be more dignified, clapped his hands and sat down
again, pursing his lips incredulously beneath that vast nose.

The noise had barely abated when our hard man, John
Kay, a tiny nugget of aggression who used to prove his
hardness by eating the antiseptic cubes from the urinals in
pub toilets, nailed Vinnie Jones. It was a stupid, nonsensical
foul, one you suspected Kay had been saving up all game,
biding his time, waiting for his opportunity. It conceded a
free-kick just outside our box, but it didn't matter; we knew
they were shot, and the foul was greeted with a roar almost
as loud as the winner had been: a real fuck-you of a tackle.

At the final whistle, fans poured deliriously from the
stands. A huge red-and-white banner, maybe 30 yards long

and 15 yards across, rare in English football in those days, was stretched out across the top of the Fulwell End and passed hand over hand down the terrace to be paraded across the pitch. In one of those inexplicable moments of a crowd finding, as one, spontaneous inspiration, the chant struck up: "Malcolm Crosby's red-and-white hankie." It was his finest hour.

I queued overnight with my dad for tickets to the semi-final against Norwich, which we won 1-0 with a John Byrne header. That persuaded the board at last to give Crosby the manager's job on a permanent basis, but we were well-beaten by Liverpool in the final. The next season started badly, made all the worse by Newcastle's rise under Kevin Keegan. Crosby was sacked a year to the week after he'd got the job, with the club seventeenth, exactly where they'd been when he took over. Bafflingly, it was a postponed game at Tranmere that the pools panel recorded as a home win that proved the final straw.

Back then, nineteen years without a trophy seemed an awfully long time. There was a sense we were due a good run. The terrifying thing is that longer has passed since that night against Chelsea than had passed between the Cup final and that night and still we're waiting for a comparable experience – beating Sheffield United 1-0 to reach the semi-final in 2004 wasn't quite the same. I hope we do get our moment in the sun again – although such is the diminished stature of the FA Cup, I'm not sure anything on the scale of 1973 is ever going to be possible – but I hope it doesn't come too soon. My dad was thirty-five when Sunderland won the Cup, the age I am now. I saw how the second half of his life as a fan was blighted by the sense that he'd already seen the best football had to offer, so if we could win something – just one trophy – in my lifetime, I'd quite like it to be in another thirty years or so. Let me be young enough to enjoy it, but not so young I have decades of anti-climax to follow.

# Afterword

## Marc Watson

Passion. That's this book, and football, condensed into a single word. I've known all the writers, through their work for BT's football website, which gives the anthology its name, but they've given us a unique insight into their world. They've been bold enough to talk honestly about their allegiances, so I'll do the same. Professionally, I've been involved in the game as part of the BT team which won the rights to screen Premier League football for three years, from August 2013. Personally, it's a different matter . . .

I was born in Luton but my family almost immediately moved to Swindon. My mum and my uncle were Luton Town supporters; my great grandfather had been a director of the club in the 50s. So my memories of football began with long-anticipated trips up the M4 to Kenilworth Road. We used to walk past the terraced houses and through all the little alleyways to get to the turnstiles. Luton Town was one of the 'big-small' clubs in those days. We were regularly in the top half of the old First Division. And Eric Morecambe's constant references to his support of The Hatters did us no harm either.

I particularly remember going to Wembley to see the 1988 League Cup Final against Arsenal (the attendance was more than 95,000!). Luton took an early lead with a goal from Brian Stein, but Arsenal equalised through Martin Hayes before, three minutes later, Alan Smith gave them the lead. Arsenal were then awarded a penalty. Game over, we supposed, but instant gloom was followed by immediate euphoria when Andy Dibble saved Nigel Winterburn's spot-kick. We then equalised with seven minutes to go with a goal from Danny Wilson. With less than a minute left, Brian Stein scored his second goal of the match to win Luton Town's first major trophy.

My team, running round Wembley with the Cup. That's the stuff of childhood fantasy. Strangely, losing in the final in '89 has all but been erased from my memory! Football is about heartbreak, and The Hatters' fall from grace since then has taken an emotional toll. The odd promotion has helped, but the points deductions, which confirmed our relegation from League Two, still sting. We're still out of the Football League but we've got a bright new manager in Paul Buckle. I am unable to persuade BT that we should buy rights to Luton matches at this time, but who knows in the future?

I go along when I can now, and a match at Kenilworth Road, as much as anywhere else, always brings back to me the power of football to connect people. There are very few situations in which football is divisive. And where it is, it's usually down to some other factor disguised by a passion for a particular team. Football actually brings people together, men and women – and even people who support different clubs. I've seen it so many times.

For BT football works in so many ways: from taking along clients and potential clients to a match, where we can get to know each other better, to more formal meetings where a little time out is (unofficially!) allowed to discuss the week-end's events in the Premier League. Who would have thought, not so long ago that BT, the 'telephone company' would be winning the rights that will bring its customers the best matches from the greatest football league in the world? What would Buzby have made of that?!

The part that football plays in my business, BT Vision, is even more important to me because of my own upbringing with the game. As much as the technology behind BT Vision is important, it doesn't have that emotional connection of content like the 'beautiful game'. I don't gaze wistfully into the middle-distance dreaming that one day the platform we use for BT Vision will one day beat another platform in some sort of 'best platform' contest.

I wonder how, and when, Luton Town will get back into the Football League.

*Marc Watson is chief executive of BT Vision*

# Team Huddle

Football, as we all know, is a team game. Think of this as the team huddle. This is where we do the rah-rah bit. It's my job, on behalf of all the contributors, to thank the people who've helped us along the way. Principal among them is Kim Fitzsimmons at BT, who has been the driving force of the Life's a Pitch project from Day One. Kim's one of us, Real 'Wall. Mike Jarvis is a Liverpool fan. It's been heartbreaking seeing him reel from the studio, after we've delivered the latest bad news from Anfield. David Pincott, as a QPR fan, is more accustomed to such trauma. Fergus Garber, BT's Head of Production, Sikander Mal and cameraman Bill Abbott are all Spurs fans, and are made of stern stuff. Bill's fellow cameramen, Nic Holman, Nigel Dupont, and John Ryan, are brilliant to work with, as are directors James Whicher and David Baird, who whisper sweet nothings in my ear. Sound men Alistair Taylor and Matt Turner have been gentle with us, as have Martin Levingbird and Graham Brown, from BT Auditorium. The unseen work done from BT Tower by Martin McGahon, Jebb Boothby, Natalie Gilmore, Tom Grevatte, Pete Harvey, Matt Jarman,

Richard Snape Dan Warburton and Denis Yeo, is much appreciated. Matt Simpson, Mike Grady and Josh Burt, from Zone, have been central to the success of www.lifesapitch.co.uk. Thanks also, to Geoff Fisher, of CPI, for getting this show on the road, and to Getty Images, for permission to produce the cover photograph. Hope you've enjoyed the book, as much as I've enjoyed working with the team.

*Michael Calvin*